ENGLISH
FOR
MODERN
BUSINESS

ENGLISH
FOR
MODERN
BUSINESS

ERWIN M. KEITHLEY, D.Ed.

Emeritus Professor of Management
Graduate School of Management
University of California, Los Angeles

MARGARET H. THOMPSON, M.Ed.

Extension Instructor in Writing
Independent Study, University of California, Berkeley
Consultant, Office Practices and Communications
Formerly Faculty, Graduate School of Business Administration
University of California, Los Angeles

FOURTH EDITION   1982

RICHARD D. IRWIN, INC.   Homewood, Illinois   60430

Irwin-Dorsey Limited   Georgetown, Ontario   L7G 4B3

ISBN 0-256-02478-2

Library of Congress Catalog Card No. 80–85462

Printed in the United States of America

1 2 3 4 5 6 7 8 9 0 ML 8 7 6 5 4 3 2 1

088371

TO THE STUDENT:

English for Modern Business provides an opportunity to develop your skills in the use of the English language. Not only will language ability serve you well in whatever career you choose, but it will also contribute to your success in all your living experiences. When you analyze your daily activities, you will understand that most of your living is a matter of communication.

Your opportunities for a successful career in business will be greatly improved if you can construct grammatical sentences, write coherent paragraphs of understandable prose, and spell correctly the words you use. In any level of work above routine mechanical functions, you cannot escape the requirement to write and speak. A person capable of writing reasonably good English will stand out among employees.

Numerous articles by business executives, educators, and others emphasize the importance of communication skills. In one large company 40 percent of the people interviewed for jobs could not meet the company's reading and writing standards. Careful study will help you meet similar standards. "The best place to learn to write is in school. If you're still there, pick your teachers' brains," is the advice of Malcolm Forbes, president and editor-in-chief of *Forbes Magazine*. The International Paper Company emphasizes the importance of communication in these words: "Today, the printed (written) word is more vital than ever. Now there is more need than ever before for all of us to read better, write better, and communicate better." Edward T. Thompson, editor-in-chief of *Reader's Digest,* points out that there are only three basic requirements for those who want to write clearly: "First, you must *want* to write clearly. Second, you must be willing to *work hard.* Third, you must know and follow some *basic guidelines."*

Your motivation to perfect your use of language will probably be the most important element in your success. You have the opportunity to apply yourself and, with the help of your teachers, to reach a high level of success. Let us explain further our reasons for encouraging you to pursue the study of language structure—the most important basic element of correct English usage.

Most of you are well aware of communication failures in your own lives, in learning situations in school, and in organizations where you may have worked. In writing this book, we have taken the position that the sentence is the basic grammatical unit of most concern to you. Improving your ability to put together direct, clear sentences is the end result you seek. Knowledge of the structure of language is a *means* to this end.

We are saying to you with great *emphasis:* Improvement of your basic language skills will pay high dividends. There is no magic process to be discovered or revealed, however; so we urge you to keep in mind that good communication involves an intense effort to make *words work.* Clarity depends not only upon the message received but also upon the ability to analyze what is said. As a writer and speaker, you will face the need to put clauses and phrases into correct sentence patterns and to choose words appropriate to the tone and rhythm of your message.

While the instruction and practice in the textbook will require solutions in writing, we urge you to keep in mind the probable transfer of skills to other basic areas of communication. In other classes and in informal activities, attempt to use the communication guidelines you are studying. Seek to improve your skills in situations where you are both passively and actively engaged. Make acceptable usage a matter of habit. View the materials presented as constructive exercises planned to help you achieve excellence in speaking and writing. As you study, be confident of your ability to learn to communicate effectively. Test yourself to measure your improvement. Strive to do the following:

1. Compose clear sentences that convey the meaning you intend.
2. Punctuate these sentences to enhance the meaning and give the emphasis intended.
3. Develop a basic vocabulary.
4. Learn to spell correctly.
5. Edit paragraphs of written material (check content, spelling, punctuation, capitalization, and so forth).
6. Improve your communication skills by consulting the dictionary frequently and effectively.

Your determination to improve your communication skills is the basic building block in developing a discipline of putting thoughts into words. Practice to perfect your knowledge of a language structure that will give you the ability to write with clarity, simplicity, coherence, and force. It is the means of getting things done. If you are applying for a job, arguing with a neighbor, or asking for a date, *what you say* and *how you say it* will pretty much determine the success you attain.

ERWIN M. KEITHLEY
MARGARET H. THOMPSON

Contents

CONTENTS ix

The sentence

Many people call this the "age of communication." With the inventions of television, computers, instant printing machines, word processing equipment, and other rapid reproduction methods, messages are being flashed before our eyes and beamed to our ears constantly. Computers can analyze, correlate, and evaluate reams of data almost faster than we can assimilate the reports they print out. Worldwide news reaches us the minute the events happen, and almost instantaneously a commentator begins to discuss them. Consequently, we are bombarded by messages continuously. Each one of us is caught up in this constant flow of communications.

Good communication is important to businesses.

Today, businesses depend on communication to carry on their nationwide and worldwide operations. To keep information flowing, companies find it necessary to establish vast communication systems. These systems depend for their success on the ability of individuals within the system to communicate efficiently and effectively. Communication among employees, between workers and supervisors, between the company and its customers or suppliers, between the company and government agencies—all these opportunities to exchange messages must be accomplished successfully. Thus, it is necessary that each of us in business knows how to use our language efficiently and effectively when communicating.

Language is the tool of communication.

Language is the tool of communication. In a way, we are fortunate to be an English-speaking people. English is less complicated in its structure than many other languages. There are only a few guidelines to remember. The better we understand how to use our language, the easier it is to exchange ideas with other people. You are preparing to enter the business world, and it is important that you look at your language in a new way.

The sentence is the framework that supports the message.

The place to start in this study of English is with the sentence. The sentence is the framework on which we hang our messages. Our thinking, our speaking, our writing—all take the form of the sentence. By learning all you can about the use and structure of sentences, you will find that you can express yourself clearly and that your messages are understood. Master the ability to speak and write effective sentences, and you'll be on your way to a successful business career.

1

Sentences carry messages

A sentence contains a complete thought.

A sentence is made up of *words grouped together to express a complete thought.* The first word of the sentence is capitalized to indicate the beginning of the thought. A period, question mark, or exclamation point is placed after the last word to indicate the end of the thought.

The catalog was developed by the Bressler Agency.

When will you purchase the supplies?

Please answer the telephone.

Buy now!

Remember, all sentences must express *complete* thoughts. The person who hears or reads the sentence should have no questions about the message. Notice that both the preceding examples and the following sentences carry messages that are clear and complete.

IBM manufactures electronic computers.

Mr. Morgan paid his income tax.

The new copier makes five copies a minute.

Sentences should have all the words necessary for a clear and complete message.

Fragments should be rewritten as complete sentences.

You may find occasionally that a person gives only part of the thought in sentence form. In a speaking situation, you, as the puzzled listener, can ask questions to obtain the rest of the thought. The speaker then has a chance to clarify the message and say the additional words that complete the thought. In writing, however, the incomplete thought may be written as a sentence with the first word capitalized and a mark of punctuation after the last word. Just doing those two things does not make the message complete, however. You, as the puzzled reader, do not have the opportunity to clarify immediately the intended message, unless you telephone the sender and ask for clarification. Writers need to be sure that their sentences contain all the words necessary for a complete message. Sentence fragments, as incomplete sentences are called, can easily be changed to complete ones. In the following illustrations, the fragments are changed from incomplete to complete sentences.

Incomplete messages	Complete messages
Because you have all the details.	You can go ahead and write the report because you have all the details.
Until the clerk has a chance to explain.	Until the clerk has a chance to explain, we will withhold our decision.
How many miles a gallon?	How many miles a gallon does this car get?

With the addition of a few words, the fragments in the left column have been changed from incomplete to complete thoughts in the right column. Only a few words are needed to change a fragment to a sentence that contains a clear and complete thought. For understanding and communication to take place, it is important that you as the communicator express ideas in their entirety. The ability to use English well—that is, communicate with clarity in both speech and writing—is a priceless asset, highly prized in the business world.

Quick review

A review now to test your ability to identify complete sentences will be helpful. Are all the sentences below complete thoughts? Place a **C** in the column opposite each sentence that does express a complete thought.

1. Making the sales quota. _____

2. Jim was glad that he made the sales quota. _____

3. Look for that letter in the files. _____

4. Margie Foster who is a fast typist. _____

5. Margie Foster, who is a fast typist, was given the job. _____

6. The workers were given a raise in pay. _____

7. The profits based on last year's figures. _____

8. The manager took the reports home to read. _____

9. Although the company sold a million units last year. _____

10. Looking over the list and not finding the name. _____

(Answers in reverse order: - - C - C C - C C -)

Sentences can be constructed in several ways.   Several types of sentences—*statements, questions, commands, requests,* and *exclamations*—allow us to express ourselves in different ways. With them, we add variety and interest to our writing and speaking.

Statements give facts, ideas, descriptions, explanations, and many other kinds of information.

Statements declare facts, develop ideas, describe objects, explain past events, and discuss future plans. Most writing in business is accomplished with statements. They end with periods. The following sentences are examples of statements.

The enclosed brochure will acquaint you with our products.
Almost every kind of employment is covered by Social Security.
Toyota builds six truck models.
Last year the company paid a $3 dividend on common stock.
Atlas, Inc. employs 10,450 persons in ten job classifications.

Questions ask for information.

A sentence written as a *question* allows you to ask for information from another person. The direct question calls for an answer—the person to whom the question is directed is expected to reply. A question mark (?) is placed after the last word as the end punctuation. The following questions are asking for specific information.

Is Mr. Jones in his office?
What is the name of this product?
Do you make this model in other colors?
Have you a copy of the annual report?
If I learn to type, will I get the job?

An indirect question may be included in a statement.

Once in a while you may run across a sentence that appears to be a question. The message may say something like this: *Mr. Jones asked whether the meeting will be held next week.* What you have here is a statement of a fact. Someone is telling you what Mr. Jones asked. Mr. Jones asked a question previously and someone is reporting that fact. The sentence is a *statement* containing an *indirect question* and takes a period as the end punctuation. *Employees are wondering if Tuesday will be a paid holiday.*

Commands tell someone what to do.

In sentences expressed as *commands,* the person addressed is asked to perform a task. The end punctuation mark for the command is a period. Notice that the following commands use verbs of action, i.e., *take, finish,* and *send.*

Take this report to Mr. Jones.
Finish this tabulation by noon.
Please send me three boxes.

Usually the name of the person who is commanded to act is not given. The person addressed, however, is understood to be "you."

You Take this report . . .
You Finish . . .
You Please send . . .

Commands are direct and to the point. They may sound harsh and dictatorial, but they are quick ways to ask for action. The tone of the spoken voice softens most verbal commands. In writing, they do not appear to be dictating action. However, in some messages to certain persons, the writer may wish to rephrase the command as a more polite request.

Requests are courteous ways to ask that something be done.

Sentences written as *requests* are more courteous than commands. The communicator is not commanding someone to do something. However, the action requested is expected to take place. Notice that the following requests are more polite in tone even though the messages are direct and to the point.

May I borrow the report.
(I expect to be lent the report.)
Could we have your check by April 15.
(We expect to receive the check by the 15th.)
Will you please let us know your decision.
(We expect to be told the decision.)
Would you please send us a full explanation of the situation.
(We expect to receive a full explanation.)

If these requests had been written as questions, the writer would have given the reader the opportunity to answer "no." Also, if the requests had been written as commands, the writer might have antagonized the reader by making demands. What the writer expects and needs is affirmative action; therefore, the sentence style of a request is used. Requests are merely statements naming the action that the person receiving the message is to take. The polite request ends with a period just as statements and commands do.

Exclamations show strong feeling.

Sentences that convey feelings of strong emotion are called *exclamations*. The end punctuation mark for them is the exclamation point (!). They may express amazement, fear, hate, delight, relief, excitement, or some other emotion. In business these sentences are used in sales letters, brochures, advertising copy, employee bulletins, or company newspapers and magazines. Notice that the following exclamations are complete thoughts just as other sentences are.

Sales are up 23 percent!
Watch for an important announcement!
Order now!

Punctuation marks are placed after the last word in sentences.

Sentences end with one of three punctuation marks—period, question mark, or exclamation point.

1. Statements, commands, requests—all end with periods (.).
2. Questions end with question marks (?).
3. Exclamations end with exclamation points (!).

Turn to pages 290–292 for further explanation and other uses of these marks.

Quick review

Here are ten sentences to be identified. Indicate in the column whether the sentence is a *statement,* a *command,* a *request,* a *question,* or an *exclamation.* Also, place the correct *end punctuation* after the last word in each sentence.

1. May we have a reply to our letter of June 19 _____
2. Watch out for falling bricks _____
3. Place your signature on the bottom line _____
4. The economic indicators point to increased production in the 1980s _____

5. Why did you promote Mr. Clark   _____

6. Salespersons should contact at least twenty customers next month   _____

7. Will you please circulate a copy of this notice in your department   _____

8. Will John Taylor be able to attend the board meeting   _____

9. Figure out the commission on this sale   _____

10. The president asked why the matter has not been settled   _____

(Answers in reverse order: SCQRSQSCER)

Subjects and verbs are the major parts of the sentence.

The next important way to look at the sentence is to discover its parts. By knowing how the parts fit together, you can then construct your own sentences correctly. Every complete sentence has one or more *subjects* and one or more *verbs*. These two parts carry most of the message. When you are able to recognize them, you write and speak more clearly. The *subject* of the sentence may be a *word, phrase,* or *clause.* The subject names the person, place, or thing about which something is said. Subjects may be either simple (one) or compound (more than one).

Look for something that *does* or *is* something in order to find the subject.

To locate the subject, you look for something that does something or is something. The subject names who or what is performing the action or who or what is being acted upon. First, let us look at sentences that contain *simple subjects.* Notice that these simple subjects may be one word, one phrase, or one clause.

  One-word subject: *John* spoke.
  One-phrase subject: *Typing a rough draft* is necessary.
  One-clause subject: *That the metal can be cut* was proved.

In the one-word subject illustration, someone *did* something—*John* (the subject) *spoke.* In the one-phrase illustration, something *is* something—*Typing a rough draft* (the subject) *is* necessary.

A *compound subject* consists of two or more subjects, either as single words or as phrases and clauses. The compound subject is easily located if you look for the entire subject. Continue reading the words in the sentence until you find all that is performing the action or is receiving the action. The following sentences illustrate the use of two or more subjects.

  Words as the compound subject: *John, Jim,* and *Bob* spoke.

  Phrases as the compound subject: *Making corrections* and *typing a rough draft* are necessary.

  Clauses as the compound subject: *That the metal can be cut, that the cut is smooth,* and *that the drill is undamaged* were proved.

Look for all the subjects.

To find all the subjects in a sentence, it is necessary to read the entire part of the message that shows (1) who is speaking, or (2) who is spoken to, or (3) who is the person or thing spoken about. The rest of the sentence contains the verb.

To find the verb, look for the words that show action or state of being.

Verbs tell what the subject is doing or what is being done to the subject.

The second major part of the sentence concerns the *verb*. The *verb* of the sentence is the word or phrase that causes the subject to act or to express a state of being. It may be either simple or compound.

To locate the *verb,* you look for the words that tell you what the subject is doing, what the subject is, or what is being done to the subject. Verbs may indicate action taken by the subject or action received by the subject. In the sentence *The manager read the report.*, the manager performed the action of reading the report. The verb *read*, therefore, indicates the action taken by the *manager* (the subject). But in the sentence *The report was read by the manager.*, the verb *was read* points out that the subject *report* has been acted upon by the manager.

The *simple verb* may be one word or one verb phrase. Notice that all the sentences below contain simple verbs—*holds, should be typed, was puzzled.*

One-word verb: Mrs. Carter **holds** a responsible position in our organization.

Verb phrase: The report **should be typed** after lunch.
The clerk **was puzzled** about where to file the letter.

A *compound verb* consists of two or more verbs. Locating multiple verbs in a sentence is easy if one looks for the *complete verb*. Check to see how many things the subject is doing.

Simple subject/compound verb: *John **ran** and **jumped**.*
Compound subject/compound verb: *John and Jim **ran** and **jumped**.*
Simple subject/compound verb phrases: A *secretary **may handle*** telephone calls, **may make** appointments, **may take** dictation, and **may compose** routine letters.

Helping verbs are used in verb phrases.

Many verbs in the sentence are made up of two or more words. These words form the *verb phrase*. Often helping verbs, such as **could, should, would, shall, will, might, must, can,** and **may,** are used with other verbs. Helping verbs assist in expressing the thought more exactly, pointing out the time of an action or shading the meaning slightly.

The next sentences illustrate the use of the verb *count* either as a single word or as part of a verb phrase. Notice that the helping verb points out the time of an action or shades the meaning slightly. Helping verbs contribute more exact meaning to your sentences.

***Count* as a single word:**   He **counts** the inventory. (present)
He **counted** the inventory. (past)

***Count* with helping verbs:**   He **will count** the inventory. (future)

He *can count* the inventory.
  (ability)

He *may count* the inventory.
  (permission)

He *might have been counting*
the inventory.
  (time and shade of doubt)

He *should have been counting*
the inventory.
  (time and duty)

He *did count* the inventory.
  (emphasis)

To be, to have and *to do* are both main verbs and helping verbs.

The verbs *to be, to have,* and *to do* can be used both as main verbs and as helping verbs. The following outline of their forms and the examples of their use as main or helping verbs illustrate correct usage:

Verb	Its forms	
be	is, am, are, was were, being, been	**Main verb:** The office *was* large and noisy. **Helping verb:** He *was given* a promotion.
have	have, has, had	**Main verb:** I *have* several letters to type. **Helping verb:** I *have typed* several letters.
do	do, does, did	**Main verb:** We *do* our sorting at these tables. **Helping verb:** *Do come* to the meeting.

Quick review

Let's take a few minutes to see if you can quickly identify subjects and verbs. Underline the subject(s) once and the verb(s) twice in each of the following sentences.

1. Every company has an accounting department.
2. The office is the information center.
3. Most office costs are classified as overhead expenses.
4. The worker should have told his supervisor.
5. Correspondence and administrative secretaries handle many difficult tasks.
6. Mr. Jones, Mrs. Falker, and Ms. Peters spoke at the convention.
7. The mail clerk stapled, folded, and put the letters in envelopes before taking them to the post office.
8. The company manufactures and sells electronic components.
9. Mr. Jones did tell the supervisor and also wrote a grievance.
10. The nuts and bolts should be packed in plastic containers.

An extensive vocabulary is an asset in the business world.

In the business world, you will need a large vocabulary if you are to communicate your ideas clearly. Choosing the right words to convey an accurate message is important. Spelling the words correctly is equally important. Most sections in this book include vocabulary building and spelling reviews to help you add new words to your vocabulary, clarify the meaning of words, and spell troublesome ones. In Appendix 1 you will find a list of 500 words many people find difficult to spell. Master the spelling of these words and you will be well on your way to acquiring a useful business vocabulary.

Here is a hint for learning to spell correctly.

Develop the ability to *visualize* the correct form of a word. If you can see in your mind the *correct form* and the *order* of the letters in the word, you can spell it any time you wish. You are already able to visualize the correct spelling of a large number of words, and you can add more and more words to this number. Take time to *look* at a word. Note *all* the letters that are in it and the *order* in which they appear.

Some words contain silent letters.

Let's start with words that have *silent* letters. The English language has many such words. Look at the following list, see if the words are familiar to you, and pick out the silent letter in each one. (The silent letter has been italicized.)

ali*g*n	dou*b*t	*k*now	*p*neumatic
answer	g*u*ess	*k*nack	recei*p*t
autum*n*	ha*l*f	lis*t*en	We*d*nesday
de*b*t	hand*k*erchief	mor*t*gage	writing

If you know the correct spelling of all these words, your mind has recognized and remembered the silent letter or letters in each. Your mind can do the same with the new words you will be adding to your vocabulary this term. Remember: *Take time to see all the letters in each word you use.*

PART **1**

ASSIGNMENTS

Apply your knowledge of sentences

A. Sentences express complete thoughts in *statements, questions, commands, requests,* and *exclamations.* To indicate the end of sentences, periods, question marks, or exclamation points are placed after the last word. Read each of the following sentences and add the correct *end punctuation.* Also, indicate the type of sentence by writing in the right-hand column the appropriate term from the italicized list in the opening sentence of this paragraph. Use the term *incomplete* for sentence fragments.

1. A major oil field was discovered in Alaska   _____

2. We have several matters to discuss   _____

3. Examine the machine carefully before buying   _____

4. May we have your answer by Tuesday   _____

5. Word processing has eliminated much person-to-person dictation   _____

6. Our natural resources should be protected   _____

7. Will I get the job   _____

8. Trade with China is opening new opportunities for our company   _____

9. Send your check or a money order for the amount due by June 15   _____

10. Did you order the book from the publisher   _____

11. Please take a letter, Miss Jones   _____

12. Income tax forms should be filled out completely   _____

13. Buy stocks when the market begins to move up   _____

14. How much will it cost to process this film   _____

15. Hurrah, we won the contract   _____

16. The Dura Glass dealer listed in the Yellow Pages   _____

17. Are my letters back from the WP center   _____

18. The new product which I told you about   _____

19. Will you please see that this report reaches Mr. Jones   _____

20. Is our order being processed   _____

B.   Here are some more sentences to identify as you just did in Exercise A. Be sure to add the *end punctuation,* and write *incomplete* in the right-hand column for any sentence fragments.

1. Looking for a job   _____

2. Many people choose jobs that use their talents   _____

3. Do owners of shopping centers lease space   _____

4. Prepare a list of parts needed to finish the job   _____

5. Will you please send us a sample of your new soaps   _____

6. Don't expect Jones to apologize   _____

7. The person who enjoys his work is a fortunate person   _____

8. When you have finished reading the minutes, place them on my desk   _____

9. What was the question   _____

10. Watch out   _____

11. The Smithsonian displays objects made in early America   _____

12. May we please have your payment now for the entire amount   _____

13. Can you see Mr. Green tomorrow   _____

14. Where is the print shop   _____

15. A major oil field discovered in Alaska by Exxon   _____

16. Select an occupation in which you are interested   _____

17. Don't be late for the meeting because we must start on time   _____

18. Mr. Fraser said that the office would be closed on Friday   _____

19. The company that supplies the spare parts   _____

20. Many housing developments have been built in that area   _____

    C. Every sentence has either a simple or a compound subject and verb. In the following group of sentences, write the subject(s) and verb(s) in the columns at the right.

	Subject(s)	*Verb(s)*
Example: Did you list the duties of the bookkeeper?	*you*	*did list*
1. Everyone should take a vacation at least once a year.		
2. The employees leave for home at 4:30.		
3. Will you please send us a sample of your product.		
4. Select an oval picture for that wall.		
5. Most companies have their stock listed on a stock exchange.		
6. Students should investigate the many careers open to them.		
7. Mr. Jones asked whether you would prefer to hold the meeting in his office.		
8. What is the price of the computer?		
9. Every company needs to keep records.		
10. The supervisor should have been told that the parts are missing.		
11. The secretary was asked to write the letter.		
12. The white cards and plastic holders for the name tags have arrived.		
13. Reports and letters should be filed carefully.		
14. Most office costs are considered to be overhead expenses.		
15. The boxes and crates should be moved to the storeroom and should be stacked against the wall.		
16. Did Mr. Jones and Mr. Smith attend the conference?		
17. Find the broken typewriter and send it out to be repaired.		

18. Hurrah, we won the contract!   _____   _____
19. What are the dates and places for our next
    meetings?   _____   _____

20. Several men and women applied for that job.   _____   _____

D. The next group of sentences contain phrases and clauses as subjects. After you have identified the subject(s) and verb(s) in each sentence, write them in the columns to the right.

	Subject(s)	*Verb(s)*

Example: Making a speech before an audience
may be required in this job.

Making a speech   *may be required*

1. Using the telephone for personal calls is not
   permitted in this office.   _____   _____
2. Collecting the papers, coding them, and
   placing them in the files are some of your
   duties.   _____   _____
3. That new cabinets are needed soon was
   discussed at the meeting.   _____   _____
4. That Jim was disappointed could be seen from
   his reaction.   _____   _____
5. When should a dividend be declared is the
   question.   _____   _____
6. Basing your report on facts will result in
   meaningful conclusions.   _____   _____
7. Just between you and me is an expression
   often used in conversation.   _____   _____

8. Typing long reports can be a tedious job.   _____   _____
9. Being able to use the calculator is necessary in
   our department.   _____   _____
10. Finding an interesting career may take several
    years.   _____   _____

E. Now that you are learning to see all the letters in a word, you should be able to pick out misspelled words in a sentence. Look carefully at the words in the following sentences, especially those that have silent letters. If you find a misspelled word, spell it correctly in the space provided.

1. I doubt that Max can aline these pages evenly.   _____

2. My hankerchief was lost at Disneyland.   _____

3. Our company uses neumatic tools for that job.   _____

4. Please listen to the talk on morgages.   _____

5. Did you order haff a pint?   _____

Name _____

Date _____

━━━━━━━━━━━━━━━━━ **PRACTICE WRITING** ━━━━━━━━━━━━━━━━━

An employee who writes well is an asset in any company. These practice writing assignments will give you an opportunity to develop skill that will be useful in a variety of jobs. The more often you write, the easier it is to express your ideas. For this assignment, you are to compose original sentences that are examples of the types discussed in Part 1. Write about business either from your own experience or from information studied in other classes. By using business terms, you will enlarge your business vocabulary.

1. Statement _____

_____

_____

2. Question _____

_____

_____

3. Indirect question _____

_____

_____

4. Command _____

_____

_____

5. Request _____

_____

_____

6. Exclamation _____

_____

_____

PART 2

Sentences have structure

In Part 1, a sentence was described as a complete thought expressed by a group of words. Several types of sentences were illustrated; and in addition, fragments were identified. The two major parts of the sentence were also identified as the subject and the verb. These sentence parts carry the message and tell who does what or what is done by something or someone.

Clauses and phrases are used to form sentences.

In this part, other sentence elements will be examined separately so that you may learn to form more effective sentences. In any discussion of sentence structure, the *clause* and the *phrase* receive the most attention. It is impossible to form a sentence that does not contain a clause, and the addition of phrases to the sentence permits us to add descriptive information to make our messages more informative and interesting. Let us begin with clauses.

SENTENCES ARE CLASSIFIED BY THEIR CLAUSES

Sentences are classified by the number and kinds of clauses they contain. Thus, they may be called *simple, compound, complex,* or *compound/complex* according to the number and kinds of clauses in them. There are two types of clauses: dependent and independent. Being able to recognize them will help you determine the sentence classification. You will also be able to (1) write and speak with variety, (2) emphasize important ideas, and (3) punctuate for clarity.

Simple sentences have one independent clause.

The *simple sentence* expresses a single thought in one *independent clause*. The thought may be given in the form of a statement, question, command, request, or exclamation.

Independent clause

Statement:	The automobile raced away.
Question:	When can you deliver the merchandise?
Command:	Check the figures on this order.
Request:	May I call you for an appointment.
Exclamation:	We won the contract!

17

You can see that each of the examples contains one complete thought, but how do you know that the thought is expressed in one independent clause? Let us look at the structure of clauses so that you can learn to recognize when a clause is independent.

All clauses have a subject *and* a verb.

A *clause* is defined as *a word group containing both a subject and a verb.* The two types of clauses are *independent* and *dependent*.

Independent clauses can stand alone as sentences.

The *independent clause* is a principal or main clause. Its message is complete and clear without the aid of another clause. A *simple sentence* is composed of one *independent clause.*

Independent clauses
The *receptionist* **greeted** us.
We **are working** late tonight.
Your *account* **should be paid** by the end of the month.

Dependent clauses must be joined to independent clauses to form sentences.

The *dependent clause* is a subordinate or minor clause and **cannot** stand alone as a sentence. Its message must be attached to the message in an independent clause. In other words, the dependent clause adds information to the main message. Notice the information added by the dependent clause in the following sentence.

Dependent clause   **Independent clause**
When *we* **entered** the office, the *receptionist* **greeted** us.

When we entered the office is not a complete thought. Upon hearing or reading this clause, you begin to wonder what happened when they entered the office. This *when* clause calls for the addition of more information to make the message clear and complete. It is, therefore, called a dependent clause. These clauses are always introduced by small words, called *subordinators,* such as one of the following:

after	before	so that	until	who
although	if	that	when	whoever
as	in order that	though	where	whom
because	since	unless	while	whomever

Some dependent clauses introduce the main clause; others are placed within the main clause; and some come at the end of the main or independent clause.

Introductory dependent clause
If you need the current figures, please see the accountant.

Interrupting dependent clause
The Magnun XL100, *which is a foreign-made car,* has a high-powered engine.

Concluding dependent clause
The report will be circulated to all supervisors, *although some of them are not involved in production.*

As we continue the study of sentence structure, you will notice that simple and compound sentences are made up of independent clauses. Complex and compound/complex sentences are made up of both independent and dependent clauses.

Compound sentences have two independent clauses.

Compound sentences use conjunctions with commas or semicolons.

The *compound* sentence contains two closely related ideas in two independent clauses. In other words, two simple sentences are joined to form the compound sentence. The two independent clauses of the compound sentence may be separated by (1) a comma and a conjunction, (2) a semicolon, or (3) a semicolon with a conjunction. The most frequently used conjunctions are *and, but, or, nor, for,* and *yet.*

In the compound sentences below, observe that the independent clauses are joined in three different ways—comma plus *and,* semicolon alone, and semicolon plus *and.*

Sometimes the semicolon is used alone in a compound sentence.

The machines arrived today, **and** we plan to install them next week.

The machines arrived today; we plan to install them next week.

The drill press, the lathe, and the buffer arrived today; **and** we plan to install them next week.

In the first example, the comma is used with the conjunction *and* to show the reader that the writer has joined two closely related independent ideas. If you choose to omit the conjunction as the second example illustrates, you must use a semicolon between the two independent clauses. In the third example, a series of three items in the first independent clause are separated by commas. Because of this inside punctuation and to tell the reader where the second independent clause begins, a semicolon is used with the conjunction.

Commas and semicolons help make the message clearer.

These uses of the comma and the semicolon show the reader where the second main idea begins. You are alerting your reader to the fact that you attach equal importance to each idea you have joined together to form the compound sentence.

Quick review

Let's take a few minutes to see if you can recognize the difference between simple and compound sentences. At the end of each of the following sentences, write *S* for simple sentence or *C* for compound.

1. All office files are kept in a central area. _____

2. Does Mr. Wiggens want a complete report? _____

3. When will you take the package to the post office, and when do you expect to return? _____

4. Take this letter to Mrs. Davis, and ask her to make a copy of it. _____

5. The employees' picnic will be held in Central Park. _____

6. Our new product sells for $5, or $60 a dozen. _____

7. Vacations may be taken between May and October, and employees must fill out a request form a month in advance. _____

8. Complaints from customers should be sent to Mrs. Cooper, and she should answer them by letter. _____

9. Income taxes are levied against wages and salaries by the federal and state governments. _____

10. Please give me your estimate now, and send me a written confirmation by next week. _____

(Answers in reverse order: CSCCSSCCSS)

Complex sentences contain both independent and dependent clauses.

The *complex* sentence has one independent clause and one or more dependent clauses. The important idea in the message is expressed in the independent clause. This idea is then enlarged or modified by the dependent clause. In the following sentence, the minor idea in the dependent clause comes first. Observe that a comma follows this introductory clause in order to separate it from the independent clause that contains the important part of the message.

Dependent clause	**Independent clause**

If you desire additional information, please sign and return the
enclosed card.

The next illustration has two dependent clauses and one independent clause. One dependent clause introduces the message, and the other is placed in natural order at the end of the sentence. A comma comes after the introductory clause, but one is usually not needed before a dependent clause at the end of a sentence.

Dependent clause	**Independent**

If you desire additional information, please sign and return the

Clause	**Dependent clause**

enclosed card *before the free trial offer expires.*

As you can see from these examples of complex sentences, the message becomes more complicated as descriptive information is added to the main clause.

Quick review

A short exercise at this point in our discussion will show you how easy it is to recognize simple, compound, and complex sentences. First, determine the structure of each sentence below by writing *S*, *C*, or *Cx* (for complex) after each one. Then **underline** the independent clause or clauses.

1. If appearance and personality are important, can a good impression be ruined by careless speech? _____

2. Our company needs administrators who can write clearly and concisely. _____

3. As the cost of living rises, labor unions claim that wages should increase in the same proportion. _____

4. Please order more stationery, and send some to our sales office in Sacramento. _____

5. An employee may deduct travel expenses when a personal car is used to drive between one plant and another. _____

6. Does that company stress research and development? _____

7. Supervisors should have frequent talks with a trainee during the course of job training, and they should compliment the trainee for good work. _____

8. When counseling is a part of the follow-up of a new employee, the personnel department usually handles the interview. _____

9. What is the definition of a compound sentence? _____

10. As we stated in previous correspondence, these visitors wish to observe your manufacturing process. _____

(Answers in reverse order: CxSCxCSCxCCxCxCx)

Compound-complex sentences contain two or more independent clauses and one or more dependent clauses.

The *compound-complex* sentence is composed of two or more independent clauses and one or more dependent clauses. This type of sentence is mainly a compound sentence. However, at least one of the parts is a complex unit having both a dependent and an independent clause. A compound-complex sentence tends to be a long message. These sentences are not written too often in business because most communicators try to keep their sentences short. Note the structure of the following compound-complex sentence.

Independent clause + Independent clause with dependent clause

The reprographics department can make clear copies, but you should consult a printer *when you want a professional printing job.*

You may join the three basic sentence structures—simple, compound, complex—in a variety of ways. As you can see in the preceding example, a simple sentence is joined to a complex sentence to make a compound-complex sentence. Now let us join two complex sentences to make another compound-complex sentence.

Independent/dependent + Independent/dependent

Employees are expected to park in the space *that has been assigned them,* and they are reminded *that there is a penalty for using someone else's space.*

Quick review

Here are three compound-complex sentences. Underline the independent clauses with a straight line, and draw a wavy line under the dependent clauses.

1. When you write, remember to include all the necessary information; for if an important detail is omitted, the communication is not clear.

2. You would have little confidence in a lawyer who did not know the meaning of a legal term, and your employer will have little confidence in you if you do not know the vocabulary of business.

3. As companies become larger, workers are separated from management; consequently, they find it difficult to understand that the job must be done a certain way.

Punctuation within sentences is often necessary.

Punctuation marks are used to separate sentence parts when necessary to aid understanding. The trend in business is to use as few marks of punctuation as possible. Punctuation usage is explained and illustrated in detail in Section 6; turn to pages 297–302 and 311, if you need to check proper usage. Some specific uses of the comma and the semicolon in simple, compound, and complex sentences are explained here.

Commas help to make the message clear.

Commas (,) are used to establish the correct association of ideas within the sentence. They help the receiver of the message to understand it.

In compound sentences.   Use a comma to separate two independent clauses in a compound sentence when the clauses are joined by a conjunction (*and, but, for, nor, or, yet*).

Send a check or money order with this card, **and** we will pay all postage and handling charges.

If the clauses are short and the meaning clear, the comma may be omitted, as illustrated below.

Look at the recommendation and give me an opinion.

In complex sentences.   Commas are used in three situations in complex sentences to separate certain dependent clauses from the independent clause.

Introductory dependent clauses.   All dependent clauses that come first in the sentence are followed by a comma.

If you have all the figures, please finish the report.

Interrupting dependent clauses.   Only *nonrestrictive* dependent clauses that interrupt the independent clause are surrounded by commas.

Mr. Jones, *who works at ABC Corporation,* will speak.

A nonrestrictive clause simply adds additional information to the sentence, but it is not needed to complete the thought. It could be left out of the sentence, and the message would be clear. The clause in the following sentence cannot be left out because it restricts the word *typists*.

Typists *who learn to use the word processor* will be promoted.

Only those typists who go to school to learn to use word processing machines will be promoted. The other typists will not be promoted. You will study restrictive and nonrestrictive elements in Section 2.

Concluding dependent clauses.   Most dependent clauses that come after the independent clause and thus end the sentence do not need commas. Occasionally a nonrestrictive clause may end the sentence, and it is then necessary to use the comma before it. The following sentence contains a nonrestrictive clause at the end.

The manager hired three workers for the night shift, *even though several machines are shut down for servicing.*

Semicolons add clarity to a sentence.

Semicolons (;) indicate a stronger degree of separation than commas do. They can be used in place of conjunctions, and they can be used in place of commas being used with conjunctions when the sentence already contains other commas.

In compound sentences without conjunctions. Use a semicolon to separate independent clauses closely related in thought and *not* connected by a conjunction.

> The invoice arrived yesterday in the afternoon mail; our check was mailed this morning.

> Mr. Porter has been asked to make the audit; he plans to start next Monday.

In compound and complex sentences with conjunctions and internal punctuation. Use a semicolon before the conjunction in compound and complex sentences to separate the independent clauses when commas are used internally in either clause. Notice in the following examples that semicolons are necessary because commas are used with both independent clauses. The first example has a series separated by commas in one clause and an introductory dependent clause in the other.

> These changes will reduce staff, overhead costs, and inventory; and although the savings will be minor at first, they should amount to a substantial sum in a few years.

In the second example, commas are used to separate four items in a series in one independent clause; and they are also needed to set off an interrupting word in the other independent clause. A semicolon, therefore, is used with the conjunction.

> Our department ordered pencils, pens, envelopes, and stationery; but the supply clerk forgot, unfortunately, to place the order.

Why not take time now to study the ways to use commas and semicolons to the best advantage in your writing. When you can apply easily the usages just discussed, you will be well on your way to becoming an effective communicator.

SENTENCES HAVE PHRASES IN THEIR STRUCTURE

Phrases are groups of closely related words. They do not contain subjects. They cannot stand alone but must always be part of a sentence. You are familiar with verb phrases that consist of the verb and its helpers— *could have been, will be going, do take.* Other types of phrases are used as nouns, adjectives, or adverbs. They are introduced by prepositions, verbal nouns, infinitives, and participles.

Phrases are always part of a sentence.

It is important that you are able to distinguish a phrase from a clause because phrases can be used in several ways within the sentence. For instance, some can be used as subjects of clauses. You can see that phrases are very special word groups. You will find it easy to recognize them after you study the following descriptions of the four types.

---

24 THE SENTENCE

Some phrases are introduced by prepositions.

The *prepositional phrase* is composed of the preposition with its noun or pronoun object and any modifiers. Some common prepositions are *in, from, for, with, by, like, to, between,* and *at.* (See Section 5, pages 277–281, for a complete list.) To find the object of the phrase, ask *what?* after the preposition. The phrases listed here will help you recognize the parts of a prepositional phrase.

Preposition	Modifiers of its object	Its object
in	the front (what?)	office
from	the old (what?)	records
behind	the green (what?)	cabinet

The dictating machine was left *in the front office.*
Please take the names *from the old records.*
The picture fell *behind the green cabinet.*

Occasionally, a prepositional phrase may be used as the subject of a sentence.

Beyond the blue is a term used to refer to a distant place.

For a complete discussion of prepositions and prepositional phrases see Section 5, Part 4, and Appendix 3.

Phrases may be introduced by a verbal noun—the *ing* form of the verb.

The *verbal noun* (also called *gerund*) *phrase* is often used as the subject of sentences. Such phrases allow you to write in an interesting style. A verbal noun is the *ing* form of the verb that becomes a noun that names an action.

Verb	Verbal noun	Verb	Verbal noun
type	typing	whisper	whispering
talk	talking	help	helping
check	checking	write	writing

Verbal noun phrase can be used as subjects.

A verbal noun phrase consists of the *ing* form of the verb, its object, and modifiers of its object. Verbal nouns and verbal noun phrases can be used in the same way nouns are used. In this discussion you will see how these phrases are used as subjects of sentences. Later, in Section 3, you will study other uses of verbal nouns. Let us see how the following verbal noun phrases—*finding the office building, hanging the picture, polishing the car*—may be used as subjects.

Finding the office building **took** longer than we expected.
Hanging the picture **should be** an easy task.
Polishing the car **takes** several hours.

Like prepositional phrases, verbal noun phrases have an object. To find the object, ask *what?* after the verbal noun. For instance, the object in the phrase *finding the office building* is *building. The* and *office* are adjective modifiers that describe *building.*

Verbal noun	Modifiers	Object
finding	the, office	building
hanging	the	picture
polishing	the	car

Infinitives and infinitive phrases can be subjects of sentences.

Infinitives and *infinitive phrases* may also be used as subjects to add variety to your writing. To identify the infinitive, look for the word *to* in front of the verb, for instance, *to run, to talk, to sit, to tabulate*. An infinitive phrase is formed by the infinitive, its object or complement, and modifiers. Because infinitives and infinitive phrases may function as nouns, they can serve as subjects of sentences.

An infinitive as a subject
To learn is a challenge.

An infinitive phrase as a subject
To learn programming is a challenge.

Additional uses of infinitive phrases will be presented in detail in Section 3, Part 6.

Participial phrases are adjective modifiers.

Participial phrases are used as *adjectives* to modify or qualify nouns and pronouns. They are phrases that you should learn to recognize in order to distinguish them from verbal noun phrases. Participial phrases are *never* used as subjects of sentences. Either the present or the past participle form of the verb is the first word of the phrase.

The *present participle* is the verb with an *ing* ending. As you have just learned, the verbal noun ends with *ing* also; thus, it is necessary to determine how the *ing* word is used in the sentence before you can identify it as either a participle or a verbal noun. Some people call these participial phrases *verbal adjectives* in order to remember their use in the sentence. In the following illustrations, notice that the participial phrases are used as adjectives to describe or limit the subject of each sentence.

The young man *polishing the car* attends college.

The correspondence secretary *using the word processor* will store the report in the computer for later recall.

Mr. Yates, *dictating rapidly,* stumbled over several words.

The *past participial phrase,* like the present participial phrase, modifies nouns and pronouns. Most *past participles* end in *ed* (hunted), *d* (sold), *en* (chosen), *n* (begun), and *t* (felt). Both past and present participial phrases are used in the following illustrations.

Past participial phrase modifying *desk*: The new desk, *built in Grand Rapids,* arrived yesterday.

Past participial phrase limiting *plan*: The architectural plan *designed by Ted Andrews* will be accepted.

Present participial phrase modifying *architect*: The architect, *having completed the plan,* started on a new project.

Present participial phrase limiting *typist*: The typist *making the fewest errors* will receive a promotion.

All the participial phrases above are used as adjectives, but you will notice that two are enclosed in commas and two are not. The two phrases without commas are *restrictive* because they not only modify the words but also limit them. For instance, in the last illustration, the only person to receive the promotion is the *typist making the fewest errors.* None of the other typists will receive a promotion. When you *limit* a word, the participial phrase that modifies it is *essential* to the message; and no commas are placed around it. If, however, you are merely adding information that is descriptive and *not essential* to the meaning, you must enclose the *nonrestrictive* phrase in commas. In the *architect* illustration, note that the phrase *having completed the plan* is a bit of extra information. The important message is that the architect started on a new project.

Nonrestrictive phrases are set off by commas.

ACCURATE WORD CHOICE DEPENDS ON A LARGE VOCABULARY

One way in which the extent of your education will be judged is by the size and accuracy of your vocabulary. To increase the size of your vocabulary, continue to add new words in everyday speaking and writing. To pinpoint accurate use of words, be sure of definitions. The two goals to keep in mind are (1) increase your vocabulary and (2) refine the meaning of words you use.

Increase your ability to use words accurately.

Here are some words that are often confused and used inaccurately. Review their definitions, and practice using them correctly in your conversation and writing. The hints and illustrations that accompany these words will show you how to use them more accurately.

above, the above   Avoid these vague expressions. Use more specific words.
the preceding idea
the paragraph written above
the deductions listed previously

advise   Use only when giving advice. Better to use *say, tell, inform.*

affect, effect   *Affect,* always a verb, means to influence, to produce a change.
The change in policy **will affect** our marketing procedures.
The new information **affected** his decision.
Effect, the noun, means result or outcome.
The **effect** of that advertisement was unpredictable.
Effect, the verb, means to bring about, to accomplish.
The committee **effected** a change in the plans.

all (of)   Usually *all* is used by itself as an adjective to modify a noun. In these instances, the preposition *of* is not needed.
Mr. Jones talked to **all** the sales personnel.
All of may be used with plural pronouns: *all of them* and *all of us.*
Send it to **all of them.**
All of us are needed in the payroll office.

all right   *All right* is always written as two words.
He said that it is **all right** to wait until tomorrow.

already, all ready *Already,* an adverb, refers to an event that took place before some particular time.

> The package had **already** been mailed by the time the letter arrived.

All ready, an adjective phrase, means completely ready or prepared.

> The supervisors are **all ready** to discuss the union agreement.

amount, number *Amount* refers to things that can be weighed or are bulky.

> We need a large **amount** of steel.

Number refers to things that can be counted.

> The **number** of letters to be mailed is in the 100s.

> A **number** of documents are missing from the safe.

(*Number* as a collective noun may be either singular or plural. Notice that *the number* is singular and takes the singular verb, whereas *a number* is plural and takes the plural verb.)

balance Use *balance* only when referring to a bank balance or a bookkeeping balance. Use *rest* or *remainder* when referring to someone or something left over.

> The **balance** in the account is $1,542.76.

> The **rest** of the correspondence will be taken care of tomorrow.

because *Because* means *for the cause that* or *for the reason that.* It is incorrect to use ". . . reason is because . . ."

> **Illogical:** The *reason* I took this course *is because* I wanted to learn about economics.

> **Better:** The reason I took this course is **that** I wanted to learn about economics.

> **Or:** *I took this course because* I wanted to learn about economics.

between, among *Between* is used when referring to two persons or things.

> Please choose **between** Miss Jones and Miss Davis for the promotion.

> The district should be divided equitably **between** the two women.

Among is used when referring to three or more persons or things.

> The bonus will be divided **among** the employees.

can, may Both words may be used to indicate *possibility.*

> The security analyst **can** attend the seminar.
> (The person is physically able to.)

> The security analyst **may** attend the seminar.
> (The person may or may not; it is possible that the person will attend.)

Only *may* is used to denote *permission.*

> Security analysts ***may*** attend the seminar.
> (They are permitted to attend.)

**canvas,
canvass**

Canvas is a heavy, strong cloth of various grades and is used for sails, paintings, or embroidery.

> Before you start to paint, be sure to stretch the *canvas.*

Canvass as a verb means to examine or solicit information, votes, orders. As a noun, *canvass* means an examination or detailed inquiry.

> They ***canvassed*** the neighborhood to find out how many people buy orange juice.
>
> A ***canvass*** was made of the registered voters in Marin County.

**capacity,
ability**

Capacity is the innate power of a person *to receive ideas or knowledge.* It may also mean *the power to produce a certain quantity in a given period.*

> That person has the ***capacity*** to learn shorthand.
>
> The factory has the ***capacity*** of 1,000 pieces a day.

Ability is the power of a person or thing to do something.

> She has the ***ability*** to take dictation at 120 words per minute.

**capital,
capitol**

Capital, the noun, names the place in which the seat of government is located. It is also used when talking about financial resources.

> The ***capital*** of Texas is Austin.
>
> We will need additional ***capital*** to finance the expansion.

Capital, the adjective, means principal, main, outstanding.

> That is a ***capital*** idea!

Capitol refers to the building in which the U.S. Congress or a state legislature meets.

> The Assembly allocated the funds to paint the ***capitol.***

**Some words are
pronounced the
same but spelled
differently.**

Be sure to take time to go over these words again and *visualize* their correct form. Note the *order* of the letters in each word so that you will be able to spell it correctly. You will notice that some pairs of words are pronounced alike but are spelled differently.

2

Apply your knowledge of sentence structure

A. You have just learned that your ability to classify sentences as *simple, compound, complex,* or *compound-complex* will help you write better sentences and punctuate them correctly. Read the following sentences, and classify them as to type in the column at the right.

Example: The office will be closed Friday because it is a national holiday.   *complex*

1. The crates will be shipped next week.   _____

2. Our new product is being designed by a well-known artist.   _____

3. Keep the doors closed.   _____

4. When will our invoice be processed?   _____

5. Please order more stationery, but tell the supplier that we do not want delivery until next month.   _____

6. The sales report, a copy of the president's speech, and the most recent profit and loss statement will be handed out at the board meeting.   _____

7. A credit card allows you to charge purchases, but you must pay the account in full at the end of the month.   _____

8. Send this report to John Jones.   _____

9. The records manager is an executive who knows about the company's operations.   _____

10. Many private companies have destroyed old file records.   _____

11. Recently, the federal government saved $6 million by destroying material in 1,600,000 file cabinets.   _____

12. Please put a copy of the press release in the mail.   _____

13. Please check all the pages, and make any necessary changes.   _____

14. When you return the material, send back only the pages on which there are corrections.   _____
15. Federal, state, and local governments ask for documents to support information on tax statements.   _____

16. Several tasks have been designed to train workers on the new machine.   _____

17. After you have completed the report, present it to the operations manager.   _____
18. To prepare for your next assignment, start immediately to review the programming manual.   _____

19. Try to find at least one hundred pieces of the metal.   _____
20. While it is not mandatory, it would be wise to talk to your supervisor first; and then you can take the matter up with the personnel department.   _____

B. You have probably found it easy to tell the difference between *clauses* and *phrases* after studying the text. Just to make sure, however, that you have the difference between the two clearly in mind, define *clause* and *phrase* on the lines below. Turn to their definitions in the text if you need to review.

A clause is _____

_____

A phrase is _____

_____

Now, for the clauses and phrases listed below, write **C** for *clause* or **P** for *phrase* in the first column. In the second column, indicate the type of clause—*independent* or *dependent* OR the type of phrase—*verb, prepositional, verbal noun, past participial,* or *infinitive.*

		Kind	*Type*
1.	begun last year	_____	_____
2.	at the door	_____	_____
3.	he left the company	_____	_____
4.	taking a letter	_____	_____
5.	manufactured by Lockheed	_____	_____
6.	after the meeting	_____	_____
7.	when you see him	_____	_____
8.	whether you like it or not	_____	_____
9.	between you and me	_____	_____

10. as soon as you know   _____   _____

11. riding on the freeways   _____   _____

12. to start tomorrow   _____   _____

13. must have been written   _____   _____

14. to the files   _____   _____

15. depending on the advice of counsel   _____   _____

16. to explain our delay   _____   _____

17. when can you start work   _____   _____

18. from him   _____   _____

19. with her experience   _____   _____

20. are asking   _____   _____

   C. To give you more practice in identifying clauses and phrases, the following sentences have been composed. Draw a straight line under each clause and a wavy line under each phrase. You will have identified nine clauses and eight phrases, if you locate all of them.

Example: The application for employment should be filled in, and the applicant should be asked to sign it.

1. Mary Stephens, who is a talented architect, spoke at the meeting.
2. The machine parts ordered by the supervisor arrived Saturday when the plant was closed.
3. If the weather is warm and sunny, the company picnic will be held in Slope Park.
4. Take good care of your tools.
5. Sales are 20 percent higher this month; but according to the sales manager, our backlog of orders is the lowest since 1972.

   D. It is important to be able to recognize *dependent clauses* because they often call for the use of commas and semicolons. All the sentences in this exercise contain dependent clauses, which you are to underline with a wavy line. While you are picking them out, be sure to notice the commas and semi-colons that have been used. Try to recall why they have been placed in the particular spots you find them. If you cannot recall why a particular comma or semicolon has been used, turn back to pages 22–23 to refresh your memory.

1. When you interview an applicant for a job, you should describe the job in detail so that the applicant knows all the requirements.
2. The company treasurer, who is James Gordon, left the merchandising field to work for us.
3. If you have a complaint, please see the adjustment department because it handles all exchanges.
4. Before you make a decision, you should talk to a counselor; another position may be open soon that you are qualified to fill.
5. The car that was repaired yesterday should be driven before it is released to the owner.

E. Add commas and semicolons to these sentences where needed to make the message clear. Commas and semicolons help you do the following.

1. Separate independent clauses and show that the ideas in each one are equally important.
2. Separate introductory dependent clauses from the main clause.
3. Set off nonrestrictive clauses and phrases that merely add information to the message in the main clause.

Select the reason for adding the comma or the semicolon from the above list, and place its number in the right-hand column. Leave the column blank if no punctuation is needed.

Example: Not only should a good investment be safe but it should also offer a satisfactory rate of return.   _1_

1. Is John Smith who is the owner of the building expected to pay the premium? _____

2. The newspaper published yesterday carried the story of the merger. _____

3. Because the cover should be attractive ask the art department to design it. _____
4. Frank Tucker designed the form for the survey but he forgot to include space for sales figures. _____
5. XYZ Corp. has agreed to sell Hoops, Inc. the manufacturing company that it has owned for ten years to Manufacturers, Ltd. _____
6. News publishing is one of the most profitable industries and its journalists earn high salaries. _____
7. When Mr. Jones, Harold Opel, and Clancy Smith left for the convention their offices were cleaned. _____
8. The desks, cabinets, and chairs arrived last week and they were immediately placed in the proper offices. _____
9. The annual report showed a slight drop in sales the profit on sales, however, was larger than last year. _____
10. The changes in procedures should be explained to managers, supervisors, and workers for we want things in the company to run smoothly. _____
11. The stock of Buckeye, Inc. is listed on the New York Stock Exchange and any broker in our city can buy and sell it for you. _____
12. Our common stock and preferred stock listed on the Pacific Stock Exchange are selling at 48½ for the common and 102 for the preferred. _____
13. Our new products which are described in the enclosed leaflet will be in the department stores next month. _____

14. If you need additional information just write Mr. Jones in New York. _____
15. Take a look at this letter and let me know whether you find the message clear and concise. _____

16. What is the message you wish to tell the president before he leaves? _____
17. Air fares are as low or lower than other means of transportation and flying reduces overseas traveling time from days, even weeks, to hours. _____
18. The sales manager who attended Michigan State University has designed a new sales campaign. _____

19. The vertical roaster is the newest way to cook chicken it costs only $11.95. _____

20.   After you have changed the ribbon on the typewriter please clean the machine and then take it to the shipping department where it will be crated and sent to our Phoenix office.   _____

   F.   It is important in today's business world that words are used correctly. Read the sentences in this exercise, and choose the word that accurately conveys the meaning. Draw a line through the incorrect word.

1.   The (number, amount) of accounts that our firm processes is staggering.
2.   The (balance, remainder) of your grade will be determined by the final examination.
3.   Will the new law (effect, affect) our firm's plan to merge with ACE, Inc.?
4.   I discussed the new project with (all, all of) the engineers.
5.   The reason we received the account is (because, that) our firm is recognized as a leader in industry.
6.   The secretary asked, "(Can, May) I take a coffee break now?"
7.   It is (alright, all right) for you to hire a night watchman for the warehouse.
8.   Can you order by Monday a large (amount, number) of cable for the new installation?
9.   Our (capitol, capital) assets are increasing slowly.
10.   It is (already, all ready) too late to make a change in the product.
11.   (Between, Among) you and me there is agreement.
12.   Customers can make their selection (between, among) the 20-inch, 18-inch, or 12-inch televisions.
13.   The (capital, capitol) building in Washington can be seen for miles.
14.   Please select a candidate who has the (ability, capacity) to make interesting speeches.
15.   The new printing machines have the (ability, capacity) to turn out 500 newspapers a day.
16.   The maintenance crew will put (canvas, canvass) over the boxes stored outside.
17.   Please (advise, tell) the others that we will leave in ten minutes.
18.   The (affect, effect) of the government's decision will be a decrease in the rate of inflation.
19.   If you wish to order, select the item from the (above, list in the second paragraph).
20.   Mr. Jones said that he needed (all, all of) us to work on Saturday.

Name _____

Date _____

—————————— **PRACTICE WRITING** ——————————

You have just learned to recognize sentences by their structure. Now you will have a chance to compose your own sentences in the structures you studied: simple, compound, complex, and compound-complex.

1. Simple sentence _____

_____

_____

_____

2. Compound sentence _____

_____

_____

_____

_____

3. Complex sentence _____

_____

_____

_____

_____

4. Compound-complex sentence _____

_____

_____

_____

_____

Sentences have patterns

You have seen in our study of the sentence so far that a variety of patterns are used to string words together. The main goal in selecting a particular pattern is to communicate a clear message. For clarity, words should be placed in correct order. Each sentence is built upon a framework that is recognized and understood by most people: the actor followed by the action. Have you noticed that the subject or actor comes first in the majority of sentences? The position of the subject first and the verb or action second is one of the basic structures of the English language. This arrangement of the major parts of the sentence is called the normal word order. Who does what and who is what are the clear messages of sentences.

There are three basic sentence patterns.

Most sentences you come across fall into one of three patterns. Learn to recognize these patterns and to use them to write interesting, factual, and informative messages.

Pattern I sentences contain a subject and an intransitive verb.

Pattern I. The first sentence pattern is the easiest. It has two parts: the *subject* followed by an *intransitive verb*. An intransitive verb signifies a complete, finished action; or it links the subject to an adverb or noun modifier. In this type of sentence, the subject may act all by itself; and the intransitive verb shows completed action.

Subject	Intransitive verb
Susan	laughed.
The clock	stopped.
The door	closed.

Many intransitive verbs, like the ones above, show action; but no other words are needed for a clear message because the action is already accomplished.

The intransitive verb may have modifiers.

In other sentences, the intransitive verb may link the subject to modifiers, such as adverbs and adverbial phrases or clauses; but it never requires an object to complete the message. Observe in these sentences that the modifiers could be omitted and the thought would still be complete and clear.

35

Subject	Intransitive verb	Adverbial modifiers
Susan	laughed	merrily.
The clock	stopped	at 3:10 p.m.
The door	closed	when he touched it.

The intransitive verb may also be followed by a noun modifier. The state of being verb *to be* and many other verbs when used intransitively are often modified by nouns that tell *when* or *where* something happened.

Subject	Intransitive verb	Noun modifier
He	is	home.
The president	returned	Tuesday.
John	worked	last night.

Pattern II sentences contain a subject, a transitive verb, and an object.

Pattern II.   The second sentence pattern has three parts: the *subject,* the *transitive verb,* and the *object.* In these sentences, the action is transferred from the subject to the person or thing acted upon. In the examples that follow, the message would be incomplete unless the action of the verb is explained in more detail.

Subject	Transitive verb	Object
He	said	nothing.
Mr. Jones	held	a meeting.
The company	will purchase	the machines.
The employees	voted	to strike.

Transitive verbs always have objects.

A transitive verb requires a word or words to complete the meaning or to receive the action. These words that complete the meaning are called *objects.* To find the object, ask *whom?* or *what?* after the verb. The transitive verb forms a pathway along which the action moves from the subject to the object.

Many verbs can be either transitive or intransitive. The sentence *The employees voted.* expresses a complete thought without an object, and the verb *voted* in this instance is intransitive. In the sentence *The employees voted to strike.,* however, the verb *voted* is transitive because the object *to strike* (an infinitive) receives the action and answers the question *what?.* Thus, the verb *vote* may be intransitive or transitive, depending on its use in the sentence. Your dictionary will tell you whether a verb is transitive or intransitive or both. If it may be both, the difference in meaning for each usage will be explained.

The next examples illustrate the use of the questions *whom?* or *what?* to locate the object of the transitive verb.

Subject	Transitive verb	Object
The supervisor	complimented (*whom?*)	Nancy.
The office manager	bought (*what?*)	a typewriter.
Mrs. Schmidt	hired (*whom?*)	another correspondence secretary.
The fan	was blowing (*what?*)	the papers off my desk.

Sentences with objects may also have indirect objects.

Two important variations occur in Pattern II sentences. In one variation, the object of the verb is transferred by the subject to someone else, called the *indirect object.* You will see how indirect objects are used in the following illustrations.

Subject	Transitive verb	Indirect object	Object
The typist	gave (*what?*)	Mr. Ortega	the report. (*to whom?*)
(You)	Send (*what?*)	IBM	the word processor. (*to whom?*)
The company	gave (*what?*)	the employees	a bonus. (*to whom?*)
Sears	shipped (*what?*)	her	the dining room set. (*to whom?*)

By asking the questions *for whom?* or *to whom?* after the object, you can easily locate the indirect object. Note that in sentences of this type, the indirect object comes *before* the object. The sentences may be rewritten through the use of a prepositional phrase and still say the same thing. When rewritten, the phrase comes after the object.

The typist gave the report to Mr. Ortega.
Send the word processor to IBM.
The company gave a bonus to the employees.
Sears shipped the dining room set to her.

The preposition *to* indicates the relationship of *Mr. Ortega, IBM, the employees,* and *her* to the rest of the sentence. These words are now objects of the preposition.

Sentences with objects may also have complements that name or describe the object.

In the second variation of Pattern II, the object is either named or described through the use of a noun or an adjective. A noun or adjective used in this manner is called a *complement.* Complement means *that which completes by adding a characteristic or quality.* A complement may be a word or a word group. The following sentences contain complements that complete the objects by naming or describing them.

Subject	Transitive verb	Object	Complement
He	painted	his car	gold.
The company	made	James White	manager of the loan department.
The supervisor	found	the workers	enthusiastic.

In the first example, *gold* is an adjective used as a complement to describe *car.* In the second one, *manager* is a noun used as a complement to name *James White. Workers,* in the third example, are described by the adjective complement as *enthusiastic.*

Quick review

Let us stop here to identify the patterns of the following sentences. Place in the column either a *I* for a sentence containing an intransitive verb or *II* for a sentence containing a transitive verb followed by an object.

Pattern

1. The driver parked the truck across the street.   _____

2. The salesperson arrived this morning.   _____

3. The executive wrote Mr. Jones a memorandum.   _____

4. The company sent its customers the new catalog.   _____

5. The supervisor found the new employee reliable.   _____

6. The cracks in the wall happened last year.   _____

7. The machine broke several plates.   _____

8. The computer broke yesterday.   _____

9. The strike occurred last week.   _____

10. The personnel officer mailed her the application blank.   _____

(Answers in reverse order: II,I,I,II,I,II,II,II,I,II)

Three of the sentences in this **Quick review** have indirect objects. Rewrite them so that the indirect objects become objects of prepositions.

_____

_____

_____

_____

One of the sentences in the **Quick review** has a complement. Place the number of that sentence here: _____.

Pattern III sentences have a subject, a linking verb, and a complement.

Pattern III. The third sentence pattern has three parts: the subject, the linking verb, and the complement. In these sentences, no action takes place; the subject is merely described in a state of existence. You are already familiar with the most common linking verb—*to be*—and its forms. The verbs of the senses and a few others are also used as linking verbs. These are listed below along with sentences that illustrate their use.

Linking verbs

appear	smell	am, are, is
become	taste	was, were
feel	seem	been, being
look	sound	

Subject	Linking verb	Complement
The men	are	employees.
Mrs. Garcia	is	the cosmetics buyer.
The authors of this textbook	are	Keithley and Thompson.
The delivery clerk	looks	cold.
The budget	seems	sound.
The workers	appear	happy.

Linking verbs show the connection between the subject and the word that follows the verb.

The two points to remember are (1) the linking verb does not show action and (2) it is never followed by an object. The function of the linking verb is simply to show a connection or to form a link between the subject of the sentence and the word that follows the verb. Sometimes the word following the verb, the *complement,* is the same in identity as the subject. At other times, the complement describes some quality of the subject. The complement, therefore, may be either a naming word (noun or pronoun) or a descriptive word (adjective).

As you can see in the next illustration, the linking verb expresses a state of being or condition. It does not show action. Notice that when it connects the subject with a pronoun, the *pronoun* is in the *nominative case* (*I, we; you; he, she, it, they*). You will study *case* in Section 2, Part 5.

Subject	Linking verb	Complement
It	is	I.
The receptionists	are	busy.
The speakers	were	Mrs. Smith and he.
The new employee	is	an experienced machinist.

Complements that follow linking verbs are nouns, pronouns, or adjectives.

When the word following the linking verb describes the subject, it must be an *adjective.* Only adjectives may modify nouns and pronouns. For this reason some complements are called *adjective complements.*

Subject	Linking verb	Complement
The comedian	was	entertaining.
Your report	appears	correct.
The computer	seems	large.
The new perfume	smells	sweet.

When reading the last sentence, you probably noted that it would be incorrect to say *The new perfume smells sweetly* when you mean *sweet perfume* not *sweetly perfume. Sweet* is an adjective; *sweetly* is an adverb.

Quick review

These next sentences are examples of all three patterns. Indicate whether they are *I*, having an intransitive verb; *II*, a transitive verb; *III*, a linking verb by placing the appropriate roman numeral in the right-hand column.

Pattern

1. The directors marched out.   _____

2. The tone of her voice was polite.   _____

3. The company sold a million parts.   _____

4. The employees worked on Saturday.   _____

5. The annual audit seems accurate.   _____

6. The bank appointed Mrs. Tucker a vice president.   _____

7. Henry Potter became the attorney.   _____

8. Workers in this department must be efficient.   _____

9. The shipping clerk received a promotion.   _____

10. Take the supervisor a copy of this report on wages. _____

(Answers in reverse order: II,II,III,III,II,III,I,II,III,I)

VARIATIONS OCCUR IN THE BASIC SENTENCE PATTERN

The natural sentence order is subject first, verb second, object or complement third.

The natural order of the basic sentence is (1) the subject, (2) the verb, and (3) the object or the complement. This order is not followed in several kinds of sentences.

In *there* sentences the subject follows the verb.

There sentences.   In *there* sentences, the subject is displaced to a position after the verb. The filler *there* is followed by the verb and then by the subject. In such sentences, it is necessary to locate and identify the subject before it is possible to determine the verb form to use with the displaced subject. Forms of verbs are discussed in Section 3, where the importance of subject/verb agreement is stressed. The skill to develop now is the ability to locate the subject in *there* sentences.

Filler	Verb	Subject
There	goes	Harry.
There	are	the reports.
There	is	the office manager.

As you can see, the filler is merely used to get the message started. In your own writing, you should use *there* sentences sparingly. Most business writers consider sentences in which the subject comes first followed by the verb to be the best way to get the message across.

It sentences also place the subject after the verb.

It sentences.   The *it* sentence also displaces the real subject to a position after the verb. The pronoun *it,* however, can be considered the subject of the sentence. The third-person singular form of the verb is determined by the displaced subject. Note the difference in emphasis between the following pairs of sentences when the displaced subject is used before the verb in the natural position of subjects.

Subject	Linking verb	Complement	Displaced subject
It	is	important	to be on time.
To be on time	is	important.	
It	was	necessary	to investigate the matter.
To investigate the matter	was	necessary.	

It	was	the president's decision	to postpone the project.
To postpone the project	was	the president's decision.	
OR			
The president's decision	was	to postpone the project.	

Notice in this illustration that either the displaced subject or the noun complement can be used as the subject in the natural order. If the writer decides that it is important to stress the fact that the president made the decision to postpone the project, he or she will begin the sentence with *the president's decision* as the subject.

When used occasionally, the *it* sentence adds variety and informality to business writing. When used too often, the ideas being presented are weakened.

Questions do not follow the natural word order.

Questions.   The *question* is another variation of the basic sentence pattern where the natural word order is changed. To identify the sentence pattern and to find the subject and verb of a question, rearrange the words in their natural order.

When can we expect to hear from you?

Rearranged: *We **can expect*** to hear from you when?

Will our recommendation be put into effect?

Rearranged: Our *recommendation **will be put*** into effect?

Did the auditor suggest changes?

Rearranged: The *auditor **did suggest*** changes?

Do you want to see the report?

Rearranged: *You **do want*** to see the report?

Commands follow the natural word order: subject then verb then object and/or complement.

Commands.   The *command* follows the natural word order and may be constructed in all three basic patterns. Simply remember that the subject of commands is always *you* and would come before the verb if it were actually stated.

Pattern I: Leave.

Pattern II: Sign this letter.

Pattern III: Be careful.

In requests the subject is placed within the verb phrase.

Requests.   The *request* is used when the command might seem too dictatorial, and the courteous use of an implied question would be more acceptable to the reader or hearer. These sentences, which are similar to questions, end with a period because compliance with the request is expected. The following sentences illustrate two ways to write a request. You will notice that the verb phrase surrounds the subject.

***Will** you* please **check** this information.

May** we **hear from you by Tuesday.

Requests need to be rearranged and the words placed in natural order to find the subject and the verb. The two requests illustrated above have been rearranged as follows:

Pattern II: *You **will** please **check** this information.*
Pattern I: *We **may hear** from you by Tuesday.*

ACCURATE WORD CHOICE DEPENDS ON A LARGE VOCABULARY

Continuing the study of accurate word choice, here is another group of words that are often used incorrectly. You can learn to use them correctly when you know their definitions. The accurate use of words results in a message that is understood by the receiver in exactly the way the sender intended.

As you study these words, remember the goals set in the last lesson: (1) increase your vocabulary, and (2) refine the meaning of words you use. In this lesson, let us add a third goal: (3) learn to spell correctly. Being able to spell a word correctly is helpful in both speaking and writing. When you know how a word is spelled, you can pronounce it; and you can write it correctly in a communication.

Increase your ability to use words accurately and spell them correctly.

cereal, serial
Cereal is an edible grain.

Most of our employees eat dry **cereal** for breakfast.

Serial means appearing in successive parts or order.

Please list the **serial** numbers of the bonds.

confident, confidant
Confident indicates one is self-reliant and has trust or belief in a person or thing.

I am **confident** he will investigate the incident.

Confidant is a person to whom secrets are entrusted.

The clerks in the department find her a **confidant** they can trust.

confirm, conform
Confirm is to verify or make certain.

His explanation was **confirmed** by the others.

The order was **confirmed** by telegram.

Conform is to adapt or make consistent.

Are you willing to **conform** to our standards of dress?

continual, continuous
Continual refers to a happening that is repeated often.

Mr. Jones **continually** parks his car in the lot reserved for visitors.

Continuous refers to a happening that goes on without interruption.

Our production line is a **continuous** operation.

cover
Cover is a word that is often incorrectly used.

When used as a verb, it means to place something *over* an object.

My desk is **covered** with papers.

Choose another word in sentences that have other meanings.

Instead of: The enclosed check *covers* your expenses for March.

Say: The enclosed check is *for* your expenses for March.

Instead of: Here are pamphlets *covering* the operations of the machine.

Say: Here are pamphlets *explaining* the operations of the machine.

data, criteria, analyses

These words are the plural forms of Latin words. When using plural words, be sure that you use plural verbs and/or prouns with them.

These criteria will have to be checked for application to the problem.

His *analyses were made* at the end of each month.

The *data were collected* by several investigators.

Data, however, may be used in both the singular and plural sense. When used to refer to a *body* or *unit* of statistics or findings, the singular is preferred.

This data is being analyzed by our finance department.

Use the plural with *data* when you think of the individual units that comprise the data.

They gathered *data* and classified *them* according to geographical location.

devise, device

Devise means to think through or invent.

The foreman *devised* a new system for the production line.

A *device* is an implement or invention.

That *device* was tested three years ago.

When will the new *device* be perfected?

disinterested, uninterested

Disinterested means that one is impartial or unselfish.

The manager chose a *disinterested* employee to settle the argument.

Uninterested means that the person is *not* interested.

The workers were *uninterested* in having a company picnic.

don't, doesn't

These contractions for *do not* and *does not* must be used with the correct person.

1st: I *don't*   **2d:** you *don't*   **3d:** he *doesn't*
                                            she *doesn't*
                                            it *doesn't*

due to

Due to is an adjective; therefore, the phrase that it introduces must modify a noun or a pronoun.

The cancellation of that product line was **due to** its poor sales record.

(The *due to* phrase modifies the noun *cancellation*.)

Due to should be replaced by *because of* or *owing to* if the phrase modifies a verb.

Because of my lack of skill, I lost my job.
(The phrase modifies the verb *lost*.)

Owing to my lack of knowledge on the subject, I was not invited to the meeting.

etc. *Etc.* should be used sparingly in writing. It is incorrectly used when it ends a series introduced by *such as*. *Such as* tells the reader that you will name only a few. Also, never use *etc.* with *and*—e.g., *saws, hammers, pliers, etc.*

I intend to discuss topics **such as** taxation, risk bearing, and investments.

farther, further Many writers use these words interchangeably. In the business world, however, you will find people who prefer that you use *farther* when indicating physical or measurable distance. *Further* indicates degree or quality.

Is it much **farther** to the factory?

We went **further** with the discussion than I intended.

fewer, less, smaller *Fewer* refers to number of items that may be counted, and it should modify a plural noun.

Lockheed has **fewer** employees than it had five years ago.

Less refers to quantity, degree, or bulk.

Thompson, Inc., made **less** profit in 1980.

Smaller refers to size.

The vice president's office is **smaller** than the president's.

formally, formerly *Formally* means in a conventional or formal manner.

The proposal will be **formally** presented to the stockholders.

Formerly means earlier, previously.

He **formerly** worked for the National Bank.

former, latter *Former* refers to past time or the *first* mentioned of two.

Please see that the **former** instead of the latter statement is printed.

Latter refers to something of more recent date or the *second* of two things being considered.

His **latter** statement proved that he had studied the situation.

got, gotten   These past tenses of the verb *to get* should be used sparingly. Other verbs, such as **have, receive, buy, purchase,** and **find,** should be used instead.

I **bought** a new tire yesterday.

He said that he hadn't **received** a reply yet.

guess   This word is loosely used as a verb. *Guess* means to form an opinion based on uncertainty. Many times a specific verb should be used in its place.

I **think** he has the report on his desk.

I **intend** to visit the stock exchange.

hardly, scarcely, only, but   Do not use these adverbs with a negative.

I **hardly ever** see you in the cafeteria.

(**Not:** I hardly never see you . . .)

The bulletin was so cluttered with art work that you **could hardly** read it.

(**Not:** . . . couldn't hardly . . .)

He **could scarcely** finish his work in time.

You are supposed to leave early **only** on Friday.

PART 3

ASSIGNMENTS

Apply your knowledge of sentence patterns

A. Your ability to recognize the pattern of a sentence depends on your being able to pick out the *subject,* the *verb,* and the *object* or the *complement* in the sentence. You have studied these parts of the sentence in previous lessons. In this exercise, you will be able to test how well you are able to recognize them. Underline the *subject once* and the *verb twice* in each sentence that follows. If a sentence has an *object,* an *indirect object,* or a *complement,* enter the word in the correct column.

	Object	Indirect object	Complement
Example: The secretary gave Mrs. Fuller the letter.	*letter*	*Mrs. Fuller*	
1. The production worker made several copies of the blueprint.			
2. The new computer is a light green.			
3. Mary Nash received a promotion.			
4. You should know the illegal uses of photocopiers.			
5. A credit card allows you the privilege of buying now and paying later.			
6. The government can impose a penalty for copying citizenship or immigration papers on a photocopier.			
7. Clear your use of the copying machine with co-workers.			
8. Place the "curl" side of the paper on the tray.			
9. How many business publications did you read last month?			
10. To achieve your professional potential should be your goal.			

47

11. The president gave John Zimmer the information on the company seminar. _____ _____ _____

12. Will you please make an announcement at the next meeting. _____ _____ _____

13. Did he give Jim the report? _____ _____ _____

14. Tell the committee the news about our new product. _____ _____ _____

15. After you have read the article, please make an appointment to see me. _____ _____ _____

16. Adaptability is vital to success in any position. _____ _____ _____

17. Our branch offices are located in seven major cities. _____ _____ _____

18. You will gain self-confidence if you read books and articles on business. _____ _____ _____

19. Miss Rolph seems confident in her ability to handle the matter. _____ _____ _____

20. Apparently, the supervisor told him the reason for the delay. _____ _____ _____

B. Our study of sentence patterns reveals that each pattern calls for a particular type of verb.

Pattern I: Subject + Intransitive verb
Pattern II: Subject + Transitive verb + Object
Pattern III: Subject + Linking verb + Complement

In the following sentences, first determine if the sentence is an example of Pattern I, II, or III. Place the number in the appropriate column. Next, circle the verb in the main clause and check its classification in the correct column.

	Pattern	Intransitive verb	Transitive verb	Linking verb
Example: Accountants (handle) ledgers, balance sheets, and profit and loss statements.	II		✓	
1. Did you appoint her captain of the tour guides?				
2. It seems logical to assume that the interest rate will go up.				
3. The chair seems sturdy.				
4. Vital records of the company are kept in a locked file.				
5. People who work under pressure are often irritable.				
6. If you have free time and a co-worker has a big job to get out, offer your help.				
7. Real friends are rare.				

8. Take time to be polite to visitors.   ___ ___ ___ ___

9. Bank tellers meet the public every day.   ___ ___ ___ ___

10. The members of the committee left early.   ___ ___ ___ ___

11. Did the shipment arrive yesterday?   ___ ___ ___ ___

12. You should develop a system for sorting the incoming mail.   ___ ___ ___ ___
13. The supplies needed when sorting mail are a letter opener, a red pencil for marking the date of arrival, paper clips, and transparent tape for mending tears.   ___ ___ ___ ___
14. After opening an envelope, check it to make sure you removed all the contents.   ___ ___ ___ ___

15. Mark on the letter its date of arrival.   ___ ___ ___ ___
16. Enclosures listed on the incoming letter should be stapled or clipped to it.   ___ ___ ___ ___
17. If an enclosure is missing, note this information on the letter.   ___ ___ ___ ___
18. Collect the files that pertain to the incoming correspondence.   ___ ___ ___ ___
19. Each letter should be clipped to the outside of the correct file folder.   ___ ___ ___ ___

20. Place the mail in order of importance on your boss's desk.   ___ ___ ___ ___

C. Underline the true, displaced, or understood subject in each of the following sentences, and write the word(s) in the right column.

Example: Please *you* call me for an appointment.   *you*

1. How does your workday begin?   _____

2. There is no reason for you to wait.   _____
3. It is a good idea to put your work station in order when you first arrive at work.   _____

4. When should I go for the mail?   _____

5. Use paper clips to attach several pieces of paper together.   _____

6. It is the president's plan to call a board meeting for next month.   _____

7. It is impossible to make delivery before Tuesday.   _____

8. There are several workers in that department who deserve a raise.   _____

9. Ask for a day off to handle your personal business.   _____

10. Where did you hear that? _____

11. It is our policy to guarantee our products. _____

12. Place an advertisement in the local papers. _____

13. Will Mr. Smith give the bonus to you? _____

14. Briefly but clearly describe the situation. _____

15. Whom does she plan to tell? _____

16. There should be a guard at the entrance. _____

17. Include all the information necessary to justify the claim. _____

18. There is a need to state the problem precisely. _____

19. Have the parts arrived yet from Chicago? _____

20. There are many changes in the specifications to record. _____

D. Continuing our study of correct word usage, read the sentences in this exercise and then select the word that accurately expresses the intended meaning. Draw a line through the inappropriate or incorrect word.

1. Did you see the television (serial, cereal) on the cosmos?
2. Our firm finally (confirmed, conformed) to the principles discussed at the policy conference.
3. The computer operates (continually, continuously) night and day.
4. My paycheck is hardly enough (to cover, for) all my expenses for the month.
5. We rechecked the (data, criteria) compiled by the finance department.
6. Mr. Butler developed a (devise, device) that will count the particles more accurately.
7. Our department has (smaller, fewer, less) employees than any other in the firm.
8. I just received a letter from Jones and Smith. The (latter, former), Mr. Smith, was a (latter, former) employee of ours.
9. The arbitrator in the dispute was (an uninterested, a disinterested) party.
10. At the company breakfast, you may have either cold or hot (cereal, serial).
11. Are you (confident, confidant) that the matter will be investigated?
12. This (analysis, analyses) was made last year.
13. Several new (devices, devises) were tested in the laboratory.
14. The workers appear to be (uninterested, disinterested) in the trip to the amusement park.
15. Please order stationery items, such as (pencils, pens, envelopes, etc.; pencils, pens, envelopes).
16. I heard him say that he (don't, doesn't) like the supervisor.
17. The new parking lot is (farther, further) from the plant than Lot 6.
18. I (guess, think) I will take my vacation in July.
19. Did Jim (get, receive) a raise last month?
20. The truck driver (could hardly, couldn't hardly) lift the crate.

E. When you read the following sentences, you may find that a word has been used incorrectly. Cross out the word and write the correct one in the right-hand column. In some sentences, a word may need to be deleted.

1. Our firm has gone farther toward achieving its goals than any other in our industry.   _____

2. The president mentioned that the budget was based on the analysis made monthly last year.   _____

3. The foreman hardly never explained the instructions.   _____

4. Outside my office window I could see trees, flowers, green grass, and etc.   _____

5. Our internal audit is a process that goes on continually.   _____

6. Jerry is considered to be a close confident of the vice president.   _____

7. Our company makes less products now.   _____

8. Do you guess our sales policy can compete with our competitor's?   _____

9. The new director formally taught at Stanford University.   _____

10. Our product got a good commendation from the consumer laboratory.   _____

11. Due to our high bid, the company was not awarded the contract.   _____

12. Many tools will be needed on this job, such as drills, hammers, pliers, etc.   _____

13. Please conform the location of the meeting.   _____

14. He cancelled the stock sale due to the rise in the stock market.   _____

15. The report covers our operations for the past year.   _____

Name _____

Date _____

PRACTICE WRITING

Write *two* original sentences for each sentence pattern outlined below. Refer to the discussion of sentence patterns you have just studied, if you need to refresh your memory.

1. Subject + Intransitive verb

_____

_____

_____

2. Subject + Intransitive verb + Modifier (adverb, phrase, or clause)

_____

_____

_____

3. Subject + Transitive verb + Object

_____

_____

_____

_____

4. Subject + Transitive verb + Indirect object + Object

_____

_____

_____

_____

5.   Subject + Linking verb + Complement

_____

_____

_____

6.   Filler + Verb + Subject

_____

_____

_____

7.   *It* + Verb + Displaced subject

_____

_____

_____

PART 4

Sentences have many variations

Knowing the rules of grammar will make you an effective communicator.

You have come across several grammatical terms in the study of the sentence thus far. These terms have been used only to help you see how words are laced together to express ideas. Some grammatical terms you will remember; others you will forget. It is not necessary to remember all of them in order to write clearly, concisely, and effectively. What you will have acquired, however, is an inner understanding of how effective sentences sound and how certain constructions help you communicate.

One of America's well-loved communicators, Mark Twain, wrote in his autobiography in 1924 his memory of grammar:

> . . . I know grammar by ear only, not by rote, not by the rules. A generation ago I knew the rules—knew them by heart, word for word, though not their meanings—and I still know one of them: the one which says—which says—but never mind, it will come back to me presently.

So you see, to be a good communicator, one does not need to remember all the rules; but one does need to study them sufficiently before leaving school so that correct usage is automatic. That is why definitions of grammatical terms and rules are kept to a minimum in this text. If you wish to find the definition of a particular term, you can turn to Appendix 4, where there is a complete glossary of grammatical terms. Use this glossary to clear up any confusion you may have as you proceed through this course. Make as many of these terms as possible part of your understanding of the language.

Sentences are made up of combinations of clauses and phrases.

Based on what you have just studied, you should now look at the many combinations of clauses and phrases that can be used to construct sentences. You have learned to recognize clauses and phrases and to understand how they are used in the sentence. The next step is to study the combinations that can be used when constructing sentences with them. Notice that the first illustration has one independent clause. Each succeeding combination adds clauses and phrases to the original independent clause.

Sentence = Independent clause

This firm manufactures office furniture.

Mr. J. T. Jones will speak.

Our accountants studied data processing.

Sentence = Independent clause + Independent clause

This firm manufactures office furniture, and sales have been rising steadily.

Mr. J. T. Jones will speak, but his talk will take only 30 minutes.

Our accountants studied data processing, and then the company bought computers.

Sentence = Independent clause + Phrase

This firm manufactures office furniture *of the latest designs.*

Mr. J. T. Jones will speak *at the annual meeting.*

Our accountants studied data processing *for two semesters.*

Sentence = Independent clause + Dependent clause

This firm manufactures office furniture *when orders are received.*

Mr. J. T. Jones, *who is president,* will speak.

When our accountants were students, they studied data processing.

Sentence = Independent clause containing a phrase + Dependent clause containing a phrase

This firm manufactures office furniture *of the latest designs* **when orders** *above $100,000* **are received.**

Mr. J. T. Jones, **who is president** *of our company,* will speak *at the annual meeting.*

When our accountants were students *in college,* they studied data processing *for two semesters.*

As you will notice, only one combination for the compound sentence has been illustrated. All the other combinations could be doubled to make compound and compound-complex sentences. The last two examples, if doubled, would probably result in sentences that would be too long and too complicated for easy understanding. Business writers try to use as few long sentences as possible so that their messages are clear.

Sentences may show action.   Another way to look at sentences is to notice that either action takes place or something is acted upon. In most sentences, someone or something does something: someone or something *acts*, as in the following sentences that indicate action.

He mailed the letter.

The machine cut a hole in the tube.

Our company employs lathe operators.

Take the chair into the next room.

In the first example of action statements, *he* did something—*he **mailed.*** In the next examples, the *machine **cut,*** our *company **employs,*** and (*you*) *take.* These action statements are the most powerful sentences. Action appeals to each of us; we like to see something happening. In businesses, most communications contain action sentences.

Sentences may be passive statements.

In other sentences, something is acted upon. This type of sentence results in a passive or inactive statement. Another way to describe a passive statement is to say that the subject of the sentence is not performing the action but is receiving it. The following illustrations show that the subjects are receiving the action.

The supervisor was told by the manager.
The letter was mailed by the office clerk.
The meeting is to be chaired by the vice president.
The speech will be given by Mr. Richard Smith, our sales manager.

Let us turn these four sentences from passive statements into action statements, so that you can readily see the difference between them.

The manager told the supervisor.
The office clerk mailed the letter.
The vice president will chair the meeting.
Mr. Richard Smith, our sales manager, will give the speech.

Notice how much clearer and more direct the action statements are because they tell **who does what.** Of course, there are times when the passive statement should be used. A good communicator, however, knows the difference between an action statement and a passive one and can select the right one for the occasion and the message being sent.

The parts of a sentence can be arranged in several ways.

A third way to approach sentence structure is to be aware of the many ways to arrange sentence parts. A simple statement can have something—another idea or bit of information—added to it. The placement of this additional material can be at the beginning of the sentence, in the middle, or at the end.

Statement: The company manufactures computers.

Addition to the *front* of the statement: **When enough orders are received,** the company manufactures computers.

Addition to the *middle* of the statement: The company, **whose president is John Smith,** manufactures computers.

Addition at the *end* of the statement: The company manufactures computers, **although it is planning to add copiers to the product line.**

Statement added to statement: The company manufactures computers, and it sells them all over the world.

Professor A. M. Tibbetts of the University of Illinois, who focuses on sentence structure in writing classes, has listed the shapes of sentences, as follows:

(a) **Statement**

(b) Opener, **Statement**

(c) **State,** Interrupter, **ment**

(d) **Statement,** Closer

(e) **Statement,** and **Statement**

Notice how easily you can identify the units in these five ways to arrange sentence parts, and also how easy it is to see where the punctuation goes. Being able to picture in your mind how sentences can be arranged and punctuated helps you improve your writing skill.

Some grammatical terms are important to know when studying sentence structure.

To round out this in-depth study of the sentence, let us review the grammatical terms that are most often used when discussing sentence structure. A review of these terms will increase your understanding of how words are laced together to express ideas. When you are able to construct sentences that get the point across, you will be prepared for challenging jobs in business.

Read the following terms and their definitions carefully. You already are familiar with them; take time now to know and understand what they mean.

Sentence.   A *sentence* is a group of words expressing a complete thought. The five types are statements, questions, commands, requests, and exclamations. In its simplest form, a sentence is made up of two parts: simple subject and simple verb.

The sentence	
Simple subject	**Simple verb**
Mr. Jones	***spoke.***
Machines	***hum.***

Subject.   The *subject* of a sentence tells who or what is being discussed. The complete subject in a more elaborate sentence consists of the subject plus all words related to it.

Verb.   The *verb* of a sentence tells what action or state of being applies to the subject. The complete verb consists of the verb plus all words controlled by it.

Complete subject	**Complete verb**
The finance *committee*	***will meet*** next Tuesday at three o'clock.
The *elevator* in this building	***goes*** to the 41st floor.

Clause.   A *clause* is a group of words that *includes both a subject and a verb.*

Independent clause.   Some clauses are independent and can stand alone as sentences.

Mr. Jones **dictated** the letter.

The *men* **loaded** the truck.

Dependent clause.   Other clauses are *dependent* (cannot stand alone) and must be linked to independent clauses to form sentences. There are three types of dependent clauses.

Introductory. An introductory dependent clause comes first in the sentence and is followed by a comma.

> If you **have** all the figures, please finish the report.
> When Mrs. Baker **returns** the merchandise, she should be given a credit voucher.

Nonrestrictive. A *nonrestrictive* dependent clause adds information to the sentence that is *not needed* to complete the thought. It is set off by commas because it could be left out without changing the meaning of the message. It usually follows the word it modifies in the middle or at the end of the sentence.

> Mr. John Jones, *who works for ABC Corporation,* will speak at the convention.
> The president talked to Ms. Edwards, *who handles public relations for XYZ Corp.*

Restrictive. A *restrictive* dependent clause adds information *needed* to complete the message in the sentence. It is not set off by commas because it cannot be left out.

> Salesmen *who are on the road by 8:30 a.m.* will make their quotas.
> The package contains several parts *that fit the Xerox copier.*

Phrase. A group of closely related words without a subject is called a *phrase*. It is always part of a sentence.

Verb phrase. A verb with its helpers is called a *verb phrase—should have been working, were typing, did count.*

Prepositional phrase. A preposition with the words it controls is known as a *prepositional phrase—after the committee meeting,* **behind** *the olive green cabinet, at the airport.*

Verbal noun phrase. A *verbal noun phrase* used in place of a noun or a pronoun is composed of the *ing* form of the verb plus all the words controlled by the verbal—*checking the invoices, operating the drill press, talking to the client.*

Infinitive phrase. *Infinitive phrases* are formed by the infinitive form of the verb and all words controlled by it—*to think through the problem, to capture the idea, to write a report.*

Participial phrase. A *participial phrase* begins with the present or past participle form of the verb and includes other words controlled by it. It is used to describe or modify nouns and pronouns.

> The man *operating the electric calculator* works in sales.
> The instructions *repeated by the supervisor* may be found in the manual.

Object. The two types of *objects* we are concerned with here are the *direct object* that follows the transitive verb and *the indirect object*.

Object, also called direct object.   The object of the transitive verb is a noun or pronoun that completes the action. The transitive verb transfers the action of the subject to the object.

The secretary gave the *letter* to the customer.

The copier prints by a photographic method six *copies* a minute.

Indirect object.   The indirect object is a noun or pronoun that receives the person or thing named by the object. In other words, the object is passed on to someone or something.

The secretary gave the *messenger* the letter.

The supervisor handed the *worker* the operating manual.

Complement.   The *complement* follows the linking verb and may be a noun, a pronoun, or an adjective. Sometimes the complement is the same in identity as the subject and is therefore a noun or a pronoun. At other times, the complement describes the subject and is an adjective.

The new employee will be the *manager* of the store.

The new manager is *tall.*

ACCURATE WORD CHOICE RESULTS IN CLEAR MESSAGES

Continue to study the accurate use of words.

In the last few lessons, you have been studying words that are often used incorrectly. Are you now able to use them more accurately in your conversation and writing? Take every opportunity in your daily life to use these particular words. By the end of this course, you will have added several hundred words to your vocabulary, if you take time to master the word-building sections.

Remember that your goals are to increase your vocabulary, to refine the meaning of words you use, and to spell them correctly.

imply,
infer

Imply means to suggest or hint at a meaning. It is always the writer or speaker who *implies* something.

The supervisor **implied** that he is worried about production.

Infer means to deduce something from the suggestion or hint. It is always the reader or listener who *infers.*

The workers **inferred** that the supervisor felt that the output was too low.

its,
it's

Its is the possessive case of the pronoun *it* and is used to modify or show possession.

Each letter is in **its** folder.

It's is the contraction of *it is.*

It's my opinion that your idea is good.

Do you think that **it's** clearer to them?

kind,
sort

These two words are singular when used as nouns. Be sure to use the singular *this* or *that* to modify *kind* and *sort.*

I ordered **this kind** of paper.

That sort of outline will help you prepare a talk.

Remember that *kind* and *sort* are used to indicate a group or class possessing the same characteristics.

What **sort** of person is he?

What **kind** of typewriter did you buy?

leave,   *Leave* means to stop, quit, or depart.
let

Please **leave** the table where it is.

Did he **leave** by the side door?

Let means to permit or allow.

Let him take the adding machine to his office.

Shall I **let** her see the telegram?

liable,   *Liable* refers to legal requirements when a person is
likely   answerable or responsible.

We are **liable** for our actions.

A driver is **liable** for damages to the property of others.

Likely means probable, apparently true, to be expected.

We are **likely** to have a meeting this afternoon.

loan,   *Loan* is commonly used as a noun. It is preferable
lend   to use *lend* as the verb.

Mr. Carr asked the bank for a **loan.**

Please **lend** her your pencil.

lot,   These words are overused. Choose another word
lots   that means exactly the amount or number you are discussing.

Vague: *Lots* of people came to the meeting.

Better: **Approximately fifty** people came to the meeting.

majority   *Majority* refers to items that can be counted or numbered. Do not use *majority* when referring to a part of or portion of something.

A **majority** of the people voted for him.

More than half of the report is typed.

(**Not:** The majority of the report is typed.)

may,   *May* refers to permission or likelihood.
might   *Might* implies possibility.

You **may** leave now. (*permission*)

He **might** wish to attend the seminar. (*possibility*)

In a dependent clause, use *might* when the verb in the main clause indicates *past* time.

The director **reported** last month that we **might** expect an increase in profits.

Use *may* in the dependent clause when the verb in the main clause indicates present or future time.

The director **reports** that we **may** expect an increase in profits.

pair, set
These words are singular; their plural forms are *pairs, sets.* Be sure to use the plural when the meaning is plural.

He purchased three **pairs** of shoes.

I ordered another bookkeeping **set.**

party, person, people
A *person* is *not* a *party* except in legal documents.

The **parties** to the contract signed their names.

Mr. Weaver is the **person** who ordered the Xerox.

Use *people* when the individuality of each person is not considered.

The office was full of **people.**

The committee consists of five **persons.**

passed, past
Passed is the past tense and past participle of the verb *pass,* meaning to go by, to transfer from one to another, to adopt, to go through a trial and succeed, and many other meanings.

She **passed** the CPA examination.

He watched until the man had **passed** the corner.

Past refers to elapsed time, to something that has gone by or is over.

Our 50th anniversary is now **past.**

The clerk walked **past** her desk.

Our **past** records will show the number of times they defaulted.

per
Per is most often used in Latin expressions such as *per annum* and *per diem.* It is used in *miles per hour* and *words per minute,* but preferred current usage is *miles an hour* and *words a minute.* Do not use *per* with English words to form phrases.

Your salary will be $200 **a week.**
(**Not:** . . . per week.)

The new wage rate is $3.10 **an hour.**
(**Not:** . . . per hour.)

I will stop at the printer **as you requested.**
(**Not:** . . . per your request.)

percent, percentage
Percent is used with the exact numerical statement.

Profits were 12.2 **percent** of net income.

Percentage indicates a part of the whole.

What **percentage** of the employees received a raise?

PART **4**

ASSIGNMENTS

Apply your knowledge of sentence variations

A. You have found that sentences are made up of various combinations of clauses and phrases. In the following sentences, test your ability to recognize clauses and phrases by underlining the clauses with a straight line and the phrases with a wavy line.

Example: You will not want to miss this issue with its wealth of information on events that are taking place around the world.

1. Please send your approval on the enclosed form before you misplace it.
2. Do you want a suit that will fit you like a glove?
3. Come in soon, Mr. Knox, and let us show you the wide assortment of patterns that are available.
4. As you already know, hundreds of companies maintain one or more planes for the use of their technical, sales, and executive staffs.
5. These companies have found that it pays off in higher efficiency, in time saved, and in travel costs.
6. If you want information on how little it costs to own a plane, just return the enclosed card.
7. The manager of the laboratory has written many articles that have appeared in leading medical journals.
8. I must report that Don Lyons, sales manager of the Export Division, has resigned.
9. The employees of Jennings Enterprises were offered an opportunity to buy stock in the company and to pay for it from their earnings through payroll deductions.
10. If you want to take advantage of the special introductory offer, return the enclosed card before the end of the month.

B. As you saw in Exercise **A,** phrases are sentence parts that occur in almost every sentence. You will recall that they are groups of words that do not have subjects. However, prepositional, verbal noun, and infinitive phrases may be used as subjects of sentences. The participial phrase is always used as a modifier. In this exercise, underline all phrases including verb phrases. If any phrase is used as a subject, place a check mark in the column.

Subject

1. Writing an effective letter takes skill and practice. _____

2. To organize your ideas before a meeting is better than to arrive unprepared. _____

63

3. Giving a worker a list of duties and discussing them should be done on the first day on the job. _____

4. Serving member banks is the chief function of Federal Reserve banks. _____

5. To hear Mr. Jones talk, you would think he owned the company. _____

6. Our new factory, designed by Brock & Brock, won an architectural award in 1980. _____

7. Getting a raise in pay often requires a persuasive talk with your superior. _____

8. Computing the sales figures for the first quarter took me all day. _____

9. The bookkeeper finished first should start on accounts receivable. _____

10. Finding a job in this city is easy if you go to an employment agency. _____

C. You have just learned that sentences may be active or passive statements. In a sentence showing action, the subject acts; and in a sentence that is passive, the subject is acted upon. Identify each of the sentences in this exercise by writing *active* or *passive* in the right-hand column.

1. The talk will be heard by the stockholders at the annual meeting. _____

2. Will you please fill out the enclosed form, and return it without delay. _____

3. A membership in the association was taken by Mr. Owen. _____

4. Payment will be made by our accountant next week. _____

5. We have shipped your order of March 16 via express. _____

6. The president told the staff to finish their reports by Friday. _____

7. It is Mrs. Johnson's plan to visit the factory next Tuesday. _____

8. Sign the letter before you mail it. _____

9. Dictators in our office use the telephone to reach the machines in the word processing center. _____

10. The office manager wrote a memorandum about the coming holiday. _____

D. You have found in this lesson that there are a few grammatical terms it is important to know by name and definition. See if you can supply the grammatical term for each definition given below.

1. A group of words expressing a complete thought is known as a _____.

2. The _____ tells who or what is being discussed.

3. The _____ tells what action or state of being is taking place.

4. A _____ is a group of words that includes both a subject and a verb. There are two kinds: _____ and _____.

5. A _____ dependent clause adds information that is not needed to complete the thought. It is set off by _____ because it could be left out without changing the message.

6. A _____ dependent clause adds information needed to complete the message.

7. A group of closely related words without a subject is called a _____.

8. The verb with its helpers is called a _____ _____.

9. Verbal noun and infinitive _____ can be used as subjects of sentences.

10. Some verbs are followed by _____ that receive the action.

11. Some sentences have _____ _____ that receive the thing named by the _____.

12. The _____ follows the linking verb and names or describes the subject.

13. A mark of punctuation, called a _____, should be placed after the last word in an introductory clause.

14. A _____ is used to separate two independent clauses without a conjunction, such as *and*.

15. A nonrestrictive phrase or clause should have _____ before and after it, if it is in the middle of the sentence.

   E.   In the following sentences, choose the word that conveys the correct meaning from the pair in parentheses. Cross out the incorrect word.
   1. Didn't you (infer, imply) from what was said that the test failed?
   2. I think (the majority, more than half) voted for three weeks' vacation.
   3. What (kind, sort) of person is the treasurer?
   4. Our department recently purchased four (pair, pairs) of bookcases.
   5. The board of directors is composed of 12 (people, persons).
   6. I would appreciate it if you would (loan, lend) me your pen.
   7. (Lots of, Several) boxes were shipped yesterday.
   8. I calculated our interest rate to be 5.4 (percentage, percent).
   9. Most of our salesmen earn $250 (per, a) week.
   10. A large (percent, percentage) of the parts were defective.
   11. I will finish this job by noon (per your request, as you requested).
   12. Ellen was upset when Mrs. Tucker (inferred, implied) that she wasn't thinking.

13. In (passed, past) years the employees were given an extra day off at Christmas.
14. The office manager ordered several (pair, pairs, set, sets) of maps.
15. Were the bonus checks (passed, past) out yesterday?
16. It was reported in the company paper that sales (may, might) be down next quarter.
17. Be sure to (let, leave) the manager see those figures.
18. A certain (percent, percentage) of our production goes to the Common Market.
19. The new branch bank will open (its, it's) doors on Monday.
20. Our departmental staff is (liable, likely) to have to work on Saturday.
21. I have (lots of, eight) letters to type before noon.
22. Did your supervisor say that (its, it's) all right to leave at four?
23. If you ask her today, she (may, might) be willing to collect the data for the report.
24. Miss Williams (inferred, implied) that she will review the matter again.
25. The truck that just (passed, past) belongs to XYZ Corporation.

Name _____

Date _____

PRACTICE WRITING

This writing practice will help you learn to express your ideas in a variety of subject-verb patterns. Use material from your favorite business course for these sentences. Compose the types of sentences asked for below.

1. A sentence containing a one-word subject and a compound verb

   _____

   _____

   _____

2. A sentence containing a phrase as the subject and a simple verb

   _____

   _____

   _____

3. A sentence containing a clause as the subject and a simple verb

   _____

   _____

   _____

4. A sentence containing several single words as the compound subject and either a simple or a compound verb

   _____

   _____

   _____

5. A sentence containing a nonrestrictive clause

   _____

   _____

The connectors

Connectors are the joining words in our language. You learned about them in Section 1, Part 1, where you studied compound subjects and verbs, and in Parts 2 and 3, where you studied compound sentences and complex sentences with dependent clauses. These particular words are used to connect words, phrases, and clauses. They make it possible for us to name two or more persons or objects, to show the relationship of two or more ideas, and to compare and contrast two or more things. A connector holds the parts of the sentence together and aids in making our message mean exactly what we want it to mean.

Connectors fall into two general groups—coordinate and subordinate. In Part 1 we will discuss coordination, the joining of things of equal rank or value. In Part 2 the discussion will consider subordination, the joining of items of unequal rank or value. Through this study, you will learn to use connectors more precisely so that your sentences will show the comparative importance of facts and ideas.

Coordinate conjunctions join items of the same type

Conjunctions join items that are of the same type and the same grammatical structure.

Coordination as defined for the study of grammar is the joining together of items of the same type or class. These items are words, phrases, and clauses of equal value and parallel construction. For example, nouns are joined to nouns, verbs to verbs, adverbs to adverbs, adjectives to adjectives, prepositional phrases to prepositional phrases, dependent clauses to dependent clauses, independent clauses to independent clauses, and so on. *Coordinate conjunctions* are *and, but, for, or, nor, so,* and *yet*.

In Section 1, Part 2, page 19, you saw conjunctions used in compound sentences and read a list of them. Also, the text discussed the uses of the comma and the semicolon with them. On pages 21–22 of Part 2, the conjunction was used in compound-complex sentences. In Part 1, pages 6–7, conjunctions were used with two or more subjects and verbs. Thus, you are somewhat familiar with them already. First, let us review what you studied in Section 1 about the conjunction.

Two or more subjects joined by one of the coordinate conjunctions listed above

Fords, Chevrolets, *and* Chryslers are manufactured in America.

Coding by name *and* sorting by alphabetic sequence are important steps in filing.

When you write them *or* when you telephone them, will be time enough to ask for Mr. Smith's home address.

Two or more verbs joined by a conjunction

The machine stamps *and* labels the pieces.

The attorney filed the brief with the court *and* asked for a calendar date for the trial.

John finished the report *but* did not mail it.

Two or more independent clauses joined by a conjunction

Most job openings are in office-related work, *for* there is a great demand for clerks and secretaries.

Will you take your vacation in June, *or* will you wait until October?

Other equal items in a series

The office contains a desk *and* a chair.

Take Mr. Bennett three yellow pads, five pencils, *and* two pens.

I plan to send Jim Jenkins *or* Paul Mayer to the seminar.

A silver *and* red car is parked across the street.

Drive slowly *and* carefully past that obstruction.

Did you say the letter is in the drawer *or* under the blotter?

The last three illustrations show adjectives, adverbs, and prepositional phrases joined by conjunctions. These three modifiers will be presented in Section 5, where all aspects of modifying words and phrases will be discussed in detail. They are included here to show items of the same class or type joined by the coordinate conjunction.

Items in a series should have the same grammatical structure.

It is important to learn how to use these coordinate conjunctions effectively. If you make sure that each item in a series is of the same grammatical structure, you will be able to compose sentences that are correct and thus effective. The illustrations that follow will show you how to change a poorly written sentence into an effective one.

Weak: The parts of the machine were found *in the drawer, in the closet,* **and** *lying on the desk.*
(Unequal items joined by **and.** The first two are prepositional phrases, and the third *lying on the desk* is a participial phrase.)

Effective: The parts of the machine were found *in the drawer, in the closet,* **and** *on the desk.*

Weak: *Writing, telephoning,* **and** *to talk* face to face are three ways to communicate.
(Unequal items joined by **and.** *Writing* and *telephoning* are verbal nouns, whereas *to talk* is an infinitive.)

Effective: *To write, to telephone,* **and** *to talk* face to face are three ways to communicate.

Or: *Writing, telephoning,* **and** *talking* face to face are three ways to communicate.

The next group of sentences shows the use of coordinate conjunctions to join two or more parts of the sentence. Remember that these parts must be of equal value and parallel form.

Subjects: *Ethel* **and** *Cynthia* plan to go shopping on Saturday.

Verbs: Mr. Jones *worked* late **and** *finished* the job.

Objects: You will find a *pen* **or** a *pencil* in the drawer.

Indirect objects: The secretary did not send the *president* **or** *me* a report.

Dependent clauses: *When you arrive in town* **but** *before you go to the meeting,* please call me.

Independent clauses: *Days are short* **but** *nights are long in January.*

Adjectives:	The office chairs were upholstered in *brown and* white checked material.
Adverbs:	The clerk counted the items *carefully and quickly.*
Phrases:	The works manager, *walking briskly and smiling broadly,* came into the factory.

Some conjunctions emphasize the comparison of two items.

When the conjunctions *and, or, nor,* and *but* are paired with other words, they are called *comparative conjunctions.* Become familiar with the following comparative conjunctions as pairs.

either . . . . or	both . . . . and
neither . . . . nor	whether . . . . or
not only . . . . but also	

Comparative conjunctions are pairs of words.

These pairs are used to emphasize comparison between two things or two ideas. Each part of the comparative conjunction should be placed immediately before the idea or thing to be compared. In the following sentences, notice that the comparative conjunctions join elements that are parallel in value and construction.

He *not only* purchased a ticket to New York *but also* bought one to Boston.
(Two verbs are compared.)

Whether listening to the discussion *or* presenting your ideas, you should watch the reaction of the audience.
(Two participial phrases are compared.)

You will notice in the next sentences that the comparative conjunction *either/or* joins two independent clauses. The comma, therefore, precedes the *or.*

Either I will pick up the letter, *or* John will stop for it on his way home.

Either the meeting will be held on Friday, *or* it will have to be postponed until the following Monday.

The next sentences illustrate the agreement of the verb in person and in number with the subject nearer it. When two subjects are joined by a comparative conjunction, use the verb form that agrees with the subject closest to the verb. You will study about verbs in Section 4, "Action and Being Words."

Not only the clerk *but also* you **are** to report to the pay window.
(Two subjects compared. *Is* should be used with *clerk,* but *you* is closer to the verb position. Therefore, **are** must be used.)

Either Mr. Green *or* all the board members **were** to attend that meeting.
(A singular and a plural subject compared. Mr. Green . . . was; members . . . were.)

Some words are used as sentence connectors.

Conjunctions are sometimes confused with *sentence connectors,* called *conjunctive adverbs* by some people. The following words are examples of sentence connectors that may be used to connect two independent clauses.

however	moreover	thus
therefore	nevertheless	too
consequently	likewise	hence

A semicolon comes before a sentence connector and a comma follows it.

When these words are used as connectors, they take a stronger mark of punctuation than a conjunction requires. In the following compound sentence, a *comma* precedes the conjunction *and*.

The clerk counted the supplies, *and* the foreman listed them on the stock sheet.

Note, however, that when a sentence connector is used in a compound sentence, it is preceded by a *semicolon*. A comma usually follows it.

The clerk counted the supplies; *however,* the foreman listed them on the stock sheet.

The preliminary work was completed on Tuesday; *consequently,* the meeting will be held on Wednesday.

ACCURATE WORD CHOICE AIDS UNDERSTANDING

The main reason for trying to improve your ability to use words accurately is to secure the complete understanding of the one who receives your message. The ability to communicate clearly is a skill highly prized by the business community. If you possess this skill, you will find many challenging positions open to you.

Increase your ability to use words accurately.

In this last set of words often used inaccurately, you will find definitions and illustrations that will show you how to use the words more accurately. Take time to learn their definitions so that they become a part of your growing vocabulary.

personal, personnel
Personal refers to characteristics belonging to a particular person.

My ***personal*** opinion is contrary to yours.

Please give this matter your ***personal*** attention.

Personnel refers to a group of people employed by an organization. It may by used as an adjective or a noun.

adj
What are your ***personnel*** policies for sick leave?

n
Will you see that the entire ***personnel*** is informed of the change.

postal card, postcard
The U.S. Postal Service issues a *postal card* with the stamp impressed on it. A person or a company may design and use its own *postcard* to which a stamp must be affixed.

Please buy 500 ***postal cards*** today.

We should enclose a return ***postcard*** for an immediate answer.

practicable, practical
Practicable means usable. Things can be practicable, but people cannot.

This solution does not seem **practicable.**

A **practicable** approach would be to gather the facts first.

Practical refers to a plan that, when put into practice, is workable or useful.

Please arrive at a **practical** solution to the problem.

He has **practical** knowledge about our operations.

proceed, precede

Proceed means to go ahead, to carry on.

Mr. Smithers will **proceed** with the experiment.

Precede refers to something that came before.

Jane **preceded** me in line.

Note the spelling of the derivatives of these words:

proceed—proceeded, proceeding, proceeds, procedure

precede—preceded, preceding, precedent, precedence

quite

Quite should be used to mean *completely* or *entirely.* It is a colloquial word when used to mean *very* or *considerable.*

His understanding of the accident is **quite** correct.

A **large number** of the employees are covered by group insurance.

(**Not:** Quite a number . . .)

real

Real is an adjective; it cannot be used in place of an adverb.

Most of our assets are in **real** property.

As used in the sentence above, *real* means *real estate,* such as houses, buildings, and land.

When an adverb is needed, choose one that is descriptive.

He did an **exceedingly** good job.

He did a **very** good job.

recent, resent

Recent refers to something that just happened or is of late occurrence.

The **recent** fire caused $200,000 damage.

Resent means that someone considers he or she was insulted or injured.

He **resented** the remarks of the superintendent.

respectively, respectfully

Respectively refers to single happenings in a particular order.

Mr. Mortenson and Mrs. Holcomb, **respectively,** are vice president and secretary of our company.

Respectfully means in a courteous manner.

She **respectfully** asked to be excused from the meeting.

run Do not use *run* to mean *manage, direct, operate.*

> The workers **operate** the power machines.
>
> Miss Harvey **manages** the file department.

Run means to move quickly or, when used as a noun, a continuous movement.

> The employees are to **run** outside when the alarm sounds.
>
> Take a **run** up to Detroit to visit the factory.
>
> I hope I have a **run** of good luck this year.

so *So* is used mainly to indicate in this, that, or such a manner or degree.

> He talked **so** fast that his words were jumbled.

Do not use *so* as an intensifier or modifier in place of *very* or *extremely.*

> The new office building is **extremely** modern.
> > (**Not:** . . . is *so* modern.)

Be careful to use *so that* when joining a dependent idea to an independent or main idea.

> They checked the report again **so that** all errors were found.

So is used occasionally as a conjunction to mean *therefore;* a precise writer, though, places the minor idea in a dependent clause.

> **Not:** The meeting was postponed, *so* we will have to decide on another date.
>
> **Better:** *As* the meeting was postponed, we will have to decide on another date.

some *Some* should not be used as an intensive adjective or in place of an adverb.

> That is a streamlined car.
> > (**Not:** . . . *some* car.)
>
> The janitor certainly cleaned this office thoroughly.
> > (**Not:** The janitor certainly gave this office *some* cleaning job.)

superior, inferior *Superior* means higher in position or authority and greater in value or amount. *Inferior* means lower in order or rank and lower in quality or value. Both these words are followed by *to,* **not** *than.*

> The new machine is **superior to** the old one.
>
> Mary's calculator is **inferior to** John's.

then, than *Then* means at that time, soon afterward, at another time, therefore.

> The speaker **then** talked about government regulations.

Than is a subordinate conjunction used to introduce a clause of comparison.

I would rather go now **than** wait for him.

This product is better **than** the one we sampled yesterday.

therefor,   *Therefor,* used in legal work mainly, means *for it.*
therefore   *Therefore* is a conjunctive adverb meaning *as a result* or *consequently.*

The money **therefor** is to be paid within 60 days.

I plan to be in your city next week; **therefore,** I will discuss the matter then.

ASSIGNMENTS

Apply your knowledge of conjunctions

A. Coordinate conjunctions join sentence elements of equal value in parallel construction. The following sentences contain such compound elements. Underline the compound elements in each sentence. Then indicate in the right-hand column how these compounds are used by writing the number from the list below to explain their function in the sentence.

1. Subjects
2. Verbs
3. Clauses
4. Phrases
5. Other words

Example: The <u>brown and beige</u> rug goes in Mrs. Fuller's office.   *5*

1. An executor of an estate must be stated in the will or in a codicil to the will.   _____

2. A contract grants rights and obligations.   _____

3. The old but respected law firm had great rapport with its clients.   _____

4. Take these messages to the law clerk, and wait for answers to them.   _____

5. The legal secretary was asked to sort, to code, and to file all the data regarding the case.   _____

6. Jim and Mary instructed their lawyer to file suit immediately.   _____

7. The terms of a written contract should be stated clearly and should contain all necessary details.   _____

8. In some contracts, unskilled work or labor may be delegated.   _____

9. Seeing the jury and realizing the strength of justice, visitors to the courtroom often renew their faith in democracy.   _____

10.   Consent of the principal and of the agent is necessary to create an agency.   _____

11.   The judge gave not only John but also me instructions in courtroom procedures.   _____

12.   The attorney drafted and filed the claim against the company.   _____

13.   If the appeal is granted and if the court adjourns, the defense will be pleased.   _____

14.   Jones and Martin are authors of the law manual.   _____

15.   To prepare good copy or to draft effective letters, one needs imagination.   _____

   B.   The following sentences use coordinate and comparative conjunctions and sentence connectors.

1.   Underline these connecting words in each sentence.
2.   If punctuation is needed, insert the correct marks.

Example: Disorderly conduct is hard to define;<u>hence,</u>it is hard to defend.

   1.   Law is based on reason and justice consequently it protects the basic rights of all of us.
   2.   The law not only protects the individual but it also protects society as a whole.
   3.   The three fundamental rights you have are security of person security of property and personal liberty.
   4.   The violation of the right to security of person or property is called a tort.
   5.   Examples of tort are libel slander assault negligence and fraud.
   6.   A tort may be intentional but intention is not essential in proving that a tort exists.
   7.   Crime is classed as a public wrong and it must be committed intentionally.
   8.   Either the plaintiff or his/her lawyer must be present.
   9.   Neither the courts nor the laws are infallible.
  10.   Not only did the plan work better but it also proved to be very popular.
  11.   We should view the case objectively however forgetting personal views may be difficult.
  12.   Would this accident be classed as a crime or a tort?
  13.   The manual states the facts nevertheless it does not present sufficient details.
  14.   The Supreme Court session began on time furthermore the gallery was packed.
  15.   The most common examples of felonies are murder theft and arson.

   C.   You have just learned that coordinate conjunctions join items of the same type or class. Read the following pairs of sentences carefully to find the words, phrases, or clauses that are joined. Then, select the one sentence that correctly illustrates the joining of equal sentence elements in parallel construction. Place the letter opposite the sentence in the column at the right.

Example: (a)   I like filing letters and to take dictation.
           (b)   I like filing letters and taking dictation.   *b*

   1.   (*a*)   Our new supervisor is tall, handsome, and has wavy hair.
        (*b*)   Our new supervisor is tall and handsome and has wavy hair.   _____
   2.   (*a*)   I'd like to work for your company for three reasons: your diversified product line, your international sales organization, and because you are a leader in the oil industry.
        (*b*)   I'd like to work for your company for three reasons: your diversified product

line, your international sales organization, and your leadership in the oil
industry.   _____

3. (a) Government statistics show the number of employed and unemployed in the
labor force.
   (b) Govenment statistics show the number of employed and those without jobs in
the labor force.   _____

4. (a) Our storeroom has neither a good stock of file boxes or labels.
   (b) Our storeroom has neither a good stock of file boxes nor labels.   _____

5. (a) Mr. Thompson is undecided whether to hire Ms. Willows today or maybe
waiting until Monday.
   (b) Mr. Thompson is undecided whether to hire Ms. Willows today or to wait
until Monday.   _____

6. (a) Either one or two carbons would be acceptable.
   (b) Either make two carbons or one would be acceptable.   _____

7. (a) In junior college, Marc studied business law, economics, and accounting.
   (b) In junior college, Marc studied business law, economics, and took several
accounting courses.   _____

8. (a) When the parts are finished and having them inspected by Mr. Stewart, please
deliver them by messenger to the Babcock Company.
   (b) When the parts are finished and have been inspected by Mr. Stewart, please
deliver them by messenger to the Babcock Company.   _____

9. (a) Making personal phone calls and talking loudly are not permitted during
working hours.
   (b) Making personal phone calls and loud talking are not permitted during
working hours.   _____

10. (a) The office building was painted beige or with some color called desert sand.
    (b) The office building was painted a color called desert sand but resembling beige.   _____

D. In the sentences below, choose the word(s) from the pair in parentheses that demonstrates correct word usage. Write your choice in the space provided.

1. The workers _____ the section leader's know-it-all attitude. (recent, resent)

2. The new computer is far superior _____ the one we _____ had. (to, than)
(formerly, formally)

3. The final inspection has been postponed; _____, you will have to work _____

_____ planned. (therefor, therefore) (later, latter) (then, than)

4. Our department is _____ with great efficiency. (run, managed)

5. Check the books once again _____ all possible errors will be found. (so, so that)

6. I thought Harry explained the process _____ thoroughly. (real, very)

7. Should our firm _____ with plans to increase its share of the market? (proceed, precede)

8. Your idea seems to be a _____ solution to our problem. (practicable, practical)

9. Did you know that the _____ in our department _____ raises? (personnel, personal) (got, received)

10. He told me that his department is doing much better _____ it did in the _____. (than, then) (past, passed)

11. When you mail those packages at the post office, buy 25 _____. (postal cards, post-cards)

12. The new method is inferior _____ the one we've been using. (to, than)

13. The luncheon _____ the program should take approximately forty minutes. (pro-ceeding, preceding)

14. The finance manager _____ asked to be excused from the meeting. (respectively, respectfully)

15. We have no reason to _____ the change in management. (recent, resent)

16. Please design a _____ for our direct mail campaign. (postal card, postcard)

17. Are you _____ sure of your facts? (quite, very)

18. The painters are doing _____ job in redecorating the halls. (a real good, an ex-cellent)

19. Mary Smith and Jean Cohen, _____, are the second-place and the third-place winners in the word processing contest. (respectively, respectfully)

20. The new IBM computer is _____ machine. (some, a versatile)

Name _____

Date _____

———————————— **PRACTICE WRITING** ————————————

The ability to connect items of the same type and of similar construction is one you should develop. See how well you can use the coordinate and comparative conjunctions in your own sentences. Follow the directions given for each sentence.

1. Write a sentence using a coordinate conjunction to connect *two or more words*.

    _____

    _____

    _____

2. Write a sentence using a coordinate conjunction to connect *two independent clauses*.

    _____

    _____

    _____

3. Write a sentence using a conjunction to join *two subjects*.

    _____

    _____

    _____

4. Write a sentence containing *several items in a series*.

    _____

    _____

    _____

5. Write a sentence using a *sentence connector* (conjunctive adverb) to join *two independent clauses*.

    _____

    _____

    _____

6. Write a sentence containing *two* closely related *independent clauses* connected by a coordinate conjunction.

_____

_____

_____

7. Write a sentence using *however* as the connector.

_____

_____

_____

8. Write a sentence using a coordinate conjunction to join *two verbs*.

_____

_____

_____

9. Write a sentence with *three subjects*.

_____

_____

_____

10. Write a sentence using *either/or*.

_____

_____

_____

PART **2**

Subordinators join dependent clauses to independent clauses

In Section 1, Part 2, you learned about subordinators that introduce dependent clauses, and on page 18 there is a partial list of them. Further on in Part 2 the discussion of complex sentences included many illustrations that show how these words introduce dependent clauses. Also, on pages 56–59 in Part 4, there are additional illustrations. In this section, we will study these important words in more detail.

Subordinate connectors join dependent clauses to independent clauses by showing the logical relationship between the clauses. As you learned in Section 1, sentences containing independent and dependent clauses are called complex sentences—a minor idea added to a major idea. Subordinators introduce the minor idea in the dependent clause. These minor clauses are either adjective or adverb clauses.

Some subordinators introduce adjective clauses.

Some dependent clauses are known as *adjective clauses* because they describe or modify nouns and pronouns. These adjective clauses are introduced by subordinators known as *relative pronouns: who, whom, which, that, what, whoever,* and *whomever.* They describe and add additional information about the nouns and pronouns they modify.

The car *that is parked at the curb* belongs to the secretary.
(The *that* clause is necessary to identify the car and, therefore, does not have commas. It is a *restrictive* clause.)

Mr. Davis, *who is chairman of the board,* spoke to the security officers.
(The *who* clause is *nonrestrictive* and is set off by commas. It is not necessary because Mr. Davis is identified by name and his title could be discovered easily.)

As you can see from these illustrations, sentences containing adjective clauses must be punctuated carefully. A *restrictive* adjective clause limits the noun or pronoun it modifies—it is necessary to the correct understanding of the message. Therefore, no punctuation is necessary. If, however, the informa-

Commas are used with nonrestrictive adjective clauses.

tion given in the adjective clause is merely an additional thought or fact, the clause is *nonrestrictive*. These nonrestrictive clauses are set off by commas to indicate to the reader that they are *not* essential to the correct understanding of the message. Adjectives and their uses are presented in detail in Section 5.

Who, whoever, whom, and *whomever* clauses are used quite often in business writing. Your problem is to decide whether to use *who/whoever* (nominative case) or *whom/whomever* (objective case). The best approach is to isolate the entire clause first; then determine how the *who/whom* is used in the clause. Many times it is helpful to reword the clause. This principle will be discussed in detail in Section 3, Part 5. Because the use of *who/whom* seems to present problems to many people, a brief discussion of the proper use of *who/whom* is included here. By the time you have studied these pronouns again in Section 3, you will be able to use them correctly in all your communications.

Here is a sentence where it is necessary to decide whether to use *who* or *whom* in the adjective clause.

He did not know *who/whom* the applicant was.

Reworded, the clause would read, *the applicant was who/whom.* Now you can see that the linking verb *was* needs a complement in the nominative case. The correct choice is the word *who.* Linking verbs are discussed on pages 38–39.

He did not know *who* the applicant was.

Study the next sentence.

Who/Whom do you think is the best programmer?

Reworded, the sentence reads, *You do think who/whom is the best programmer.* The dependent clause, *who/whom is the best programmer,* needs a subject. All pronoun subjects are in the nominative case. *Who* therefore, is the pronoun needed. The sentence should read:

Who do you think is the best programmer?

In the next sentence, determine how the pronoun is used.

Our new president, *who/whom I know personally,* will head the charity drive.

Reworded, the clause reads, *I know personally who/whom.* You have already determined, no doubt, that the verb **know** takes an object. Objects of verbs are in the objective case; therefore, your choice should be *whom.*

Our new president, *whom* I know personally, will head the charity drive.

Subordinate connectors introduce adverb clauses.

Another type of dependent clause introduced by subordinators is the *adverb clause.* These dependent clauses are used as adverbs to modify the verb in the main or independent clause. They are introduced by subordinators that are adverbs. Here is a list of adverbial subordinate connectors.

after	in order to	whether
although	if	whereas
as	since	unless
as if	until	than

as though	when	provided
because	while	inasmuch as
before	where	so that

A comma follows an introductory adverb clause.

In the following sentences, notice that the adverb clauses modify the verbs in the independent clauses. The sentences also illustrate an important use of the comma. Adverb clauses that introduce the sentence have a comma immediately after them. Those that end a sentence ordinarily do not need a comma preceding them.

Sam immediately unpacks the office supplies *when shipments arrive.*

If we receive the supplies by tomorrow, we can fill all the orders.

A comma comes before a nonrestrictive adverb clause at the end of the sentence.

No punctuation is used in the first sentence because the adverb clause *when shipments arrive* is a restrictive clause telling when Sam unpacks the boxes. It is needed to complete the meaning of the independent clause. When, however, the adverb clause introduces a sentence, as in the second example, it is *always* followed by a comma. When an adverb clause ends a sentence, check it to determine whether it is restrictive or nonrestrictive. If it is nonrestrictive, place a comma before the clause.

Please decide immediately if you want the job, *inasmuch as we have other applicants.*
(a bit of additional information)
You can buy Samson toys at the ABC Department Store, *as they handle them exclusively.*
(an additional fact)

Connectors show how things and ideas relate to each other.

Connectors establish the relationship of ideas. To become an effective communicator, therefore, you should choose them carefully. When two or more closely related ideas are joined in a sentence, decide whether both are of equal importance or whether one is of less importance than the other. Consider the ideas in the following sentence.

The Ellis Company manufactures electronic equipment and should be successful in today's electronic age.

Are the two ideas of equal importance? They do not appear to be; therefore, the sentence should be rewritten to indicate which of them is more important. Notice below how the important message is highlighted by being placed in the independent clause.

The Ellis Company, which manufactures electronic equipment, should be successful in today's electronic age.

The descriptive adjective clause *which manufactures* . . . is a nonrestrictive dependent clause surrounded by commas. If the two ideas had been of equal importance, the use of the coordinating connector *and* would have been correct.

Try to avoid the constant use of *and, but,* and *for.* Instead, look for the best subordinate connector to show the importance of each idea and to show the relationships of *cause, comparison, time, sequence,* and *contrast.* See Section 7, "Writing Effectively."

Learn to use these connectors correctly.

Here is a list of troublesome connectors. Study them so that you can use them correctly in your speaking and writing.

And should not be used when an infinitive is needed.

> Try *to answer* the letter today.
>> (**Not:** Try and answer . . . You are not *both* trying and answering.)

But, for, since are used as connectors and prepositions.

> Everyone went to the meeting *but* John.
>> (preposition)
> The president attended the meeting, *but* the secretary stayed in the office.
>> (connector)
> The report was typed *for* Mr. Hughes.
>> (preposition)
> The stenographer worked late, *for* she had two reports to type.
>> (connector)
> The factory had been shut down *since* Monday.
>> (preposition)
> *Since* the material is needed immediately, please phone the factory today.
>> (connector)

Like is a preposition or a verb but **never** a connector. Instead of *like,* use *as, as if, as though* to join clauses. The preposition *like* means *similar to.*

> Do the job *as* I do.
> This painting looks *as though* it were the work of an amateur.
> The new building looks *like* the old one.
>> (preposition)
> The manager *would like* to launch a campaign in April.

Provided (not *providing*) is preferred as the subordinate connector to join a clause to the sentence.

> I shall promote him *provided he demonstrates initiative.*

Etc. may be used in some writing for *and so forth.* An additional *and* before it is unnecessary.

> We mailed letters, brochures, postcards, *etc.*
> She requisitioned paper, pencils, pens, *etc.* for the supply closet.

That or *whether* should be used to introduce clauses following such verbs as *say, think, know,* and *ask.*

> He said *that* he would make his decision later.
> Do you think *that* Walter will come?
> Did he ask *whether* Mr. Temple had said that the report should be rewritten?

That/which. Careful writers use *that* to introduce a restrictive clause and *which* to introduce a nonrestrictive one.

> The calculator *that* is in my office needs repair.
> Mr. Peters' calculator, *which* is a Friden, needs repair.

Whether should be used to introduce clauses indicating an alternative. The alternative may be expressed or understood.

I do not know *whether Mr. Jones will approve the change.*
Please tell us *whether you received the tool.*
Please tell us *whether or not you received the tool.*
(*or not* may be added for emphasis.)

So should be used sparingly as a conjunction. Instead use one of these sentence connectors—*therefore, accordingly, consequently, hence, thus*—to introduce clauses of result.

I told John about the case; *consequently,* he is aware of the possible outcome.

(**Weak:** . . . about the case, *so* he is aware . . .)

As . . . *as* is used to show equality.

Our capital is *as* large *as* it was two years ago.

So . . . *as* is used to show inequality or negative comparison.

Our capital is *not so* large *as* it was two years ago.

ACCURATE CHOICE OF WORDS IS IMPORTANT

The group of words presented here are called *homonyms*. Look carefully at the word *homonym*. Do you see two *m*'s and one *n*? If you do, you are learning to visualize the correct form of a word. This ability will make it possible for you to spell words correctly. Be sure to take time to *look* at a word so that you *see* all the letters and the *order* in which they occur.

Some words sound alike but are spelled differently and have different meanings.

Homonyms cause trouble because they sound alike but have different meanings and spellings. The English language contains many such words. Take a good look at each pair of words in the following list, and learn the definition for each spelling. Use your ability to visualize the letters that are different in the words.

aloud	Loudly; with a speaking voice.
allowed	Permitted; granted.
ascent	An upward slope.
assent	To agree; to admit a thing is true.
calendar	A record of time.
calender	n. A finishing machine used in the manufacture of paper or cloth.
	v. To press paper or cloth between rollers to make it glossy.
canvas	A heavy, closely woven cloth made of hemp or flax.
canvass	To solicit; to seek orders.
grate	To fret, to irritate, to make a rasping noise; a frame.
great	Large in size, most important, much higher in some quality.
here	In this place.
hear	To perceive by the ear.
hole	A hollow place; a pit.
whole	Entire; not broken; intact.
packed	Packaged; arranged compactly; crammed.
pact	An agreement.

{	past	Pertaining to a former time.
	passed	Gone by; elapsed.
{	role	A part, or character, performed by an actor.
	roll	To revolve by turning over and over; that which is rolled up.
{	seem	To appear.
	seam	The line formed by sewing two pieces of cloth together.
{	weighed	Past tense of *to weigh* (to gauge heaviness).
	wade	To move by stepping through water; to go forward with difficulty.
{	wave	To swing back and forth; to motion with the hand.
	waive	To give up a claim to.
{	whose	Possessive of *who*.
	who's	Contraction of *who is*.

ASSIGNMENTS

Apply your knowledge of connectors

A. Because connectors are of several types, you must be able to recognize each type in order to punctuate sentences for the reader's understanding. Underline both coordinate and subordinate connecting words in the following sentences. Also, punctuate each sentence where necessary.

1. The financial statement is current accurate and complete.
2. You have a good traffic record therefore your insurance will be renewed.
3. If you appeal to the courts they will help you obtain justice.
4. You should either make a settlement or bring suit through proper legal channels.
5. Because you handle administrative duties you need a large vocabulary consequently you should add new words every day.
6. Communication often fails because people define words differently.
7. We should obey a law even if it seems unreasonable.
8. A data sheet is often necessary for securing a job but even if it is not needed it is a valuable tool to prepare one for the interview.
9. Be careful how you spend your money otherwise you may not be able to pay your bills.
10. The forms should be filed neither alphabetically nor geographically but they should be filed chronologically.

B. Select the appropriate word from those in parentheses, and write it in the column at the right.

1. Please send me another widget (like, as) the one you sent last week. _____

2. This report looks (like, as if) it were a complete study of the problem. _____

3. The accountant should try (and, to) have the balance sheet ready by Tuesday. _____

4. The manager should take a day off (and, to) go to the seminar on motivation. _____

5. Your speech not only is well written (but, but also) is extremely forceful. _____

6. Mr. Jones found the speeches interesting, (and, but) he thought he learned more from the question-and-answer sessions. _____

7. We have not heard from the applicant (since, after) the inteview.   _____

8. It will be unnecessary for you to appear in court (providing, provided)
    you pay the parking fine.   _____

9. Please let us know (whether, if) you will attend the law seminar.   _____

10. The clients have been notified by mail; (so, consequently), they should
    be aware of the difficulties that may arise.   _____

11. The car (that, which) is parked across the street belongs to the
    caretaker.   _____

12. The budget, (which, that) I worked on yesterday, will be presented
    Friday to the finance committee.   _____

13. Do you know (that, who, what) Bob Fischer plans to retire next month?   _____

14. The census figures were not (as, so) large as they were last year.   _____

15. Our profit for this year is (as, so) large as it was last year.   _____

16. We ordered the following items: paint, brushes, canvas, thinner, (and
    etc., etc.)   _____

17. The office manager will order the supplies (providing, provided) you can
    show a need for them.   _____

18. Try (and, to) telephone your message soon.   _____

19. (Who, Whom) will take this report to Mr. Sheldon?   _____

20. You should keep your clients informed of meeting dates (like, as) I do.   _____

C. Read carefully the following complex sentences, and underline the dependent clauses. Then add punctuation where needed to make the meaning clear to the reader.

1. Businesses should employ people who will work in harmony together.
2. After a check is cashed it is returned to the issuing bank.
3. The attorney should be put on a retainer if the client wishes additional help.
4. Mr. Smith who is the president of the Chamber of Commerce presided at the meeting.
5. When the application was received, it was given to the counselor.
6. The firm where the tool was manufactured is located in the South.
7. This is the first program that we feel will meet our needs.
8. The personnel director whose office is on the second floor will see you today.
9. As your account is long overdue we should like payment immediately.
10. I will hire Mr. Jones whom you chose.
11. We have read your report with a great deal of interest inasmuch as we are specialists in direct-
    mail selling.
12. The book that was written by our governor was published in January.
13. If you would like to make an appointment fill out the enclosed card.
14. The worth of the product will be judged by the number of people who return the coupon.
15. Mr. Burns answered the phone while his secretary talked to the visitor.

16. When a project is being terminated the government will require records to support claims for work performed.

17. Government contracts carry a clause that gives the federal government the absolute right to terminate contracts.

18. When a contract is terminated for convenience the contractor is allowed to recover all reasonable and allocable costs that were incurred up to the point of termination.

19. Jack Jones who is your most qualified and experienced worker should be named termination coordinator.

20. Costs that you incur after the termination date are reimbursable as settlement expense.

D. Complete the following sentences by selecting the correct *homonym* from those in parentheses. Write your choice in the space provided in the right-hand column.

1. The box is _____ (packed, pact) and _____ (weighed, wade) for shipment by air.

   _____

   _____

2. The company will _____ (wave, waive) its right to sue.

   _____

3. In _____ (passed, past) years an exta day off at Christmas was _____ (aloud, allowed).

   _____

   _____

4. Did you _____ (here, hear) about the proposed _____ (pact, packed) between them?

   _____

   _____

5. Smoking is not _____ (aloud, allowed) in the laboratory, and neither is thinking _____ (aloud, allowed) acceptable.

   _____

   _____

6. _____ (Whose, Who's) papers are those on the receptionist's desk?

   _____

7. It _____ (seems, seams) that Mr. Wilton _____ (past, passed) Mrs. Childers in the hall without speaking.

   _____

   _____

8. Please purchase a large _____ (role, roll) of cellophane tape.

   _____

9. Our company is planning to order _____ (calendars, calenders) as gifts for our customers.

   _____

10. Please find out _____ (whose, who's) responsible for the purchase of the _____ (canvas, canvass) used in this suitcase.

    _____

    _____

11. Did that noise _____ (great, grate) on your nerves?

    _____

12. I plan to _____ (weighed, wade) through these complaints before the meeting.

    _____

13. Please bring the package _____ (hear, here).   _____

14. _____ (Whose, Who's) going to the convention?   _____

15. Does Mr. Jones _____ (ascent, assent) to the plan to raise rates?   _____

16. The mill uses its _____ (calendars, calenders) to make
    glossy paper.   _____

17. The women have a _____ (great, grate) deal of respect for
    higher education.   _____

18. The _____ (ascent, assent) from the parking lot to the
    main building is too steep.   _____

19. Please take the machinist the _____ (hole, whole) sheet of
    metal.   _____

20. All the _____ (seems, seams) in the new drapes in the presi-
    dent's office are coming apart.   _____

Name _____

Date _____

—————————————— **PRACTICE WRITING** ——————————————

By writing sentences that contain unequal clauses (dependent and independent), you will develop your skill to tie minor ideas to major ideas. Think of your main or most important idea *first;* put it in the independent clause. Then select additional information that is less important but that will add interest; put this less important information in the dependent clause. In writing the five sentences called for below, see that you place the important part of your message in the independent clause. Follow the illustrations on pages 83–85.

1. Write a sentence containing a *nonrestrictive which* clause.

    _____

    _____

    _____

2. Write a sentence containing a *restrictive that* clause.

    _____

    _____

    _____

3. Write a sentence containing an *adverb* clause that *introduces* the sentence.

    _____

    _____

    _____

4. Write a sentence containing an *adverb* clause at the *end* of the sentence.

    _____

    _____

    _____

5. Write a sentence containing a *nonrestrictive who/whom* clause.

    _____

    _____

    _____

    Write three more sentences containing either *restrictive* or *nonrestrictive* clauses. Be sure to punctuate them correctly.

6. _____

    _____

7. _____

    _____

8. _____

    _____

Naming elements

The naming words in our language constitute the largest portion of the half a million or so words listed in an unabridged dictionary. This group expands daily as new words are borrowed from other cultures and languages. New words are also being formed to meet new needs, especially those resulting from scientific discoveries and inventions. Modern technology also adds new words to the business vocabulary.

The phenomenon of the 1960s and 1970s has been the addition of a host of words assigned new meanings by young people. They are said to have a language of their own, incomprehensible to those of an older generation. New words are constantly being coined; old words are being modernized and changed.

Ours is a viable, living language through which learning is acquired of all other subjects. It is appropriate that we begin our study of individual words used in sentences with the naming elements, nouns and pronouns.

Nouns have important roles in sentences

Each word in a sentence is called by a special term. The term for those words that name many kinds of things is *noun*. Because of their large number, nouns are the basic words in our language. They point out the persons, places, ideas, qualities, or things being talked about. When you identified one-word subjects in the previous section, the word chosen was a noun or a pronoun. In sentences nouns may be subjects, but they are not complete thoughts. To complete a thought something must be told about the subject. Naming what you are talking about and telling something about it gives you a sense of completeness. As a person interested in business, you want to know how to transmit precise information from one person to another. This study of nouns will show you that the careful choice of the noun and its correct use assist in the transmission of an accurate message.

Nouns are words that name. These words that name things allow your mind to visualize a picture or to think about the idea named. For instance, your mind can see a building, a machine, a pen; and you can think about confidence, absenteeism, cooperation. Notice also that some of these nouns are concrete; that is, they name things that can be touched. Some are abstract; they name things that can only be thought about. Most nouns are common nouns and begin with small letters. Some that name specific persons, places, or things are proper nouns and begin with capitals.

Study the list below. It will orient you to the detailed discussion that follows.

Persons—man, secretary, employee, supervisor

Places—city, county, harbor, district

Things—desk, eraser, ribbon, typewriter

Qualities or ideas—loyalty, reliability, democracy, policy

Groups (collective nouns)—committee, team, pair, jury

Specific places and persons (proper nouns)—Linda, Chicago, The Crawford Corp., Chevrolet

Nouns have different positions in a sentence.

Another helpful way to identify nouns is by the position they occupy in a sentence. They serve as subjects, objects of the verb, complements, objects of prepositions, and appositives.

As a subject, nouns name the person, place, idea, or thing being talked about.

The *employees* applauded.

The *city* is congested.

Accuracy is essential.

Computers help business.

As an object, nouns name the person, place, idea, or thing receiving the action.

He fired the *supervisor.*

We visited the *country* last summer.

I respect your *loyalty.*

Sally needed the *eraser.*

As a complement, nouns name the person, place, idea, or thing completing the subject.

Miss Jamison is our *bookkeeper.*

My favorite place is the *beach.*

Her strength of character is her *honesty.*

My first large purchase was my *car.*

Remember that the complement may be either a noun or an adjective. The complement is a noun if it names another identity of the subject. If it describes some quality of the subject, it is an adjective, such as the word *confusing* in the following sentence.

His message was *confusing.*

As an object of a preposition, nouns name the person, place, idea, or thing completing the prepositional phrase. (Prepositional phrases will be studied further in Section 5, Part 4.)

He is a relative of the *supervisor.*

The center of the *city* is congested.

Members of a *democracy* should exercise their voting privilege.

The cost of the *typewriter* was $300.

As an appositive, nouns name the person, place, idea, or thing that further describes the noun or pronoun they follow.

Harold Kuntz, a management *professor,* has written several books.

Washington, a beautiful *state,* is usually green.

He lacks an important trait, *dependability.*

I'd be lost without my office aid, *Liquid Paper.*

An *appositive* is a noun or pronoun, often written with modifiers, that explains the noun or pronoun it follows. It is set off from the rest of the sentence by commas because it is not necessary for sentence completeness. The message is complete without it. Notice in the sentences above that the appositives may easily be omitted.

Nouns may be common or proper.

A *common noun* names a member of a general class. The words *state, country, theater, vice president,* and *store* are common nouns.

A *proper noun,* written with a capital letter, is one that fits only one particular person, group of people, place, or thing. Some of the words used in the paragraph above become proper nouns when used to name specific people or places.

Common	Proper
state	State of California
country	Italy
theater	Bay Theater
officer	Vice President Samuels
store	Barnes Drug Store
place	Oswego Country Club

Section 8, Part 3, contains numerous illustrations of capitalization rules. Refer to it if you have questions about when to capitalize a noun.

Nouns have gender.

Gender refers to the use of nouns and pronouns to identify sex or a lack of it. Sex and gender, however, are not the same things. Gender relates to language; sex relates to biological structure. We frequently refer to things that have no sex as masculine or feminine—*he* or *she;* for instance, a ship is often referred to as feminine *she* or *her.* The following examples will help you understand gender.

A noun is of the *masculine gender* if *he* or *him* substitutes for it.

The *man* rode a bicycle.

He rode a bicycle.

An automobile hit the *man.*

An automobile hit *him.*

A noun is of the *feminine* gender if *she* or *her* substitutes for it.

Miss Cohen acted as secretary at the conference.

She acted as secretary at the conference.

The computer is operated by *Mrs. Fasman.*

The computer is operated by *her.*

A noun is *neuter gender* if *it* substitutes for the noun.

The manager checked the *computer.*

The manager checked *it.*

The *elevator* stopped between the 11th and 12th floors.

It stopped between the 11th and 12th floors.

Masculine and feminine gender will cause you little difficulty in sentence structure. Keep in mind that masculine-feminine make up one group of words for which you can substitute *he, she, him,* and *her,* and neuter gender includes the group of words for which you can substitute *it.*

There are specific words for some masculine and feminine forms, such as *man, woman, husband, wife, aunt, uncle.* In other instances gender is shown by a change in the word ending, such as *actor, actress, heir, heiress.* In business situations, one form is frequently used for titles for either male or female: *author, director, manager, attendant.*

Verbs can change into nouns.

Verbal nouns (or *gerunds*) change verbs into nouns by giving names to actions. A verbal noun, the verb plus *ing,* can occupy any of the noun positions.

Subject:	*Typing* is fun.
Object:	I admire neat *typing.*
Complement:	My greatest skill is my *typing.*
Object of preposition:	They proofread the copy before *typing.*
Appositive:	The clerk's present job, *typing,* requires little supervision.

Note that the same word can also be a verb. As a verb, it *expresses* action rather than *naming* an action.

The stenographer *is typing* the report.

Collective nouns name a group of persons or objects.

Some nouns, called *collective nouns,* name groups of persons, objects, or parts of groups. Here are some examples of collective nouns.

committee	board	majority
senate	commission	number
audience	jury	company

When the designated collection is thought of as a whole or a unit, the noun takes a singular verb.

The staff *is* to meet in the board room.

The committee *favors* early adoption of the plan.

When each individual of a designated collection is considered, the noun takes a plural verb.

The majority *were* not *agreed* on the verdict.

A number of cars *were* defective.

The group *give* their consent for an outside appraisal.

Subject-verb agreement is discussed in more detail in Section 4, Part 2.

ACCURATE CHOICE OF WORDS IS IMPORTANT

You have learned to take time to look at a word in order to see all its letters. Also, you have learned that many words pronounced the same are spelled differently. How can you attack these words so that you may become an accurate speller? One of the best methods to use for mastering words is a four-step routine: **see, say, spell, write.**

See the whole word and all its letters; visualize it in your mind.

Say the word correctly.

Spell the word out loud.

Write the word legibly; check it; write it again.

		Write	
		First time	*Second time*
capitol	Official state house; the building occupied by the U. S. Congress.	_____	_____
capital	Accumulated wealth; principal; main; city or town official seat of government.	_____	_____

cede	To yield; to grant.	_____	_____
seed	That from which anything grows.	_____	_____
complement	That which fills up or completes.	_____	_____
compliment	A flattering speech or attention.	_____	_____
faze	To disturb; to worry.	_____	_____
phase	A state of development or change.	_____	_____
forth	Forward; onward.	_____	_____
fourth	Ordinal number, following _third_.	_____	_____
instance	Occasion; step in an action.	_____	_____
instants	Moments; very brief periods of time.	_____	_____
loan	That which is lent or borrowed.	_____	_____
lone	Solitary; single.	_____	_____
mean	Vicious; unmanageable; bad; average.	_____	_____
mien	Bearing; demeanor.	_____	_____
pair	Two of a kind; a couple.	_____	_____
pare	To shave off; to cut off.	_____	_____
pear	A fruit in the same family as the apple.	_____	_____
piece	A fragment separated from the whole.	_____	_____
peace	State of tranquility or quiet.	_____	_____
presents	Gifts; things given.	_____	_____
presence	State of being present.	_____	_____
stationary	Fixed in a certain place.	_____	_____
stationery	Articles used in writing, as paper and envelopes.	_____	_____

ASSIGNMENTS

Apply your knowledge of nouns

A. The following sentences contain many nouns. Place each noun you find in the proper column at the right according to its use in the sentence.

	Subject	Appositive	Object or complement	Object of preposition
Example: Mr. Diaz, the director, gave the checks to his secretary.	*Mr. Diaz*	*director*	*checks*	*secretary*
1. A well-managed store operates on sound policies.				
2. One generally sound policy is selling on credit.				
3. Consumer credit is often short-term credit.				
4. The most common form of retail credit is charge accounts.				
5. Investment credit, long-term credit, extends payments over several years.				
6. No down payment is asked in the traditional charge account.				
7. Installment transactions, another form of retail credit, involve contracts.				

8. A person in debt, a debtor, must use caution when spending. _____ _____ _____ _____

9. Your total debts should probably not exceed 20 percent of your take-home salary. _____ _____ _____ _____

10. Knowledge of personal finance is meaningful to people with income. _____ _____ _____ _____

B. Compose new sentences by selecting other nouns for the ones given in the following sentences. Try to use a few verbal nouns in your sentences. The abbreviations used here are *s* (subject), *o* (object), *c* (complement), *op* (object of preposition), and *appos* (appositive).

Example: The _____*papers*_____ on the _____*desk*_____ need _____*signatures*_____.

The _____*comments*_____ on the _____*report*_____ need _____*clarification*_____.

The _____*folders*_____ on the _____*cabinet*_____ need _____*labels*_____.

1. _____*Mr. Allen*_____, our _____*salesman*_____, asked for a _____*raise*_____.

_____, our _____, asked for a _____.

_____, our _____, asked for a _____.

2. My _____*boss*_____ is a _____*person*_____ of _____*principle*_____.

My _____ is a _____ of _____.

_____ is the _____ of _____.

3. _____*Tom*_____ sent the _____*letter*_____ to our New York _____*office*_____.

_____ sent the _____ to our New York _____.

_____ sent the _____ to our New York _____.

4. _____*Complaining*_____ distracts the _____*supervisor*_____.

_____ distracts the _____.

_____ distracts the _____.

5. The _____*chairman*_____ of the _____*committee*_____ is _____*Mr. Phillips*_____.

The _____ of the _____ is _____.

The _____ of the _____ is _____.

C. Underline each noun in the following sentences. Write each noun in the proper columns at the right, indicating that it is a common, a proper, or a collective noun.

	Common	*Proper*	*Collective*
1. Americans have consistently adhered to habits of thrift.	_____	_____	_____
2. The resulting capital has been channeled into productive facilities.	_____	_____	_____
3. This capital has made the United States an advanced industrial country.	_____	_____	_____
4. Industrialized countries tend to channel savings into productive activity.	_____	_____	_____
5. Individuals must save for emergencies or opportunities for personal advancement.	_____	_____	_____
6. An American family should have three months' salary saved for emergencies.	_____	_____	_____
7. The California Legislature regulates some savings institutions.	_____	_____	_____
8. The commission publishes figures on gross annual savings of individuals in the United States.	_____	_____	_____
9. Generally, deposits in commercial banks are insured by the Federal Deposit Insurance Corporation.	_____	_____	_____
10. Many people fail to save because they fail to trim their wants to their income.	_____	_____	_____

D. Name the position in the following sentence of the underscored nouns. (Note: Position in a sentence may be subject, object, complement, appositive, or object of preposition.)

	Dr. Merry	*instructor*
Example: Please see <u>Dr. Merry</u>, my <u>instructor</u>.	*object*	*appositive*
Please talk to my <u>instructor</u>, <u>Dr. Merry</u>.	*appositive*	*object of prep.*
<u>Dr. Merry</u> is an excellent <u>instructor</u>.	*subject*	*complement*

	Mrs. Matson	*auditor*
1. Mrs. Matson, the auditor, will be here tomorrow.	_____	_____
2. Our auditor, Mrs. Matson, will be here Tuesday.	_____	_____
3. To the best of my knowledge, Mrs. Matson is our auditor.	_____	_____
4. As I told you, Mrs. Matson is the name of our auditor.	_____	_____
5. You should see the auditor, Mrs. Matson.	_____	_____

	English for Modern Business	*textbook*
6. *English for Modern Business* is a widely used textbook.	_____	_____
7. Mrs. Brown studied *English for Modern Business*, the textbook in her business English class.	_____	_____
8. The student learned it in her textbook, *English for Modern Business*.	_____	_____
9. Studying for her test, she nearly memorized the textbook, *English for Modern Business*.	_____	_____
10. A good business English textbook is *English for Modern Business*.	_____	_____

E.   Choose the word from the parentheses that completes the sentence. Write your choice, being careful to spell it correctly, in the right-hand column.

1. I thought the outcome of the conference provided some (capitol, capital) ideas.   _____

2. He agreed to (seed, cede) the point on taxation of inventory.   _____

3. That color will (complement, compliment) the colors of the sofa.   _____

4. I would appreciate it if you would (lend, loan) me your pen.   _____

5. Austin is the (capital, capitol) of Texas.   _____

6. The attorney's (presence, presents) was felt by everyone in the courtroom.   _____

7. Please find me a (piece, peace) of the leather used in the 1981 Ford Mustang.   _____

8. Be sure that the computer is (stationary, stationery).   _____

9. The company plans to (faze, phase) out that line by October.   _____

10. There are many (instance, instants) during the day when I pause to catch my breath.   _____

11. The (forth, fourth) door on the left is Mr. Herbert's office.   _____

12. The president received many (complements, compliments) on his
speech.   _____

13. Ask the supply clerk to order two (pairs, pares, pears) of work gloves.   _____

14. There is still time to replenish the (stationary, stationery) stock.   _____

15. For (instants, instance), the doors on the cabinet do not close tightly.   _____

16. At last, there is (piece, peace) in the machine shop.   _____

17. Our company policy says that employees cannot accept (presence,
presents) from vendors worth more than $25.   _____

18. That was a (mien, mean) trick to pull on the new draftsman.   _____

19. With the high cost of living, my (capital, capitol) seems to be drying up.   _____

20. The seniority rule gives workers (piece, peace) of mind.   _____

Name _____

Date _____

PRACTICE WRITING

Surprisingly enough, many business people have difficulty communicating with fellow workers. For a variety of reasons, the messages they send are misunderstood by the receivers. One of the reasons for the breakdown in communications is faulty sentence structure. You can profit from these Practice Writing exercises by writing clear, easy-to-understand sentences. The experience will make it easier to communicate with others in the business world.

In this exercise, compose original sentences in the spaces provided. Use the nouns given in parentheses as indicated.

Example: *(foreman;* object of preposition) *Mr. Jones spoke to the foreman about the problem.*

1. *(schedule;* object) _____

_____

2. *(meeting;* subject) _____

_____

3. *(secretary;* appositive) _____

_____

4. *(class;* subject) _____

_____

5. *(Santa Barbara;* object of preposition) _____

_____

6. *(president;* complement) _____

_____

7. *(accountant;* appositive) _____

_____

8.   (*company;* object of preposition) _____

_____

9.   (*management;* object) _____

_____

10.   (*student;* subject) _____

_____

11.   (*supervisor;* complement) _____

_____

12.   (*file;* object) _____

_____

13.   (*branch;* appositive) _____

_____

14.   (*policy;* object of preposition) _____

_____

15.   (*Richard D. Irwin, Inc.;* complement) _____

_____

Nouns may have plural forms

The regular way to form plurals of most English nouns is to add **s** or **es.** The plurals of a few nouns, however, are formed in irregular ways, by changing the spelling or changing **y** to **i** or **f** and **fe** to **v** and then adding **es.** In the illustrations that follow, you will notice that some nouns are always singular or always plural, and a few are either singular or plural depending on their use in a sentence.

Plurals of nouns are formed by adding s.

The plurals of most English nouns are formed by adding **s** to the singular form.

desk, desks	bank, banks
office, offices	idea, ideas
manager, managers	union, unions
typist, typists	document, documents
German, Germans	Buffa, Buffas

Nouns ending in **o** or **y** preceded by a vowel (*a, e, i, o,* or *u*) also form plurals by adding **s.**

portfolio, portfolios	studio, studios
radio, radios	trio, trios
attorney, attorneys	day, days
key, keys	survey, surveys

A few nouns ending in **o** preceded by a consonant form their **plurals by** adding **s.** In fact, all musical terms ending in **o,** regardless of the letter preceding the **o,** merely add **s** to form the plural.

auto, autos	crescendo, crescendos
dynamo, dynamos	piano, pianos
memento, mementos	solo, solos
tobacco, tobaccos	soprano, sopranos

Some nouns ending in **f, fe, ff** form their plurals by simply adding **s**.

proof, proofs	Keefe, Keefes
chief, chiefs	cliff, cliffs
safe, safes	plaintiff, plaintiffs
Graff, Graffs	

Some plurals of nouns are formed by adding es.

Nouns ending in **s, ch, sh, x,** or **z** (all "s" sounds) form the plural by adding **es**. The sound of the extra **e** is needed for smoothness between the two "s" sounds.

business, businesses	box, boxes
address, addresses	buzz, buzzes
branch, branches	Adams, Adamses
brush, brushes	Hendrix, Hendrixes

Nouns ending in **o** preceded by a consonant most often form their plurals by adding **es**.

echo, echoes	no, noes
embargo, embargoes	manifesto, manifestoes
hero, heroes	cargo, cargoes
motto, mottoes	veto, vetoes

Some plurals are formed by changing word endings.

Common nouns ending in **y** preceded by a consonant form their plurals by changing **y** to **i** and adding **es**.

authority, authorities	reply, replies
company, companies	lobby, lobbies
lady, ladies	quantity, quantities
facility, facilities	accessory, accessories

A few common nouns ending in **f** or **fe** change the **f** or **fe** to **v** and add **es**.

half, halves	life, lives
knife, knives	shelf, shelves
leaf, leaves	thief, thieves
loaf, loaves	wife, wives

Some plurals are formed by changing the spelling.

Several frequently used nouns form their plurals by a change in spelling.

foot, feet	mouse, mice
goose, geese	tooth, teeth
man, men	woman, women
workman, workmen	saleswoman, saleswomen
child, children	ox, oxen

Proper names may be formed into plurals by the addition of s or es.

The spelling of a proper name should never be changed. To form the plural, just add **s** or **es**.

Sally, Sallys	French, Frenches
Humphrey, Humphreys	Jones, Joneses
Wolf, Wolfs	Harris, Harrises
Henry, Henrys	Lewis, Lewises

When titles are used with a proper name, the plural may be formed by making either the title or the name plural.

Miss/Misses/Ms.	the Misses Smith or the Miss Smiths or Ms. Smiths
Mr.	the Mr. Blacks
Mrs./Ms.	the Mrs. Powells or Ms. Powells
Dr./Doctors	the Drs. Reed or the Dr. Reeds

The first method (plural title) is considered more formal. It is better to avoid this form in modern business usage. Use the second method (pluralize the name) when referring to two or more persons with the same name. Repeat the singular title with each name when referring to persons with different names.

Formal	Preferred
Misses Riley and Winston	Miss Riley and Miss Winston
Ms. Chu and Sands	Ms. Chu and Ms. Sands
Messrs. John and Harry Cole	Mr. John and Mr. Harry Cole

Compound nouns may be formed into plurals.

Compound nouns consist of two or more words that are considered single units. They may be written as single words, hyphenated words, or separate words. Use the dictionary if you do not know the correct form. (See also Section 8.)

Compound nouns written as single words make the last syllable plural.

bookcases	railways
chalkboards	salesmen
letterheads	stockholders

Compound nouns composed of two nouns written separately make the second word plural.

post offices	lieutenant commanders
purchase orders	title pages

Compound nouns composed of a noun plus another part of speech usually make the noun plural.

secretaries of state	editors in chief
courts-martial	mothers-in-law
bills of lading	notaries public

In compound nouns composed of words other than nouns, the last syllable is made plural. Such compound nouns are often hyphenated.

follow-ups	trade-ins
go-betweens	strikeovers
pay-offs	lockouts
stand-ins	setups

Nouns that end in *s* need special consideration.

Many nouns end in **s.** They should be considered separately because some are always singular, others are always plural, and a few may be considered either singular or plural.

Always singular. The following nouns are **singular** in meaning even though they end in **s.**

| athletics | electronics | molasses | physics |
| civics | mathematics | news | politics |

When used as subjects, these nouns require singular verbs. (See Section 4, Part 2.)

Mathematics *is* a difficult subject for me.

The news *was* more reassuring today.

Fortunately, politics *attracts* many fine leaders.

Always plural.   Some nouns do not have a singular form. They are always considered to be *plural.*

| auspices | premises | remains | thanks |
| headquarters | proceeds | riches | trousers |

When such nouns are used as subjects, a plural verb is required.

The proceeds *are* earmarked for employee welfare.

The scissors *are* in the top drawer.

Our headquarters *were* damaged by fire.

Singular or plural.   Some nouns are spelled the same in both the *singular* and the *plural* forms.

| Chinese | gross | salmon | sheep | corps |
| deer | means | series | statistics | chassis |

These nouns are used with either singular or plural verbs, depending on the meaning desired.

The lecture series *is* well attended.

These three series on Shakespeare *are* the finest ever offered.

Although nouns ending in a silent **s** do not change their form when used as plurals, the pronunciation of the two forms differs, as illustrated below.

corps (singular) pronounced *kor.*

corps (plural) pronounced *korz.*

chassis (singular) pronounced *shasi.*

chassis (plural) pronounced *shasiz.*

Nouns from foreign languages retain their foreign forms for the plural.   Words from foreign languages form the plural by changing the singular form in the following ways:

Singular, Plural	Singular, Plural
is **to es**	
analysis, analyses	diagnosis, diagnoses
axis, axes	hypothesis, hypotheses
basis, bases	parenthesis, parentheses
crisis, crises	thesis, theses
um **to a** (some add *s*)	
addendum, addenda	medium, media (or mediums)
datum, data	curriculum, curricula (or curriculums)
stratum, strata	memorandum, memoranda (or memorandums)

us to *i* (some add *es*)
alumnus, alumni	cactus, cacti (or cactuses)
fungus, fungi	terminus, termini (or terminuses)
stimulus, stimuli	

a to *ae* (some add *s*)
alumna, alumnae	larva, larvae
vertebra, vertebrae	formula, formulae (or formulas)

on to *a* (or add *s*)
phenomenon, phenomena	criterion, criteria (or criterions)

ix or *ex* to *ices* (or add *es*)
matrix, matrices	appendix, appendices (or appendixes)
index, indices (or indexes)	apex, apices (or apexes)

Plurals of most abbreviations are formed by adding s.

These plurals of abbreviations are formed by adding **s**. (See Section 8, Part 4.)

Words	Abbrev.	Plural Abbrev.	Word	Abbrev.	Plural Abbrev.
gallon	gal.	gals.	year	yr.	yrs.
month	mo.	mos.	barrel	bbl.	bbls.
yard	yd.	yds.	pound	lb.	lbs.

For some units of weight and measurement, however, use the same form for both plural and singular.

Word	Abbrev. (sing. and plural)	Word	Abbrev. (sing. and plural)
inch	in.	foot	ft.
mile	mi.	bushel	bu.
ounce	oz.	millimeter	mm.

The plurals of *uncapitalized* abbreviations composed of *separate letters* are formed by adding an *apostrophe* and s.

c.o.d.'s   a.m.'s
p.m.'s   r.p.m.'s

Plurals for *capitalized* abbreviations are formed by adding s.

M.D.s   C.P.A.s   D.D.S.s   Jrs.   IIIs

Numbers, letters, and words as words may be formed into plurals.

The plurals for figures, symbols, letters, and words being discussed as words are formed by adding an *apostrophe* and s. Omit the apostrophe if the meaning is clear without it.

50's (or 50s)
O's (or Os)
and's, if's, but's
x's and y's
D's (or Ds)
%'s (or %s)

ASSIGNMENTS

Apply your knowledge of plural nouns

A. Write the plural form of each word in the space provided. If the word has both a foreign and an English plural form, give both forms.

1. absence _____	16. asset _____
2. analysis _____	17. business _____
3. attorney _____	18. reply _____
4. auto _____	19. referendum _____
5. belief _____	20. memorandum _____
6. bureau _____	21. loyalty _____
7. chief _____	22. medium _____
8. company _____	23. committee _____
9. corps _____	24. salary _____
10. criterion _____	25. portfolio _____
11. datum _____	26. stimulus _____
12. facility _____	27. salesman _____
13. man _____	28. editor in chief _____
14. tax _____	29. veto _____
15. variety _____	30. index _____

B.   Some of the sentences below contain incorrect plural forms. Circle the incorrect form and write it correctly in the space provided. If these are no incorrect forms in a sentence, write **C** in the space at the right.

1.   The branches of a company are sometimes called subsidiarys.   _____

2.   The shelfs of merchandise are arranged to attract housewives.   _____

3.   Handicraft is a major source of income to some familys in Europe.   _____

4.   We received two memorandums about the boxes.   _____

5.   The plaintiffs need the services of several attornies.   _____

6.   The embargos on shipments from certain countries encourage trade with friendly nations.   _____

7.   The portfolioes of some insurance companies reveal unusual risks.   _____

8.   Several packages of supply are arriving by truck today.   _____

9.   The Phillipses are both alumnuses of Oregon State College.   _____

10.   Changes in the curriculums have caused several crisis.   _____

C.   Write the correct plural form for the compound nouns that appear in parentheses in the following sentences. Since there are some errors in the singular forms given, you will need to decide whether each compound noun should be written as one word, as separate words, or hyphenated. Check a dictionary if you are uncertain.

Example: Jack designed several clever (bill board).   _*billboards*_

1.   The (chief of staff) do more than prepare budgets.   _____

2.   Please keep all your (bill of sale).   _____

3.   Savings and loan associations usually have (notary public).   _____

4.   Mr. Wright and Mr. Brubaker have requested (leave of absence).   _____

5.   Mr. Brown locked the (blue print) in the cabinet.   _____

6.   Two new (post office) will open this month.   _____

7.   Depositors must present (pass book) when making withdrawals.   _____

8.   The (tax payer) met to decide on their next move.   _____

9.   Our (show room) have been redecorated recently.   _____

10.   Industrial (work man) are referred to as blue-collar workers.   _____

D.   Change the forms of address in the following sentences to the less formal style preferred in modern business.

Example: Mmes. Kramer and Hoffman are members of the committee.

Mrs. Kramer and Mrs. Hoffman

1.   There are two Messrs. Jackson listed in the directory.

2.   Misses Joan and Nancy Taylor have accepted our invitation.

3.   The new reception room was decorated by Mmes. Frank Fulton and Robert Mills.

4.   A copy of the report will be mailed to Messrs. Carter and Smith.

5.   The reception was planned by the Misses Cartwright of Los Angeles.

6.   Please invite the Fred C. Browns, Jr., to the exhibit.

7.   The Drs. Murphy are husband and wife.

8.   Messrs. Milton Neimeyer and Beatrice Rubens have consented to be our representatives at the convention.

9.   The authors of *Management for the 70's* are Drs. James B. and Richard A. Perry.

10.   Have you asked the Walter Moores III to attend the opening?

E.   In the spaces provided, write the plural for the abbreviations, symbols, words, and dates in the following sentences.

1.   Our company experienced rapid growth during the (1960).   _____

2.   There are two (p) in appreciate.   _____

3.   The research chemists are all (Ph.D.).   _____

4.   We discussed the (pro and con) of the proposal.   _____

5. He wrote (OK) opposite all the items he approved.   _____

6. How many (%) appeared in the report?   _____

7. She has several (IOU) to collect.   _____

8. Don't use so many (however) in your writing.   _____

9. The planks were supported by (2 x 4).   _____

10. The company ordered two (TV) for the employees' lounge.   _____
11. If you will check (Vol.) 3 and 4 of *Management Digest,* you will locate that article you mentioned.   _____

12. Please count the number of (PBX) in this building.   _____
13. He is to order 35 (lb.) of sand, 10 (bbl.) of oil, and 14 (oz.) of glue.   _____

14. Most of the (M.D.) in our city belong to the A.M.A.   _____

15. How many (A) and (B) did you get this semester?   _____

16. In the (80) and (90) more computers will be needed.   _____

17. Too many (c.o.d.) are being shipped to our customers.   _____
18. He uses too many (and) and (but) when he is talking before a group.   _____
19. It is anticipated that a larger number of (B.A.) and (M.A.) will be earned next year.   _____

20. How many (etc.) did you find in that report?   _____

F.   Some of the following sentences contain errors in the usage of plurals. If the sentence is correct, place a **C** on the line provided. If the sentence is incorrect, write the correct form of the plural on the line provided.

Examples: The bones in the spinal column are the vertebra.   *vertebrae*

He bought three fezzes on his trip to Morocco.   *C*

1. I have three sister-in-laws.   _____

2. The datum are incorrect.   _____

3. The main headquarters are in Boston.   _____

4. Politics is an interesting topic.   _____

5. There are two Nancies in my class: Nancy Jones and Nancy Reed.   _____

6. Notaries public are generally honest people.   _____

7. Salmon is my favorite fish to eat.   _____

8. Salmon are a challenging fish to catch.   _____

9. Orchestras play "Rhapsody in Blue" often.   _____

10. There are several theorys of evolution.   _____

Name _____

Date _____

—————————————— **PRACTICE WRITING** ——————————————

You've been thinking about putting a stereo in your VW, and yesterday you saw the following ad in *Travel* magazine.

Car-Musak, new all-transistor stereo cartridge tape recorder for your car—5,000 already sold this year. Backed by *Good Housekeeping*. Money-back guarantee if not satisfied. Tapes included with purchase.

Write a letter to the manufacturer inquiring about all the facts. You want to know the price, number of tapes included, weight, method of installation, and number of transistors. Ask them to send you also an illustrated brochure and the terms of the guarantee.

_____

_____

_____

_____

_____

_____

_____

_____

_____

_____

_____

_____

_____

_____

_____

_____

Nouns show possession

Nouns may show that a person, a group of people, or an animal owns or possesses something by the addition of an *apostrophe* and *s* (*'s*) or by the addition of an *apostrophe only* (*'*). As illustrated below, the possessive form of nouns is used as a modifier to show ownership or some similar relationship.

Ownership:	Mary's purse	**Authorship:**	Albee's plays
Origin:	auditor's report	**Kind:**	a child's game

Nouns show possession by the addition of an apostrophe or an apostrophe and s.

It is easy to make a noun possessive, as there are no irregular possessives. Seldom are errors made in conversation. Yet in writing, many people put the apostrophe in the wrong place or forget to put it in at all. Sometimes writers add the apostrophe where it doesn't belong because they have confused plural and possessive forms. An easy way to test a possessive form is to take the "possessive" noun in question and place it in an "of" prepositional phrase:

The *union's* demands were discussed.
The demands *of the union* were discussed.

Employees' benefits were increased.
Benefits of the *employees* were increased.

The *employer's* request satisfied her staff.
The request *of the employer* satisfied her staff.

When you are sure that the noun is showing some form of ownership, you can indicate this in both common and proper nouns by applying one of the following suggestions.

1. Add an *apostrophe* and *s* (*'s*) to all nouns that end with any letter except *s.*
2. Add an *apostrophe only* (*'*) to nouns that end in *s* or a sibilant or hissing sound.

Singular nouns show possession by the addition of an apostrophe and s.

Form the possessive of *singular* nouns by adding an *apostrophe* and *s* (*'s*).

I met the *bookkeeper's* family.

Fred's car is parked outside.

When the singular noun ends in an *s* sound, you may avoid the hissing sound of an additional *s* by adding only an apostrophe.

> *Mr. Matthews'* nephew arrived yesterday.

If the noun has only one syllable or if the additional *s* does not sound disagreeable, you should add the *'s* as usual.

> my *boss's* calendar   *Mr. Morris's* account
> the *witness's* description   *Mr. Storz's* office

With singular nouns that end in *s*, you can see that you may use your discretion about whether to use *'s* or *'* (*'s* is always acceptable). You must be careful, however, to spell out the word completely, so that you won't make the mistake of placing an apostrophe before the last letter in the word. If you are discussing Mr. Holme*s*, you would write *Mr. Holmes's trip* (**not** Mr. Holme's trip).

Add only an apostrophe to plural nouns that end in s.
Form the possessive of plural nouns that end in *s* by adding an *apostrophe only* ('). To determine whether the possessive noun is singular or plural, put the possessive noun in an "of" prepositional phrase.

> The *managers'* reports are due at 4 p.m. (reports of the *managers*)
> We will count the *stockholders'* votes. (votes of the *stockholders*)
> The *secretaries'* time cards should be brought to my office. (time cards of the *secretaries*)

Add an apostrophe and s to plural nouns that do not end in s.
Form the possessive of plural nouns that do not end in *s* by adding both an *apostrophe* and *s* (*'s*). There are very few plural nouns that do not end in *s*. *Men, women,* and *children* are plural nouns that are used frequently. You should learn to form their possessives correctly.

> The *men's* bowling team meets on Wednesday; the *women's*, on Tuesday.
> We are having a sale of *children's* toys.
> Please stack the *mice's* cages.

Use possessive nouns correctly.
Separate possession.   To indicate separate possession, use the possessive form for each noun individually.

> *Mark's, John's,* and *Arthur's* desks have been moved to other departments.
> They manufacture *boys'* and *girls'* shoes.

Joint possession.   To indicate joint possession, use the possessive form for the final noun only.

> *John and Mary's* daughter will be married next month.
> *Barton & Smith's* truck just arrived.
> The *Artists and Models'* Ball will be held in October.

Possessives of compound nouns.   To show possession in compound nouns, use the possessive form for the last word only.

> This is my *father-in-law's* favorite chair.
> He is trying to locate the *secretary-general's* office.
> The *editor in chief's* duties are both managerial and editorial.

Do not confuse plural compound nouns with possessive forms.

Singular	Plural	Possessive (singular)
father-in-law	fathers-in-law	father-in-law's
editor in chief	editors in chief	editor in chief's

Possessives of abbreviations. To make an abbreviation possessive, add an *apostrophe* and *s* ('s) to the singular form. *Note:* 's follows the period when used.

National Dietary Corp.'s products	*C.P.A.'s* report
Mr. Herbert Walker, Jr.'s statement	*NATO's* forces

Add an apostrophe (') only to the plural form of an abbreviation.

Graham Bros.' displays	the *Philip Rood IIIs'* yacht
M.D.s' opinions	the *John Smith, Jrs.'* new home

Possessives of company names. Following general usage, company names show possession by adding the 's or ' to the last word or abbreviation in the title.

Shell Oil Company of Canada's explorations

Bank of America's branches

IBM's computers

Some companies and organizations omit the apostrophe from possessive nouns in their official titles. Check the organization's letterhead or official directory, and write the title as it is written by the organization.

Valley Painting *Contractors* Association

Retail *Merchants* Committee

Citizens National Bank

Possessives of nouns naming inanimate objects. It is good practice to avoid using the possessive form of nouns that name inanimate objects.

Awkward:	the *chair's* arms		the *cabinets'* color
Better:	the arms of the chair		the color of the cabinets

Possessives of nouns designating time. Nouns that designate *time,* however, are frequently used in the possessive form. The word before the *time* word indicates whether it is singular or plural possessive.

a minute's notice	*a month's* vacation	*one year's* interest
three minutes' notice	a day's receipts	two years' interest
an hour's journey	five days' receipts	three weeks' work

Location of the possessive noun. The possessive form is not always followed by the noun it modifies. For instance, the noun may be found elsewhere in the sentence.

A friend of *Mr. Johnson's* took him to lunch.
  (Mr. Johnson's friend)
The decision is the *chairman's.*
  (chairman's decision)

Or the noun modified by the possessive may not appear in the sentence but merely be understood.

> Please pick up my new suit at the *tailor's.*
>   (tailor's shop)
> Send those reports to the *printer's.*
>   (printer's shop)
> *Mary's* made the result unanimous.
>   (Mary's vote)

Possessives with verbal nouns.   A noun (or pronoun) used to modify a verbal noun should take the possessive form.

> *Shirley's* typing is excellent.
> The foreman is tired of *their* complaining.

A noun used to modify a verbal noun phrase also takes the possessive form. You should first decide whether the phrase is being used as a noun in the sentence. If it is, use the possessive form for the modifying noun.

> The *president's* changing the policy came as a surprise.

In the sentence above, the phrase *changing the policy* is used as the subject, so we know it is being used as a noun. It is therefore a verbal noun phrase, and the modifying noun *president* must take the possessive form. Here is another example.

> He approved *John's* taking the supplies.

Taking the supplies is the object of the verb *approved.* An object in a sentence is in a noun position. Therefore, *John,* as the modifier of the verbal noun phrase, must be in the possessive form.

PART 3

ASSIGNMENTS

Apply your knowledge of possessive nouns

A. Write the corresponding possessive form for the following *of* phrases. If the *of* phrase is preferred for good writing style, place a **C** in the space provided instead of writing the possessive form.

Example: the comments of the men   *the men's comments*

1.   the benefits of the employees   _____

2.   the hands of the clock   _____

3.   the sales of the subsidiaries   _____

4.   the office of Lamkin & Betz   _____

5.   the talent of the chief draftsman   _____

6.   a vacation of a week   _____

7.   the color of the room   _____

8.   the reports of the salesmen   _____

9.   the office of Mr. Andrews   _____

10.   the answer of the chief of police   _____

11.   the support of the AFL-CIO   _____

12.   the desks of Jane and Sally   _____

13.   the plans of the company   _____

14. the stage of the auditorium   _____

15. the staff of Tillson Bros.   _____

16. the expense accounts of Mr. Wilson
    and Mr. Lamb   _____

17. the votes of the vice presidents   _____

18. pay of four hours   _____

19. the decision of John Sharp, Sr.   _____

20. the transcription of the stenographer _____

B.   In the following sentences, circle any errors in usage of the possessive form and write the correct form in the space provided. If there are no errors, place a **C** in the space.

Example: The ⟨stairway's⟩ railing should be painted.   *railing of the stairway*

1. The holding company's main function is to buy and hold stock in other corporations.   _____

2. The girls' finger got caught in the electric typewriter.   _____

3. A secretaries success depends on the manager's patience.   _____

4. The speaker discussed New York's subways and Los Angele's freeways.   _____

5. Farmer's purchasing associations are similar to consumers' cooperatives.   _____

6. Samuelson and Bach's textbooks on economics are both on the reading list.   _____

7. San Francisco is only one days drive from Los Angeles.   _____

8. The electric typewriter's noise is distracting.   _____

9. He objected to Sally delivering the mail.   _____

10. The United California Banks' loan department is headed by Mr. Warren.   _____

11. The Bureau of Labor Statistic's studies confirm our statements.   _____

12. We were all pleased by Mr. Steven's promotion.   _____

13. Henry Smith has two year's experience as a supervisor.   _____

14. Our company handles all its creditor's claims promptly.   _____

15. Various insurance companys' investments require careful management.   _____

16. Mr. Atkins son, Ralph Atkins, Jr., is now a member of the firm.   _____

17. The students' primary concern should be to obtain as much knowledge as he can.   _____

18. One of the Internal Revenue Services objectives was to develop uniform audit procedures.   _____

19. The building's equipment was selected by Mr. Howard.   _____

20. Mr. Thomas' office is smaller than Mr. Buffa's.   _____

C. In this exercise, choose the correct form of the words in parentheses to make these sentences meaningful. Write your choice in the column.

1. The best suggestion is _____.
(Tom, Tom's, Toms, Toms')   _____

2. _____ and Mary's uniforms were identical.
(Betty, Betty's, Bettys, Betties')   _____

3. Our purchasing agent is satisfied with Kane _____ products.
(Co., Co.'s, Cos.')   _____

4. The chairman asked to hear the _____ report.
(treasurer, treasurers, treasurer's, treasurers')   _____

5. Billions of dollars of bank credit have been created through the _____ guaranteed bank loans.
(FHA, FHAs, FHA's, FHAs')   _____

6. The _____ dividend checks will reach them by the end of the month.
(stockholder, stockholders, stockholder's, stockholders')   _____

7. The new lighting fixture was purchased from _____ Anaheim store.
(Lyman & Lee, Lyman's & Lee, Lyman & Lee's, Lyman's & Lee's)   _____

8. We investigated four _____ incentive programs.
(company, company's, companys', companies, companies')   _____

9. _____ selecting our entry was a complete surprise.
(Edgar, Edgar's, Edgars')   _____

10. We were all amazed at Mr. _____ skillful handling of the situation.
(Morris, Morrises, Morris', Morris's)   _____

D. Write the correct possessive form—singular or plural—of each of the nouns in parentheses.

Example: (Mr. Jones) ambition is to meet his (customer) demands for convenience goods.   *Mr. Jones's*
customers'

1. The (treasurer) report is prepared for the (stockholder) meeting.   _____

_____

2. The employees' (association) demands were for greater (employee) benefits.

    _____

3. The (man) department is to be moved to the third floor where (man and woman) shoes are now located.

    _____

    _____

4. Mr. (Williams) arrival was in time for his (firm) annual meeting.

    _____

    _____

5. The (committee) report will be distributed at the (board) next meeting.

    _____

    _____

6. The (secretary) loud talking disturbed their fellow workers.

    _____

7. The (chair) arms were too high for the (clerk) comfort.

    _____

    _____

8. The (faculty) tinkering with the course schedule didn't help.

    _____

9. (Management) goals should also be the (worker).

    _____

    _____

10. (Mrs. Jones) report was helpful in obtaining the (CPA) approval.

    _____

Name _____

Date _____

————————— **PRACTICE WRITING** —————————

Write a sentence for each word or word group below, using the possessive form of the word.

Example: secretary *The secretary's proofreading is excellent.*

secretaries *The secretaries' coffee break gave them a chance to relax.*

1. company _____

2. companies _____

3. Mr. Marks _____

4. the Markses _____

5. week _____

6. weeks _____

7. manager _____

8. managers _____

9. *Bill and Steve* (separate possession) _____

_____

10. *Bill and Steve* (joint possession) _____

_____

11. *Mr. Richard Sanchez* _____

_____

12. *salesmen* _____

_____

13. *General Motors* _____

_____

14. *United States government* _____

_____

15. *CPA* _____

_____

Pronouns are substitutes for nouns and other pronouns

Pronouns are used as substitutes for nouns. What you have learned about nouns in the preceding sections will be useful in this study of pronouns. To select the correct pronoun, you must first determine its antecedent. The noun for which the pronoun substitutes is the *antecedent*. A pronoun may substitute for another pronoun also as in the third example below. Look for the noun for which the pronoun is to substitute, and select a pronoun that agrees with this antecedent in person, number, and gender. The antecedent can be a noun, proper noun, or another pronoun; it will be either singular or plural; and it will be masculine, feminine, or neuter gender. After collecting all these facts about the antecedent, you'll find it easy to pick the correct pronoun.

> The *nurse* wore *his* raincoat to the hospital.
> (*Nurse* is the antecedent of *his*.)
> *John* and *I* mailed *our* letters.
> (*John* and *I* are the antecedents of *our*.)
> *She* finished *her* work.
> (*She* is the antecedent of *her*.)

Use pronouns to avoid repetition of nouns.

We use pronouns to avoid repetition of nouns and to make writing and speaking flow more smoothly. Note the difference between the following sentences.

> *Edith* wrote to *Edith's* sister that *Edith* was sending a gift.
> *Edith* wrote to *her* sister that *she* was sending a gift.

In the first sentence the proper noun *Edith* is repeated three times. Note how much more smoothly the second sentence reads when pronouns are substituted for the proper noun.

Sentence patterns using pronouns are the same as those using nouns; that is, pronouns may act as subjects, appositives, objects, complements, or objects of the preposition. (Pronouns are rarely used as appositives.) Unlike nouns, however, pronouns frequently change form depending on the usage

131

in the sentence. In the next part, we will look into this aspect of pronouns. Right now, though, let's concentrate on identifying the various kinds of pronouns.

Use personal pronouns correctly.

Personal pronouns represent persons or things: *I, you, he, she, it, we, they, my, mine, your, yours, his, him, her, hers, its, them,* and *their.* Pronouns are divided into three persons: first person, naming the speaker; second person, naming the one spoken to; and third person, naming the one spoken about. (See page 143.)

First person: *I* study *my* lessons every day.
(names the speaker)

Second person: *You* study *your* lessons every day.
(names the one spoken to)

Third person: *They* study *their* lessons every day.
(names the ones spoken about)

Use relative pronouns correctly.

A *relative pronoun* is a connecting word that has a double function:

1. It connects a dependent clause with a main clause.
2. It serves as the subject of the dependent clause.

That, which, who, and *what* are examples of relative pronouns used in place of the name of a person or of an object. These relative pronouns have the same forms whether their antecedents are singular or plural. *That* is used to refer to persons or inanimate objects; *which* refers to inanimate objects only; *who, whose,* and *whom* refer to persons only.

I like Mary, *who* is a good worker.
(*Who* refers to *Mary,* a person, singular.)
I like men *who* are good listeners.
(*Who* refers to *men,* persons, plural.)
The desk, *which* had a maple finish, was sold.
(*which* refers to *desk,* inanimate object, singular.)
The desks, *which* have maple finishes, were sold.
(*Which* refers to *desks,* inanimate objects, plural.)
I heard a speech *that* was given by Mr. Jones.
(*That* refers to *speech,* inanimate, singular.)
I have head speeches *that* were given by Mr. Jones.
(*That* refers to *speeches,* inanimate, plural.)

Other variations of relative pronouns are compounds, such as *whoever, whomever, whosoever, whichever, whichsoever,* and *whatsoever.*

A relative pronoun should be placed close to its antecedent to avoid possible ambiguity.

Not: The *desk* had a maple finish *which* I sold.
But: The *desk* that I sold had a maple finish.

Use interrogative pronouns correctly.

Interrogative pronouns ask questions. *Who, whom, whose, which,* and *what* are the pronouns used when asking for information. The following questions illustrate their correct usage.

Who broke the chair?
The customer was *who?*

Whose dictionary is that?

Whom did you consider for president?

What is it?

Which of the checks is to be returned?

The pronouns *who, whom, whose, which,* and *what* may be either interrogative pronouns or relative pronouns, depending on their usage in the sentence.

Interrogative	**Relative**
Who paid the bill?	He is the gentleman *who* paid the bill.
Whose coat is that?	It was Mary *whose* coat was lost.
What does she do?	I don't care *what* she does.

Use indefinite pronouns correctly.

Indefinite pronouns do not name specific persons, places, or things.

all	both	none	neither	everybody	anybody
any	some	one	someone	everyone	others
each	many	either	somebody	nobody	anything

Singular indefinite pronouns. Some indefinite pronouns are always singular, and often they act as antecedents for other pronouns. A pronoun that refers to a singular indefinite pronoun must also be singular. Singular indefinite pronouns require singular verbs.

each	everybody	everyone	nobody	either
one	somebody	someone	another	neither

Each has *his* own job to do.

Everyone has *his* own job to do.

Nobody knows *her* job better than *she.*

With the recent stress on sexual equality in our language usage, it is sometimes better to avoid using singular pronouns that require sex identification. The examples above could be rewritten as follows:

Awkward: *Each* has *his/her* own job to do.

Better: *All* have *their* own jobs to do.

Awkward: Nobody knows *his/her* job better than *she.*

Improved: Nobody knows *that* job better than she.

Better: *Few* know *their* jobs better than she.

Indefinite pronouns may be singular or plural.

Some indefinite pronouns, such as *all, some, any,* and *none,* may be either singular or plural. For good usage, other pronouns referring to them must agree with them in number. Usually they are *singular* when they stand for a quantity of inanimate things and *plural* when they stand for persons.

Some of the paper *is* lost.
   (quantity of paper—singular verb)

Some of the people *were* lost.
   (persons—plural verb)

All is well.
   (quantity—singular verb)

All are well.
   (persons—plural verb)

When these indefinite pronouns specifically refer to plural nouns, they require plural verbs.

> *Some* of the papers *are* lost.
>   (*Some* is the subject—it refers to papers.)
> *All* the products *were* delivered.
>   (*All* is the subject—it refers to products.)

The plural noun may be omitted but implied.

> *All were* delivered.
> *None were* lost in shipment.

Plural indefinite pronouns require plural verbs and pronouns.

Indefinite pronouns that are always plural, such as *few, several,* and *many,* always require plural verbs and plural pronouns.

> *Several* of them *have been* invited to the meeting.
> *Many* of the orders *were* filled.

Compound indefinite pronouns are written as one word.   When the words *body* and *thing* are joined to indefinite pronouns, they form compound indefinite pronouns and are written as one word, for example: *somebody, anything, nobody, everything, something.* Compounds formed by adding *one* are also written as one word except where the reference is to each of a number of persons.

> *Someone* is coming in the room.
> *Some one* person is to blame.
> *Anyone* can play the flute.
> *Any one* of a number of people may be guilty.

Use demonstrative pronouns correctly.

Demonstrative pronouns point out specific persons or things. *This, that, these,* and *those* are demonstrative pronouns. They must refer to their noun or pronoun antecedents clearly. Demonstrative pronouns are dependent on previous statements and do not express independent thoughts.

> *That* is a strange question.
> *Those* are the best pictures.

Insertion of a noun after *this* or *that* improves the meaning where the reference may otherwise be vague. Often a writer uses *this* or *that* to refer to an idea that is not expressed in a noun or a pronoun. The following sentences are examples of vague references to antecedents.

> The group was asked to meet tomorrow. *This* is not possible.
>   (**More clearcut:** *This meeting* is not possible.)

> The sales department is on the tenth floor. *This* delays our work.
>   (**Clearer:** *This location* delays our work.)

> Mr. Jones usually takes the eight o'clock train to New York, *which* is frequently late.
>   (**Rewritten to correct the weak reference of *which:*** Mr. Jones usually takes the eight o'clock train to New York. *This train* is frequently late.)

Demonstrative pronouns may be used as adjectives. When the sentences above were rewritten for clarity, the demonstrative pronouns became adjectives as a result of inserting a noun.

This is not possible.
   (*This* is a pronoun.)
This meeting is not possible.
   (*This* is an adjective modifying meeting.)

This delays our work.
   (*This* is a pronoun.)
This location . . .
   (*This* is an adjective modifying location.)

. . . , *which* is frequently late.
   (*Which* is a relative pronoun.)
This train is frequently late.
   (*This* is an adjective modifying train.)

When demonstrative pronouns are used as adjectives, they must agree in number with the nouns they modify. The most difficult usage involves *kind* and *sort*. For a discussion of adjectives, see Section 5.

This kind of *organization* is good.
   (*This kind* agrees in number with *organization*.)
These kinds of *organizations* are common.
   (*These kinds* agrees with plural *organizations*.)
These sorts of *combinations* are possible.
   (*These sorts* agrees with *combinations*.)
We cannot permit *this sort* of *conduct*.
   (*This sort* agrees with *conduct*.)
Those kinds of *problems* are not difficult to solve.
   (*Those kinds* agrees in number with *problems*.)

ACCURATE CHOICE OF WORDS IS IMPORTANT

As you continue your study of homonyms, those sound-alike words, apply the four-step routine you learned in the previous unit. **See** the word; **say** it aloud; **spell** it silently or aloud; and **write** it once from memory. Check the spelling and **write** it the second time. Learn to spell and to define the ten pairs of homonyms listed here.

		Write	
Homonym	*Definition*	*First time*	*Second time*
council	An assembly summoned for consultation.	_____	_____
counsel	To give advice to; to recommend.	_____	_____
current	Prevailing; circulating; the present.	_____	_____
currant	A small seedless grape.	_____	_____
dew	Condensed moisture.	_____	_____
do	To perform; to place; to work at; etc.	_____	_____
due	Payable immediately; owed.	_____	_____

feat	An act of skill; a deed of courage.	_____	_____
feet	Plural of foot.	_____	_____
indict	To accuse a person of crime.	_____	_____
indite	To compose and write.	_____	_____
lessen	To decrease; to reduce.	_____	_____
lesson	Instruction.	_____	_____
miner	A worker in a mine.	_____	_____
minor	Less; smaller; not of legal age.	_____	_____
muscle	An organ that produces motion.	_____	_____
mussel	A small bivalve mollusk.	_____	_____
peer	n. An equal, as in natural gifts or social rank. v. To gaze; to look at curiously.	_____	_____
pier	A structure built out into the water.	_____	_____
plain	Free of embellishments or patterns.	_____	_____
plane	A flat or level material surface; a tool for making a smooth surface.	_____	_____

PART **4**

ASSIGNMENTS

Apply your knowledge of pronouns

A. The following sentences contain many pronouns. To demonstrate your ability to recognize this important group of words, write every pronoun you find opposite the appropriate sentence. If you find them all, you'll have 30.

1. Who will give him and me instruction? _____

2. The president told his assistant that he could expect a raise in salary. _____

3. I expect my promotion will depend on my performance. _____

4. There are several of us who worked in the department before it grew so large. _____

5. Did you recommend to your department head his change of plans? _____

6. There are those who prepare their lessons daily. _____

7. Those were excellent reports that you handed in yesterday. _____

8. Who is the employee who was commended for being courteous to all whom he meets? _____

9. Everyone agrees the new treasurer is the man who

    is responsible. _____

10. Some of the secretaries want their hours reduced. _____

B. The ability to recognize the antecedent of a pronoun will help you choose the correct pronoun for any usage. To test your present ability, draw an arrow from each pronoun to its antecedent in these sentences.

1. Mr. Snyder, who is an engineer, gave a lecture before his professional group.

2. The employee put his paycheck on the table and spilled his coffee on it.

3. Jim is one who is considerate of all people about him.

4. The members of the committee submitted their opinions in writing.

5. Did Miss Sutro give her report?

6. Take the letter to Mr. Falk, and ask him to check it before he asks the president to sign it.

7. The office machines need to have their periodic cleaning, or they will require repair.

8. Several papers were misplaced, but they were found eventually on Mr. Lambert's desk.

9. Frank, Joan, and I were told that our paychecks were lost, but the manager promised to find them and get them to us before quitting time.

10. Take this tool to Joe and ask him to fix it.

C. Now that you have confidence in your ability to recognize pronouns, test that ability by choosing the correct form from those in parentheses to complete the following sentences. If there is doubt as to the gender of the antecedent, use masculine gender. Enter your choice in the column.

1. I like Bert, _____ is a good IBM operator. (who, which)   _____

2. The boss had great hopes for that system, _____ is more than I had. (who, which, that)   _____

3. Each has _____ own special job. (his, her, their)   _____

4. I told _____ to correct the error in the books (somebody, some body)   _____

5. We like _____ kinds of machines. (this, these)   _____

6. Someone is not going to get _____ work finished on time. (his, her, their)   _____

7. The office manager prefers to use _____ kind of material. (that, those)   _____

8. Will any of the secretaries talk to _____ bosses? (his, her, their)   _____

9. I like _____ sort of carbon paper. (this, these)   _____

10. Did you know that nobody has kept _____ assignment secret? (his, her, their)   _____

D. Having studied the text and worked through the previous exercises on pronouns, you are now well equipped to supply the pronouns that have been omitted from these sentences. Enter the pronoun you believe fits the context of the sentence in the blank space in each sentence.

Example: Secretaries are often asked to screen telephone calls for _*their*_ employers.

1. Some employers want to know _____ is calling, what _____ wants, and what company _____ represents.

2. Did Jim give _____ answer to the question yet?

3. Good filing is an art, and _____ should be considered as such.

4. A bookkeeper would be happier with _____ job, if _____ looked for ways to systematize the work load.

5. Every file clerk should notify _____ superior when _____ leaves the department.

6. Some members told him that _____ would back _____ proposal.

7. Did Mr. Lyons and Mr. Baker take _____ Social Security cards to Personnel?

8. Either Angela or Susan should take _____ vacation in August.

9. Every customer wants _____ purchases delivered first; but _____ should understand that first come, first served is our motto.

10. _____ kind of carbon paper is usable, but _____ kinds will make more copies.

11. Did I leave _____ coat in your office?

12. You should take _____ time when checking figures.

13. She saw the package _____ he gave _____.

14. Neither Mrs. Packard nor Mrs. Shaw voiced _____ opinion, but Mrs. Fuller freely shared _____ views.

15. The new position was given to Mr. Tate, _____ indicated _____ willingness to work nights.

E. When indefinite pronouns are used as subjects, it is always necessary to see that they agree with the verb in number. For instance, a singular indefinite pronoun takes a singular verb; a plural one takes a plural verb. Select the verbs that agree with the pronoun subjects found in these sentences.

1. Some of the punched cards (is, are) mutilated.   _____

2. Any one of the typists (is, are) qualified for the promotion.   _____

3. Several of the boxes (was, were) opened.   _____

4. Something (is, are) the matter with the radiator.   _____

5. Ail the instruments (was, were) checked for defects.   _____

6. Nobody (know, knows) what will happen at the meeting.   _____

7. Few of them (is, are) willing to share their good fortune.   _____

8. None of the oil (was, were) ready for the refinery.   _____

9. Either Mr. Babcock or Mrs. Cohn (is, are) the one for the appointment.   _____

10. Both of the new employees (need, needs) training on the keypunch.   _____

F.   Choose the correct homonym from those in parentheses to complete the following sentences. Because this is a spelling review also, be careful to spell your choice correctly.

1. The (current, currant) trend is to buy from discount stores.   _____

2. Please plan a (lessen, lesson) on filing for the new secretaries.   _____

3. The laws of this state protect (miners, minors) from unlawful seizure of their property.   _____

4. You will have to use your (mussels, muscles) to get that crate on the truck.   _____

5. Joan (piered, peered) at the strange object on her desk.   _____

6. Please find me a (plane, plain) piece of bond paper.   _____

7. Do you think they will (indite, indict) them?   _____

8. You should (council, counsel) them about the problem.   _____

9. That invoice is (dew, do, due) on the 30th.   _____

10. If you can secure the contract, it will be a profitable (feet, feat).   _____

11. Try to (lessen, lesson) the size of the package.   _____

12. The restaurant on the corner serves (mussels, muscles).   _____

13. The (council, counsel) will consider the ordinance at the next meeting.   _____

14. Those pictures (dew, do, due) make the office more attractive.   _____

15. Are there three (feet, feat) in a yard?   _____

Name _____

Date _____

PRACTICE WRITING ——

Read the following sentences. Then rewrite only that portion of the sentence where the reference of the pronoun to its antecedent is weak. It would be a good idea to check the section on demonstrative pronouns before you begin.

1. Our accounting department uses the company's new computer to process all accounts receivable. This results in a saving of both time and money.

_____

_____

2. Data processing involves recording, classifying, sorting, computing, summarizing, transmitting, and storing. These are simply part of information handling.

_____

_____

3. Our salesmen purchase their tickets months in advance, which avoids the customary last-minute rush for reservations.

_____

_____

4. The sales department is at the other end of the building. This means that customers have a long way to walk.

_____

_____

5. The decision was made to market the new motor in the Midwest first. This will delay its introduction on the West Coast until February.

_____

_____

Pronouns assume different forms

Personal pronouns assume different forms depending on how they are used in sentences. When used as the subject of a verb, the pronoun is in the *nominative case*. When used as an object of a verb or preposition, it is in the *objective case*. When it shows ownership, it is in the *possessive case*. *Case* merely means that nouns and pronouns can show their relationship to other words in a sentence by a change in the way they are spelled. You have already changed the form of nouns to show ownership, making them possessive-case nouns. There is no reason to study nominative- and objective-case nouns because they are the same. Pronoun forms, however, are different in all three cases. Because errors in pronoun usage are very noticeable to listeners and readers, you will want to avoid making them. The discussion that follows will show you how to use pronouns correctly.

Pronouns show nominative, objective, and possessive case in number and gender.

Study this table to master the changes that take place in personal pronouns as to *number* (singular or plural), *gender* (masculine, feminine, or neuter), and *case* (nominative, possessive, and objective).

	Nominative case	Objective case	Possessive case
First person			
Singular	I	me	my, mine
Plural	we	us	our, ours
Second person			
Singular	you	you	your, yours
Plural	you	you	your, yours
Third person			
Singular	he, she, it	him, her, it	his, her, hers, its
Plural	they	them	their, theirs

Note that the third-person pronoun singular also has gender—masculine (*he*), feminine (*she*), and neuter (*it*)—in all three cases. Also note that no

143

apostrophes are used with possessive forms.

ours, yours, hers, theirs, its

Remember: Never use the apostrophe with possessive pronouns. A common error is to confuse the possessive pronoun *its* (no apostrophe) with the contraction of *it is* (written *it's* with an apostrophe). Note the difference in usage in the words in the following sentences.

It's a rainy day.
    (*It is* a rainy day—*it's* is a contraction for *it is*.)

Everything is in *its* place.
    (*Its* is a possessive pronoun.)

The nominative case is used for subjects and complements.

Use the *nominative case* of the personal pronoun when the pronoun is used in the following situations.

1.   The subject of a sentence or clause.   A subject may consist of one pronoun.

I will meet you at the gate.
They may vote for the president.
We were at the meeting.

A subject may consist of two pronouns or a pronoun and a noun joined by *or, nor, and*.

She or *I* will make the trip.
Jerry and *he* will get the package.

2.   A complement.   When a noun or pronoun is joined to the subject by a linking verb (*is, are, was, were, will be*), it is called a *complement*. The complement is in the nominative case because in reality it is just another word for the subject.

It *was I* who spoke at the reunion.
If you *were she,* would you write the letter?
The outstanding workers *were* Mr. Jones and *I.*

The objective case is used for both objects and indirect objects of verbs, for objects of prepositions, and for subjects and objects of infinitives.

Use the *objective case* of the personal pronoun when the pronoun is used in the following situations.

1.   The object of a transitive verb.

The manager interviewed *me.*
The manager interviewed my brother and *me.*

The manager will hire *him* or *me.*
The manager will hire neither *him* nor *me.*

2.   The object of a preposition.

The report was proofread *by* Gladys and *me.*
Between you and *me* there should be no secrets.
The present is *for her.*

3.   The indirect object of a verb.   An indirect object in a sentence receives the thing named by the object of the verb. This receiver could be given in a prepositional phrase. Therefore, place the preposition *to* before the pronoun to determine the correct form.

> The receptionist gave *her* a book.
>   (gave to *her*)

> The girls told *her* a lie.
>   (told to *her*)

4.   The subject and object of an infinitive.   All pronouns used before and after an infinitive (*to type, to process, to write*) are in the objective case.

> The instructor expects *her to give* a speech.
> We meant *him to tell them.*
> Does Chuck wish *her to be* his secretary?

The possessive case is used to show ownership.

The *possessive case* of the personal pronoun is used to show ownership. The forms of possessive pronouns are the following.

Singular	Plural
my, mine	our, ours
your, yours	your, yours
his, her, hers, its	their, theirs
whose	whose

Agreement.   Possessive pronouns must agree with their antecedents (the person[s] to whom they refer) in number and gender.

> *John* locks *his* desk every night.
> *My book* will be published soon.
> *Bruce* and *I* gave *our* speeches.
> The *men* forgot *their* briefcases.

With verbal nouns.   Use the possessive pronoun with verbal nouns. (A verbal noun, or gerund, is an *ing* form of the verb used as a noun). A pronoun used to modify a verbal noun is in the possessive case.

> We do not object to *his talking* on the phone.
> There are no rules against *his working.*
> *Her being* present was a mistake.
> *His typing* is accurate.

Used alone.   When the noun is omitted, use *hers, ours, theirs, mine,* and *yours.* These special forms of possessive pronouns may be used as subjects, objects, and complements.

> This house is *ours.*
>   (*our house*)

> *Theirs* is the green house.
>   (*Their house*)

> We gave our money to charity. Jane kept *hers.*
>   (*her money*)

Whose.   The possessive pronoun *whose,* when followed by a noun, may be used to ask questions.

Whose book is on the table?

Whose chart has not been signed?

Pronouns must be in agreement with their antecedents.   The meaning of a pronoun is clear only if the word to which it refers can be located easily. This word for which the pronoun stands is called its *antecedent.* The antecedent may be a noun or another pronoun. Pronouns must *agree* as to *person, number,* and *gender* with their *antecedents.*

Mr. Jones stopped *Miss Smith* and asked *her* to file the papers.
(*Miss Smith* is the antecedent of *her.*)

We asked *our* neighbor to give *us* the pictures.
(*We* is the antecedent of *our* and *us.*)

Usually, the first- and second-person pronouns are easily identified with their antecedents. But third-person pronouns can cause trouble unless the antecedents are carefully placed in the sentence.

He says that *he* will write a letter to *him.*
(The antecedents are not clear.)

Bruce says that *he* will write a letter to *Bob.*
(*Bruce* is antecedent of *he.*)

Study the following common usages.

1.   Use a singular pronoun to refer to a singular antecedent. Use a plural pronoun when it refers to a plural antecedent.

The *girl* wore *her* dress too short.
(singular use of pronoun)

The *girls* wore *their* dresses too short.
(plural use of pronoun)

Notice in the two sentences above that the pronouns are possessive pronouns that modify the nouns *dress* and *dresses.* Agreement in number, of course, applies to all uses of pronouns.

2.   Use a singular pronoun in referring to these antecedents: *one, any, anyone, anybody, someone, somebody, each, every, everyone,* and *everybody.*

Everyone turned *his* head when I entered the room.
(*everyone*—singular; *his*—singular)

Each of us must think for *himself.*
(*each*—singular; *himself*—singular)

Somebody should bring *his* copy of the report.

Note that it is grammatically correct to use the masculine, *he, his,* or *him,* in referring to an antecedent if gender is not stated.

As discussed previously, however, it is becoming more popular to re-write these kinds of sentences to avoid gender identification.

All heads turned when I entered the room.

We must think for ourselves.

Somebody should bring a copy of the report.

3.   Use a singular pronoun when a collective noun stands for a group considered as a unit.

> Our track *team* won *its* fourth victory.
> (*Team* is considered a unit.)

> The *Army* displayed *its* weapons.
> (*Army* is considered a unit.)

> The *company* will celebrate *its* first anniversary.
> (*Company* is considered a unit.)

4.   Use a plural pronoun when a collective noun stands for a number of individuals considered separately.

> The *class* took *their* positions quickly.
> (*Class* is considered as many individual persons.)

> The *group* were approached for *their* viewpoints.
> (*Group* is considered as many individual persons.)

5.   Use a singular pronoun when two or more singular antecedents are joined by *or* or *nor*.

> Neither Joan *nor* Grace knitted *her* sweater.
> Either he *or* Mr. Mill should sign *his* name.

6.   Use a plural pronoun when one antecedent is singular and the other plural, and they are joined by *or* or *nor*. It is preferred that the plural antecedent be placed nearer the verb to avoid awkwardness. Thus, the pronoun is closest to the plural antecedent.

> Neither Alice *nor* her sisters mailed *their* replies.
> Neither Jack *nor* his classmates turned in *their* reports.

7.   Use a plural pronoun when two or more antecedents are joined by *and*.

> Alice *and* Marie checked in *their* uniforms.
> He *and* I have done *our* work.
> Miss Hughes *and* the other managers should have *their* dismissals listed by noon.

Learn to use *who* and *whom* correctly.

There are special ways to use *who* and *whom*. *Who* (nominative case) may be the subject of a sentence or clause, and it may be a complement following a linking verb. *Whom* (objective case) is used as the object of a verb, of a preposition, or of an infinitive.

> *Who* broke the chair?
> (*who* = subject)

> The man *who* is going to win this award will have to increase his sales 100 percent.
> (*who* = subject of clause)

> *Whom* did you consider for president?
> (*whom* = object of verb *did consider*)

> From *whom* did you get this?
> (*whom* = object of preposition *from*)

Whom do you want me to meet?
(*whom* = object of infinitive *to meet*)

To identify the correct use of *who* and *whom* in questions, change the question to a statement, as in the following sentences.

Whom did you elect for president?
(**Change to:** You did elect *whom* for president. *Whom* is the object of the verb *elect*.)

Who is president?
(**Change to:** The president is *who*. *Who* follows the linking verb *is* and is the complement.)

There are two fundamental guides to help you develop correct usage of *who* or *whom*.

1. Use *whom* wherever *him* or *her* could be substituted.

    Whom do you think I saw in my office today?
    (I saw *whom* [him, her] in my office?)

2. Use *who* wherever *he* or *she* could be substituted.

    Don't you know *who* it was?
    (It was *who* [he, she]?)

ACCURATE CHOICE OF WORDS IS IMPORTANT

Here are ten more groups of homonyms for you to master. By now you are probably able to identify the differences in homonyms more quickly than you were able to do when you first started this study. Are you noticing that your usable vocabulary is increasing? Do continue to use all the words you know in your conversation and written work. A large vocabulary is an asset, so do not be embarrassed to use it. You are preparing for a career in the business world.

		Write	
Homonym	*Definition*	*First time*	*Second time*
principal	Chief; main; highest in rank; capital sum.	_____	_____
principle	A basic law; a rule.	_____	_____
scene	A division of a drama; a landscape; any striking display of feeling.	_____	_____
seen	Past participle of the verb *see*.	_____	_____
stake	A pointed piece of wood driven into the ground as a mark or support; something wagered or risked, as a bet.	_____	_____
steak	A slice of meat.	_____	_____
steal	To take away illegally.	_____	_____
steel	A commercial form of iron.	_____	_____

straight	Not curved; direct; uninterrupted, unbroken.	_____	_____
strait	A narrow passageway connecting two bodies of water; restricted as to space; difficulty.	_____	_____
threw	Past tense of _throw_.	_____	_____
through	By way of; finished.	_____	_____
their	Possessive of _they_.	_____	_____
there	In or at that place.	_____	_____
they're	Contraction of _they are_.	_____	_____
to	In a direction toward.	_____	_____
too	Likewise; also.	_____	_____
two	A pair; a couple.	_____	_____
vain	Showing pride in one's appearance.	_____	_____
vane	Instrument used to show wind direction.	_____	_____
ware	An article of merchandise.	_____	_____
wear	To carry upon a person; to exhaust the strength of.	_____	_____

ASSIGNMENTS

Apply your knowledge of case and agreement of pronouns

A. These sentences will test your ability to select pronouns that agree with their antecedents. Read each sentence carefully, select the pronoun that agrees with the antecedent, and insert the pronoun in the sentence.

1. The telegrams came by messenger, and _____ were taken immediately to Mr. Smith. (it, they, them)

2. Our department developed _____ most important product last year. (its, their)

3. Each employee has been loyal to _____ boss. (his, their)

4. Each man is to turn in _____ time card by 3 p.m. (his, her, their)

5. It is the responsibility of every employee to attend every meeting that _____ can. (he, they)

6. Not one of the members sold _____ tickets for the raffle. (his, their)

7. Everyone clapped as loudly as _____ could. (he, they)

8. Our board of directors made _____ first appearance of the year. (its, their)

9. Each of the men except Don and Barry did _____ part. (his, their)

10. The office staff wore _____ new badges last week. (its, their)

11. Each woman should do all _____ can to help the department. (they, she)

12. Give the package to _____ so that he can take _____ to George. (he, him; them, it)

13. The professor asked his students when _____ wanted the final examination. (he, they, them)

14. All the students took _____ examinations at the same time. (his, their, theirs)

15. None of the finance committee members discussed _____ particular job. (his, their)

16. Neither Jean nor Ann has completed _____ filing. (her, their)

17. Everyone has _____ favorite TV program. (his, her, their)

18. Mr. Keill asked _____ to attend the luncheon with the visitors and _____. (I, me; he, him, them, they)

19. He asked if it was _____ who assembled the file. (I, me)

20. The chairman asked the group about _____ plans for the next meeting. (his, its, their)

B. In the blank following the noun or nouns in parentheses, write the correct pronoun substitute.

1. What does (Mr. Roberts) _____ intend to do with the drawings?

2. The supervisor gave (Terry and Irwin) _____ the tickets.

3. Did (Terry and Irwin) _____ go to the game?

4. Perhaps it was (Kathy) _____ who wrote this memorandum.

5. Joe had an order from (Miller Bros., Inc.) _____ yesterday.

6. We heard (the typewriters) _____ making copies automatically.

7. Mike asked (Phil and Margaret) _____ to his house for dinner.

8. It must have been (the men) _____ who sent the flowers.

9. The president came with (the office managers) _____ to the picnic.

10. I think it was (Richard) _____ who made the plans.

11. I am sure that (the typists) _____ will make the necessary changes.

12. Did you see (Barbara and Ben) _____ at the conference?

13. It was (the supervisor's) _____ suggestion that we inventory the supplies.

14. Give (Mr. Janis) _____ the minutes of our last meeting.

15. Did Mr. Jobes take (Mr. Jobes') _____ coffee break yet?

C. Underline the correct word in the following sentences.

1. Did you know that (yours, your's) was the only poorly organized report?
2. (Its, It's) the only car available for the trip.

3. Did you notice that (theirs, their's) were the only figures missing?
4. I can't tell you if (we, us) will be at the meeting or not.
5. You and (her, she) had better improve your customer relations.
6. Mrs. Thompson and (me, I) will review the minutes of the conference.
7. (We, Us) managers are in a better position to judge the situation.
8. It was (me, I) who told the boss about the delay.
9. The outstanding workers were Mr. Brown and (he, him).
10. The manager interviewed (he, him) and (me, I).
11. The reports were corrected by George and (me, I).
12. Just between you and (me, I), the new secretary is excellent.
13. His supervisor expected (him, he) to be on the job.
14. He invited (we, us) men to attend the awards banquet.
15. You should tell (us, we) employees the truth about the stock split.
16. We do not really object to (his, him) doing this task.
17. There are no rules against (their, them) taking too long for lunch.
18. (Whose, Who's) pencil did you find in the computer center?
19. I don't know if it's (their's, theirs) or (our's, ours).
20. It seems as though (her, hers) filing is improving.

D. Underline the correct word in the following sentences.

1. Karen cannot type as well as Mary and (her, she) can type.
2. Harry has been selling much more than John and (he, him) have sold.
3. To (who, whom) was the boss referring?
4. (Who, Whom) is going to handle that account?
5. Knowing (who, whom) to reprimand in this case is quite a problem.
6. Have you considered (who, whom) might take the vacant position?
7. He is the man (whom, who) will succeed in this position.
8. He is bringing a guest of (whom, who) we have heard him speak.
9. (Who, Whom) is the man most respected by the employees?
10. (Whoever, Whomever) wishes to apply for the opening should sign here.
11. Someone left (her, his, their) umbrella in the cafeteria.
12. The committee announced that (they, it) had reached a decision.
13. A person should not sign (her, his, their) name to a contract without reading it first.
14. Neither the mayor nor the councilmen have announced (their, his) decision.
15. Both Jim and Bob take (his, their) duties seriously.
16. Mr. Jones invited (we, us) to join the discussion.
17. Give the key to (whoever, whomever) asks for it.
18. If you were (he, him), would you accept the job?
19. Please give a copy to Mary, Helen, and (I, me).
20. (Who, Whom) did he say paid the last installment?

E. Here are a few more sentences in which homonyms are used. Pick out the one that completes the sentence, and write it in the column.

1. The (principal, principle) theme of the conference is management by objectives. _____

2. Some parts in that machine are made of (steal, steel).   _____

3. The surveyor's assistant placed (steaks, stakes) at the corners as directed.   _____

4. I plan to go (through, threw) this material at home.   _____

5. Many people sell Tupper(wear, ware) at coffee klatches in the home.   _____

6. It is (to, too, two) late for you to stop payment.   _____

7. If (their, they're, there) planning to catch the plane, they had better start right now.   _____

8. Many young men and women are (vane, vain) about their appearance.   _____

9. (There, They're, Their) are many attractive young people in the business world.   _____

10. You should (wear, ware) sensible shoes to work.   _____

11. Everyone should learn the (principals, principles) of accounting.   _____

12. Please don't make a (scene, seen) over such a minor error.   _____

13. The visitor ordered a (stake, steak) for dinner.   _____

14. If you go (straight, strait) down the hall, you will find the print shop.   _____

15. Many employees find themselves in dire (straights, straits) during a layoff.   _____

Name _____

Date _____

———————————— **PRACTICE WRITING** ————————————

    Persons who have confidence in their ability to use pronouns correctly will find it easier to express ideas fluently in both speech and writing. In this exercise, you have the opportunity to compose original sentences that contain your own thoughts in your own words. The only restriction is that you use pronouns.

    A. Write five original sentences using personal pronouns in the person, number, and case given.

Example: First person, singular, nominative *I have confidence in my ability to use pronouns correctly.*

1. First person, plural, possessive _____

_____

_____

2. Third person, singular, masculine, objective _____

_____

_____

3. Second person, plural, nominative _____

_____

_____

4. Third person, plural, objective _____

_____

_____

_____

5. First person, singular, possessive _____

_____

_____

_____

B. Write five original sentences using the word or words below and a pronoun of your own choice that refers back to it or them as the antecedent.

1. *everybody* _____

_____

_____

2. *committee* _____

_____

_____

3. *Mr. Jones and Miss Hanson* _____

_____   _____

_____

4. *Maria and the secretaries* _____

_____

_____

5. *he and I* _____

_____

_____

Action and being words

Action and being words include all forms of the verb. In our language, they signal the performance of an action, the occurrence of an event, the possession of things or attributes, and the presence of a condition. These words allow us to get movement and progress into our messages. They bring static naming words to life. Because action and being words work closely with naming words—nouns and pronouns—certain patterns of usage have been adopted over the years to ensure the accurate linking of these two elements. In this section, you will study how action and being words may be used more accurately.

Verbs have an important function

Verbs, the action and being words, are important to sentences. They add life to the message in a variety of ways. You learned to pick out subjects and verbs in Section 1, pages 6–8, of this book. To help you become an effective communicator, however, you should make a study of the many ways verbs can be used. First, though, let us review what you have already studied about them.

You recall that verbs in both independent and dependent clauses tell what action, possession, or state of being applies to the subject. Notice how the verb tells us these things in the following sentences.

The operator **turned** on the computer.

The machine **has** four blades.

The letter **is** confusing.

You also found out in Section 1 that clauses may have more than one verb or verb phrase.

Mr. Jones **read** and **sorted** the mail.

Your memorandum **is** too long and **should be rewritten.**

Before you **lock** the file and **leave** for the day, **take** this report to Mr. Smith, **ask** him to read it, and then **return** it to the file.

Quick review

To refresh your memory about verbs used with subjects, here is a review that asks you to identify both the subject of a clause and its verb or verbs. Underline subjects once and verbs twice in *all* clauses in the following sentences.

1. Please complete and return the enclosed card.
2. Speakers will discuss and illustrate a sound estate planning program.
3. Most of the people took the power outage in stride, but some sent letters of complaint.

158

4. When the repair crews are finished, they should report to head-quarters.
5. The customer ordered ten dozen hinges but sent money for only eight dozen.
6. The speaker said that the company must import low-sulfur oil.
7. Taxpayers are saving nearly $150,000 a year.
8. Plans have been made to visit the site.
9. If you need information on energy conservation, visit or call your local water and power office.
10. The book tells how to make kites and lists safety rules.

There are three groups of verbs.

Now let us review what you studied about verbs in the section on sentence patterns, pages 35–42. You found that there are three groups of verbs: *transitive, intransitive,* and *linking.*

Transitive verbs are followed by objects.

In the discussion of transitive verbs, it was pointed out that these verbs must have an *object* to complete the meaning or to receive the action of the verb. The transitive verb forms a bridge for the action to travel from the *subject* to the *object.* You learned that asking *what?* or *whom?* will help you locate the *object of the verb.* Some people use the term *direct object* when referring to the object of the verb. Once again observe how the action of the transitive verbs is carried from the subjects in the following sentences to the objects of the verbs.

Trucks *carry* heavy loads.
(Carry what? *loads*)
The pitcher *threw* the ball to first base.
(Threw what? *ball*)
Do you *know* the new branch manager?
(Do know whom? *manager*)

Pronouns used as objects of transitive verbs must be in the objective case.

It is important to know that when a pronoun is the object of a transitive verb, it must be in the *objective* case. In the section on case and agreement of pronouns, you learned that the objective case pronouns are *me, us, you, him, her, them,* and *whom.* The use of the objective case of pronouns is explained on pages 144–45.

Mr. Johns *asked* Susan and *me* to work overtime.
(Asked whom? *Susan and me*)
Whom *did* you *see* at the game?
(Did see whom? *whom*)

Pronouns used as indirect objects must be in the objective case.

Sentences containing transitive verbs may indicate the transfer of the object to someone else. The final receiver of the thing or person named as the object is called the *indirect object.* You ran across indirect objects on pages 37 and 144–45. The sentence below has an indirect object.

The typist *gave* Mr. Higgins the report.

Mr. Higgins is the final receiver of the report, or the *indirect object.* If you wish to use a pronoun in place of the person's name as the indirect object, use the *objective case—me, us, you, him, her, them,* and *whom.*

The typist *gave* him the report.

Transitive verbs may be followed by object complements.

Transitive verbs may also be followed by *object complements* that are either nouns or adjectives. Usually there is no problem in using them. The important point to remember is that the *noun object complement* is merely another *name* for the object. In the illustration below, the object of the transitive verb is *Mr. Lawler,* and the complement *chairman* is another name for him.

The group **elected** Mr. Lawler *chairman.*
He **made** Harold department *head.*
The executive committee **appointed** Mrs. Gomez branch *manager.*

The *adjective object complement* describes or modifies the object of the transitive verb. Notice in the sentence below that Mr. Soames describes the manager's attitude as cooperative. *Cooperative* is an adjective used as a complement to modify or describe the object *attitude.*

Mr. Soames **thought** the manager's attitude *cooperative.*
Mary **considered** her *frivolous.*
The decorator **painted** the walls *green.*

Intransitive verbs do not take objects.

An *intransitive* verb expresses action or state of being *without* requiring a completing element. A subject and a verb are all that are needed for a complete message. If the sentence has other words after the intransitive verb, these words merely add information. They are not needed, however, because the main thought is complete without them. The sentences below illustrate this point.

The *employees* **left.**
The employees **left** at 4:30 p.m.
(Additional information is added.)

Sentences containing intransitive verbs may be written in an interesting and informative style. The following example shows that an intransitive verb may be followed by a word, phrase, or clause that limits the action or describes the state of being expressed by it.

The *idea* **occurred** to him *while he was reading the company paper.*
(Occurred when? *while he was reading . . .*)

The phrase *to him* and the clause *while he was reading* . . . limit the action but are not objects of the verb. Ask *when?* or *where?* after a verb in order to identify intransitive verbs. The material after intransitive verbs answers those questions: *when?* or *where?*.

Our factory *will be built next year.*
(Will be built when? *next year*)
The office manager **sits** at the desk in the far corner.
(Sits where? *at the desk . . .*)

The *to be* verb may be used as either an intransitive or a linking verb. Its use as an *intransitive verb* may be seen in these sentences.

The dedication of our new office building **was** *last month.*
(Was when? *last month*)
The supervisor **is** at the conference.
(Is where? *at the conference*)

Many verbs are used both transitively and intransitively. In the sentences below, the verb *sell* is used both ways.

Transitive: The man *sells* electrical *appliances.*
(Sells what? *appliances*)

Intransitive: The man *sells* when the spirit moves him.
(Sells what? No answer. Sells whom? Still no answer.
Sells when? *when the spirit moves him*)

Linking verbs are followed by complements.

A *linking verb,* similar to intransitive verbs, never requires an object. It is, however, followed by a *complement.* The function of the linking verb is to point out that the word following it has the *same identity* as the *subject* or that the word *describes* the *subject.*

This room *smells* damp.

The new administrative secretary *is Ruth Weber.*

The work crew *seem* angry.

Tony Sanchez *has been* a *leadman* for three years.

Notice in the previous examples that you have a *damp room, Ruth Weber the new administrative secretary, angry crew,* and *leadman Tony Sanchez.*

Linking verbs show condition or state of being.

Linking verbs merely express condition or state of being. The forms of the infinitive *to be* are the most common linking verbs.

am	shall be	should have been
are	will be	must have been
is	has been	might have been
was	have been	
were		

Other linking verbs are these four verbs of the senses—*taste, smell, feel, look*—and other verbs, such as *become, appear, sound,* and *seem.* The term *linking* means that the subject is tied to other words in the sentence. For additional explanation, turn to pages 38–39.

Pronoun complements that follow linking verbs are in the nominative case.

Complement, as you learned earlier, is the general term used for nouns, pronouns, or adjectives that follow linking verbs. The noun or pronoun complement refers to the same person or thing named by the subject. The subject and the complement are the *same* in identity. Because the subject and the complement are the same, the *pronoun complement* must be in the same case as the subject. As you learned in the section on *case,* the *subject* of a sentence is in the *nominative case.* The pronoun that follows the linking verb, therefore, must be in the *nominative case—I, we, you, he, she, it, they,* and *who.*

The manager of the Sales Department *was* formerly a sales *representative.*
(*representative* = *manager;* therefore, *representative* = noun complement)

The applicants *were* Mr. James Fisk and I.
(*applicants* = *Mr. James Fisk and I;* two complements: one a proper noun, one a pronoun in nominative case)

Who was it?
(Remember to reword questions to find the subject. *it* = *who;* a pronoun complement in nominative case)

It **was** *she* and *I* who asked for time off.
(*it* = *she and I*; two pronoun complements in nominative case)

Adjective complements that follow linking verbs describe the subject.

When the word that follows the linking verb describes the subject, it is called an *adjective complement*. Only adjectives that modify nouns and pronouns can be used as complements.

Satin **feels** *cool* and *smooth* to the touch.
(It is *cool* satin, *smooth* satin.)

Your perfume **smells** *spicy*.
(It is *spicy* perfume.)

The coffee **tastes** *strong*.
(It is *strong* coffee.)

Your information **is** *correct*.
(It is *correct* information.)

You should be cautious when you are trying to determine whether a verb is a no-action linking verb. Some verbs, such as *seem, appear, sound, look, feel, taste,* and *smell,* can be used to show action. When they show action, they are transitive or intransitive verbs, and adverbs must be used to modify them.

I **feel** *strongly* about the matter.
(The adverb *strongly* modifies the verb **feel**.)

Mr. Jones **looked** *carefully* through the papers in the file folder.
(*Carefully* is an adverb that tells *how* Mr. Jones performed the action.)

In summary, a *transitive verb* shows action and requires an *object* to complete its meaning. If the object is a pronoun, it is in the *objective case*. An *indirect object* in the *objective case* might also follow the transitive verb and receive the thing named by the object. *Object complements* that name or describe the object may often be included in these sentences. An *intransitive verb* does *not* require an object to complete its message, but it may be followed by a word, phrase, or clause that limits the *action*. A *linking verb* does not show action but connects the subject with the word that follows the verb, called the *complement*. The complement may be a noun or pronoun that names the subject or an adjective that describes the subject. If the complement is a pronoun, it must be in the *nominative case*.

Quick review

Let's quickly review what has just been discussed about verbs and their objects and/or complements. Underline the subject once and the verb twice in each of the ten sentences. At the same time, write the object (direct and/or indirect) and the complement (noun, pronoun, or adjective) in the appropriate column.

		Object	*Complement*
1.	The mountains across the valley look beautiful.	_____	_____
2.	Our company conducts periodic surveys of the community.	_____	_____
3.	The president of Kiwanis is an employee of ABC Corporation.	_____	_____

4. The new machine cuts several hundred sheets an hour. _____ _____
5. She thought about the matter for several minutes. _____ _____
6. Will you please give her yesterday's minutes to read. _____ _____
7. The workers must have been happy about the hourly increase in wages. _____ _____
8. The rug in Mr. Jones' office is blue and gold. _____ _____
9. Take Gene Simons the part for his machine. _____ _____
10. Who was it that the supervisor wanted to see? _____ _____

ACCURATE CHOICE OF WORDS IS IMPORTANT

This last group of words completes your review of sound-alike words that confuse all of us. Apply the *see, say, spell, write* routine to them also. By the end of this practice, you will find that you have a better mastery of 125 words.

Homonym	Definition	*Write* First time	Second time
correspondence	Communication by exchange of letters.	_____	_____
correspondents	Plural of *correspondent:* one who writes to another.	_____	_____
coarse	Unrefined, rough.	_____	_____
course	Direction of progress.	_____	_____
led	Past tense and past participle of the verb *lead;* to guide by drawing along or going before.	_____	_____
lead	A heavy, pliable metal.	_____	_____
rain	Water falling in drops.	_____	_____
reign	To govern, usually as a king.	_____	_____
rein	To hold in check; the strap of a bridle.	_____	_____
raise	To lift; to erect.	_____	_____
rays	Beams of light.	_____	_____
raze	To tear down; to demolish.	_____	_____

residence	A place where one has his home.	_____ _____
residents	Those who reside in a place.	_____ _____
right	Correct; not mistaken or wrong.	_____ _____
rite	A ritual; form of conducting a ceremony.	_____ _____
write	To form letters or words on paper.	_____ _____
sight	The power of seeing; a view.	_____ _____
site	The seat or scene of any thing; a location.	_____ _____
cite	To quote.	_____ _____
tear	Moisture in the eye.	_____ _____
tier	A row, rank, or layer.	_____ _____

Now go back over the five lists of homonyms which sound alike (pages 87, 99, 135, 148, and 163), and isolate those pairs or triplets that you can always use and spell correctly. Have confidence in your mastery of them. Next, turn to those words that continue to be confusing. List them below. For the next several days, spend a few minutes on them until you master every word.

MY LIST OF HOMONYMS TO BE MASTERED

See	Say	Spell aloud	Write first time	Write second time
_____			_____	_____
_____			_____	_____
_____			_____	_____
_____			_____	_____
_____			_____	_____
_____			_____	_____
_____			_____	_____
_____			_____	_____
_____			_____	_____

ASSIGNMENTS

Apply your knowledge of the function of verbs

A. Read the following sentences and identify the verbs in both independent and dependent clauses. Some clauses may have more than one verb or verb phrase. Write the verbs you find in the right-hand column.

1. The new office opens tomorrow. _____

2. The sales force should call on customers five days a week. _____

3. Your duty is to train new employees. _____

4. How many new customers have been added to our list? _____

5. Please settle the dispute between Jim and Ron. _____

6. If you will ask Mr. Jones, he will explain the next procedure. _____

7. Verbs of action make a message more interesting. _____

8. Tell the supervisor to shut down at least four machines over the weekend. _____

9. These figures should be added and then entered in the proper accounts. _____
10. When a pronoun is the object of a transitive verb, it must be in the objective case. _____

11. Customers should pay their bills on time. _____

12. Will you borrow the money from the bank? _____

13. If you lose a check, call the bank and ask to have payment stopped on it. _____

14. The bank will confirm your request in writing. _____

15. The auditor checked the accounts receivable for errors.   _____

16. They will depart at noon.   _____

17. The guests will be waiting in the lobby.   _____

18. Customers complain.   _____

19. The truck driver waited impatiently for the next load.   _____

20. Should we invite the entire staff to the meeting?   _____

B. Select from the following sentences the verb, its object (if any), and its complement (if any). Write your selections in the columns provided at the right.

	Verb	*Object*	*Complement*
Example: Mr. Simpson is our new president.	*is*	_____	*president*
1. The package came this morning.	_____	_____	_____
2. Mr. Fields placed the hammer on the bench.	_____	_____	_____
3. The flowers are yellow.	_____	_____	_____
4. The new members of the board of directors are Mrs. Lewis and my superior.	_____	_____	_____
5. The company expects a profit from sales.	_____	_____	_____
6. The chairperson introduced Mrs. de los Reyes, the vice president in charge of public relations.	_____	_____	_____
7. In what states are your competitors located?	_____	_____	_____
8. Take this folder to the files and bring the one for the Parker Construction Co.	_____	_____	_____
9. Several of the trucks need new tires.	_____	_____	_____
10. Small retailers appear hesitant about opening a shop in a shopping center.	_____	_____	_____
11. The interviewer seems able to judge character.	_____	_____	_____
12. Most of our customers are people who eat at gourmet restaurants.	_____	_____	_____
13. Self-service stores have become popular in the last 15 years.	_____	_____	_____
14. The back of this violin feels rough.	_____	_____	_____

15. Finish the blueprint before you
leave.   _____ _____ _____

16. A parking lot for employees should
be built.   _____ _____ _____

17. Sara itemized the items purchased
for the customer.   _____ _____ _____

18. Send your reply by return mail. _____ _____ _____

19. If you buy this widget now, you will _____ _____ _____
save $2.50.

                                _____ _____ _____
20. The accountant prepared the charts
for the monthly report.   _____ _____ _____

C. A pronoun used as an object of the verb or an indirect object is always in the objective case
—*me, us, him, her, them,* and *whom*. A pronoun used as a complement with a linking verb is always
in the nominative case—*I, we, you, he, she, it, they* and *who*. To demonstrate that you recognize objects
and complements and know the proper case to use with them, select the correct pronoun from the pair
in parentheses, and write it in the space provided at the right.

1. Bring (I, me) the dictionary from the next room.   _____

2. Mr. Fasman, a recent retiree, asked (she, her) to send his retirement check
to the bank.   _____

3. The engineers who will attend the briefing are Bob Phelps and (I, me).   _____

4. It was (I, me) who asked for a raise.   _____

5. Mr. Tracy told (he, him) to go to the stockroom for more supplies.   _____

6. Mrs. Schwartz gave (she, her) the report to read.   _____

7. Who will show (we, us) and (they, them) how to operate the computer?   _____

8. Send (she, her) a receipt and (he, him) a copy of the letter.   _____

9. Did Jim give (they, them) instructions before he left?   _____

10. The new sales manager will be either Otto Fritzen or (he, him).   _____

11. Tell (they, them) your decision after the board meeting.   _____

12. The ones selected to go to the convention were Max Jones, Marian Hilker,
and (I, me).   _____

13. (Who, Whom) did Mr. Smith ask for the notes on the meeting?   _____

14. The customer who received a duplicate might have been (she, her).   _____

15. (Who, Whom) did you give a ride to work?   _____

D.   To demonstrate that you recognize a linking verb and know the form of the descriptive word that follows it, select the correct word from the pair in parentheses and write it in the right-hand column.

1.   The driver of the delivery van looked (foolish, foolishly) in the bright uniform.   _____

2.   Martha Perkins feels (badly, bad) about the mistake in the sales totals.   _____

3.   That material looks (soft, softly) and (pliable, pliably).   _____

4.   Secretaries who are (neat, neatly) in appearance seem (confidently, confident) in their ability to meet important visitors.   _____

5.   The noise from the factory sounds (loud, loudly) and (strident, stridently).   _____

6.   Those chemicals smell (pungent, pungently).   _____

7.   The meals in the cafeteria sometimes taste (terribly, terrible).   _____

8.   After the accident, his arm felt (sore, sorely) for several days.   _____

9.   Mr. Orr was (slow, slowly) in making up his mind to buy the panel truck.   _____

10.   The bolts on the lathe might have been too (tightly, tight).   _____

11.   This weakness seems (obvious, obviously) when you look (close, closely).   _____

12.   Our production schedule appears (difficult, difficultly) to maintain, and the works manager became (angry, angrily) when told it could not be revised.   _____

E.   Choose the word from the ones in parentheses that accurately expresses the message in the sentence. Write your choice in the space provided.

1.   Please _____ the windows in the laboratory. (raise, rays, raze)

2.   Is it _____ that we should have to work overtime? (right, rite, write)

3.   We receive so much _____ from the public and our customers that it is impossible to answer all the letters. (correspondence, correspondents)

4.   How many business _____ do you know personally? (correspondence, correspondents)

5.   You will find that file on the third _____. (tear, tier)

6.   Mr. Jones asked the attorney to _____ the first paragraph of the subpoena. (sight, site, cite)

7.   The guard _____ the agent through the courtyard to the security department. (led, lead)

8.   The new concrete walkway was made of _____ gravel. (coarse, course)

9. Give the employees free _____ within the guidelines set forth in the office procedures manual. (rain, reign, rein)

10. The _____ in this building asked for a self-service elevator. (residence, residents)

11. Please ask the machinist to see that the _____ from his torch do not hit the eyes of other workers. (raise, rays, raze)

12. That machine must be made of _____; it is so heavy. (led, lead)

13. Please _____ the company that manufactured the car for an operations manual. (right, rite, write)

14. The proper _____ to take in this matter is the one spelled out in the procedures book. (coarse, course)

15. They plan to _____ the new building as soon as they _____ that old one. (raise, rays, raze)

16. There is a ceremonial _____ often used by the Navy to launch ships. (right, rite, write)

17. Where is the _____ for the new headquarters building? (sight, site, cite)

18. The _____ has slowed down construction of the power plant. (rain, reign, rein)

19. It is an impressive _____ to see the new models coming off the assembly line. (sight, site, cite)

20. Does Mrs. Kelly _____ over her department, or does she delegate responsibilities? (rain, reign, rein)

Name _____

Date _____

—————— **PRACTICE WRITING** ——————

Here is an opportunity to construct sentences that use strong verbs to show action. Try to select colorful verbs from your own vocabulary so that your message conveys the feeling of action. Compose sentences using the types of verbs called for below.

1. Use the transitive verb with a noun object.

   _____

   _____

   _____

2. Use the transitive verb with a pronoun object.

   _____

   _____

   _____

3. Use the transitive verb with an object and an indirect object.

   _____

   _____

   _____

4. Use the transitive verb with an object and its complement.

   _____

   _____

   _____

5. Use the intransitive verb.

_____

_____

_____

6. Use the linking verb with a noun or pronoun complement.

_____

_____

_____

7. Use the linking verb with an adjective complement.

_____

_____

_____

2

Verbs agree with subjects in person and number

Because the subject and the verb work together, they should agree in both person and number. If the subject is singular, the verb should be singular. If the subject is plural, the verb should be plural. Similarly, if you use a first-person subject, you will need to use a first-person verb. Thus, you can see that before selecting the verb form to use, you will need to decide what subject or subjects should be used and whether they should be singular or plural. After the subject is selected, then the choice of the verb and its form is easy.

In your study of the sentence in Section 1, pages 35–42, you learned to recognize the subject and the verb. In this part, you will study the changes in person and number that affect the spelling of the present tense of all verbs and, in addition, the spelling of the past tense of the verb *be*. A mastery of the material here will make it possible for you to select the correct verb form for any subject you might use. Subject/verb agreement errors are frequently made in business correspondence. Unfortunately, they call attention to a writer's failure to recognize a major grammatical error. To achieve your goal of becoming an effective communicator, you should have subject/verb agreement in all your messages, both oral and written.

Verbs have singular and plural forms.

Verbs, as well as nouns and pronouns, have singular and plural forms. Use a singular verb if the *subject* is *singular*. Use a plural verb if the *subject* is *plural*.

The shipping *carton* **weighs** two pounds.
(singular subject *carton*, singular verb **weighs**)
The shipping *cartons* **weigh** ten pounds.
(plural subject *cartons*, plural verb **weigh**)

Notice in the second illustration that while the addition of *s* or *es* to nouns makes them plural, the plural verb does not end in *s*. *Cartons* is the plural subject and *weigh* (without an *s*) is the plural verb. It is in the singular form of the verb that the addition of *s* or *es* signifies that the verb is third-person singular. *Carton*, the singular subject in the first illustration, is followed by the singular verb *weighs* (with an *s*).

175

These next few examples will make subject/verb agreement in number even clearer.

Machines hum, but the machine hums.
They talk, but she talks.
Mr. Jones makes many decisions, but the employees fail to hear about them.

Verbs must agree with first-, second-, or third-person subjects.

Person refers to the relationship between subject and verb, especially when using pronouns. The subject of a sentence may be *speaking, spoken to,* or *spoken about.* The person *speaking* is called a *first-person subject*—**I** or **we.** The person *spoken to* is a *second-person subject*—**you.** The person or thing *spoken about* is a *third-person subject*—**he, she, it,** or **they.** The verb must agree with the subject-person as illustrated in the following sentences.

I *type* letters all day.
You *type* letters all day.
He *types* letters all day.
She *types* letters all day.
The stenographer *types* letters all day.

Type is both the first-person and the second-person singular of the present tense of the verb *type. Types* is the third-person singular of the present tense.

A noun is always third person.

Notice that *stenographer* takes the third-person singular form of the verb. A *noun* is always *third* person.

When plural, the first-, second-, and third-person subjects use the plural form of the verb. Notice that the plural form of a verb is written **without** an **s.**

We *type* letters all day.
You stenographers *type* letters all day.
They *type* letters all day.
The stenographers *type* letters all day.

Present tense singular and plural forms of regular verbs are the same.

The *present tense* singular and plural forms of all regular verbs are the same. Using the regular verb *walk* as an example, you can see that only the spelling of the present tense, third-person singular changes by the addition of an *s: he walks.*

Present tense

Person	Singular	Plural
First	I walk	we walk
Second	you walk	you walk
Third	he *walks*	they walk
	she *walks*	
	it *walks*	

Add s to most regular verbs to form the third-person singular.

The following rules will enable you to *spell* the third-person singular, present tense for most verbs. The first rule to remember is *to add s to the majority of regular verbs.*

asks	nominates	predicts	translates
calls	occurs	forecasts	figures
invites	precedes	computes	writes

Also, add *s* to a verb that ends with *y* preceded by a vowel.

plays   displays   obeys
employs   conveys   portrays

Add *es* to certain verbs to form the third-person singular.

The second rule to remember is *to add es to certain verbs*. Verbs that end with *y* preceded by a consonant require the *y* to be changed to an *i* and then the *es* to be added.

carries   satis*fies*   justi*fies*
tries   accompan*ies*   appl*ies*

Verbs that end in *o*, *s*, *x*, *z*, *sh*, and *ch* call for the addition of *es* when forming the third-person singular.

vetoes   fiz*zes*   address*es*   wat*ches*
zeroes   ma*shes*   fixes   lat*ches*

The spelling of the irregular verb *be* is different for each person.

Because the irregular verb *be* is used with many regular verbs, you need to review the spelling of its singular and plural forms. Other irregular verbs are discussed on pages 205–08. The forms of *be* show that both the singular present and the singular past tenses are spelled differently.

BE
Present tense

Person	Singular	Plural
First	I am	we are
Second	you are	you are
Third	he is	they are
	she is	
	it is	

Past tense

First	I was	we were
Second	you were	you were
Third	he was	they were
	she was	
	it was	

Singular items joined by *and* form a plural subject.

Here are a few important points to remember about subject/verb agreement in person and number. Singular words, phrases, or clauses joined by *and* to form a compound subject require a *plural verb* because the subject is plural. Two or more persons, places, or things are involved.

The man *and* his dog **are walking** down the street.
Mary *and* Ellen **sing** in the company chorus.
Selling appliances *and* repairing them **keep** him busy.

Singular items joined by *or* and *nor* take a singular verb.

Singular words, phrases, or clauses joined by *or* and *nor* require a *singular verb* because only one of the subjects is involved in the action of the verb.

One *or* the other of the two men **is** responsible.
(not both, just one of the men)

Neither Tuesday *nor* Wednesday *is* a suitable day for the meeting.
(only one day being considered for the meeting)

Either Jane's *or* Mary's typewriter **needs** to be repaired.
(only one typewriter to be repaired)

The subject closest to the verb determines the choice of person.

Occasionally, you may wish to use two or more singular subjects, joined by *or* or *nor,* that are in two or three different persons. In such cases, the subject closest to the verb determines the person of the verb.

Neither John *nor* I **see** the point you are trying to make.

Ellen, you *or* I **am** the person to be called next.

Either he *or* I **am going** to the labor meeting.

Singular and plural words joined by *or* or *nor* take the plural verb.

A compound subject in which *singular and plural words* are joined by *or* or *nor* requires the plural form of the verb. It is preferable to write the singular subject first so that the plural subject is closest to the plural verb. By placing the words as suggested, you avoid making one of the most common grammatical errors that occur in business writing.

Neither Marian *nor* her sisters **work** for their uncle.

As I recall, the truck *or* the automobiles **need** new tires.

Either Carlos *or* the department managers **are** to attend the board meeting.

Each and every before the subject call for the singular verb.

Sometimes *each* or *every* precedes one or both of the parts joined by *and* in the compound subject. In such sentences, the verb is *singular* even though the two subjects are joined by *and.*

Each employee and supervisor **parks** in the assigned space.

Every salesperson and *every* sales trainee **is asked** to sell twice as much next month.

Every lathe and drill **runs** smoothly.

The second *each* or *every* may be omitted or retained, as desired. If used, emphasis is obtained.

Singular indefinite pronouns take the singular verb.

Indefinite pronouns, such as *everyone, someone, anyone, anybody, everybody, one,* and *no one,* are singular in meaning and take the singular verb.

One of us **is** the person to make the final decision.

Is *someone* responsible for the food for the party?

Anyone who wishes to talk to the personnel representative **makes** an appointment first.

Find the true subject before deciding whether the verb should be singular or plural.

Sometimes finding the true subject is difficult. It may be obscured by an intervening phrase or an inverted construction. Look for the true subject and determine whether it is singular or plural. When using inverted sentences in speaking or writing, reword them in your mind first so that the subject and verb fall in the normal order. By rearranging the words, you will automatically choose the verb that agrees with the subject in person and number. Don't let this bit of extra mental work stop you from using inverted sentences. They add variety and interest to your communications.

Among our employees *is* a *person* who thinks creatively.
  (**Reworded:** A person who thinks creatively is among our employees.)

What steps *are* the *engineers taking* to correct the problem?
  (**Reworded:** The engineers are taking . . .?)

The *size* of women's hats *shows* a trend toward picturesque clothes.

In the file *are* the *folders* on the XYZ Corporation.

Some subjects appear to be plural but are really singular.

Titles of books, magazines and articles, amounts (monetary, measurement, time), and company names may include plurals or a compound structure joined by *and*. Think about what the subject represents in order to decide whether it is singular or plural. Does it represent one or many persons or things? Is the subject a unit acting alone, or are there several parts or pieces in the word with each one acting separately?

Titles of books, such as *Mathematics,* may look as if they were plural; but in reality each title represents a single book. Titles of books and similar materials are singular; and when used as subjects, they would require the singular verb. You should think of similar expressions, such as amounts and names of companies, as single units and use a singular verb with them.

Economics for Our Times is a high school textbook.
Twenty years is long enough to wait.
A hundred dollars is not too much to pay for a portable typewriter.
Fred C. Warren and Associates is located at 132 Austin Place.

In the following illustration, each part or piece in the word is being thought of individually. Each man will receive a few of the dollars that are in the total amount. Therefore, the subject is plural and so is the verb.

One hundred dollars *are being distributed* to the men.

Words meaning part or portion sometimes are singular and other times are plural.

A few words used as subjects mean part or portion of something. Whenever you use *none, some, half, one fourth,* or any other word meaning part of something, remember that these words are *singular when used alone* and take the singular form of the verb.

One tenth is the correct portion to allocate.
Half is packed in that box.
The *rest arrives* next month.

The problem of choosing the correct verb to agree with the subject in number occurs when these words are followed by an *"of" phrase*. When one of these words is followed by an "of" phrase containing a singular noun or pronoun, the verb is singular.

Half of the message *is* misleading.
Three fourths of the research *begins* next year.
Some of her work *has* to be checked.
The first of the shipment *is* damaged.

However, when the "of" phrase contains a plural noun or pronoun, use a plural verb.

Half of the telephone calls *were* for Mrs. Franklin.

Some of the parts *are* missing.
One fifth of the men *vote* to strike.
Of all the reasons mentioned, none *are* acceptable.
Some of us *are going* to the convention.

Collective nouns take either the singular or the plural form of the verb.

Collective nouns, such as *company, committee, board, audience, jury, orchestra,* and *family,* may be used as either singular or plural depending on the sense of the message. You, as the communicator, must make the verb agree with your idea of the number represented by the collective noun. If you are thinking of the collective noun as plural, use a plural verb. (See page 99 for a discussion of collective nouns.)

The committee *votes* on that issue tomorrow.
The board *disagree* on when and where to meet.
Management *decides* on policies affecting all departments.

Number, a collective noun often used in business, is singular in meaning when preceded by *the* and plural when preceded by *a.*

The number of annual reports mailed to stockholders *is* 250,000.
A number of parts *are* missing from the motor.

REVIEW THE SPELLING OF COMPOUND WORDS

Compound words can be one word, two words, or hyphenated.

Compound words are spelling problems because some are written as one connected word, others are two separate words, and still others are hyphenated. For instance, all compounds beginning with *self* are hyphenated except for two that are written as solid words: *selfless* and *selfsame.* See Section 8, Part 1.

Most compound *verbs* are written as connected words. For instance, all *under* and *over* compounds are written as one word.

underbid	overcharge
undermine	overlay
underrate	oversold
understand	overwork

A few other *verbs,* however, that are built up from two or more words that form a single thought should be hyphenated.

dry-clean	quick-freeze
dry-dock	

The hyphen is used in some *verbs* beginning with the prefix *re,* in which *re* means again. This usage distinguishes the verb from an identically spelled word with a different meaning. Study the following pairs of words with their definitions and notice the differences in meaning.

Verb	Definition	Usage
recount	To tell the particulars of.	recount a story
re-count	To count again.	re-count your change
reform	To change from bad to good.	reform a criminal
re-form	To form again.	re-form the mold

recover	To retrieve; to obtain again.	recover a loss
re-cover	To cover again.	re-cover the machine
remark	To express by speech or writing.	remark on his progress
re-mark	To mark again.	re-mark the sales tags
rebound	To recoil; to bound back.	rebound off the net
re-bound	To bind again.	book was re-bound
recollect	To remember.	recollect his name
re-collect	To collect again.	re-collect the information
relay	To forward by or provide with relays.	relay the message
re-lay	To lay again.	re-lay the bricks
retire	To separate or withdraw.	retire from the company
re-tire	To change the tire.	re-tire the wheel
restore	To bring back to a former state.	restore the painting
re-store	To store again.	re-store the supplies

Exercise care when writing compounds. If you do not know whether the word should be written as one word, two words, or hyphenated, check your dictionary for the meaning and spelling.

PART 2

ASSIGNMENTS

Apply your knowledge of subject/verb agreement

A. The subject and the verb must agree in person and number. In the following sentences, select the verb that agrees with the subject and write it in the column to the right.

1. What (is, are) the plans of the reception committee? _____
2. Either the office manager or the assistant (complete, completes) the time sheet at the end of the day. _____
3. Executive leadership, an attribute that is hard to define, (involve, involves) skill in planning. _____
4. Mrs. Fletcher (dictate, dictates) every afternoon at 1:30. _____
5. Management (is, am, are) sending three executives to the conference on investment policies. _____
6. One of the section leaders (is, are) asking for more machinists. _____
7. What changes (is, am, are) Phil Franklin making? _____
8. Either John or I (is, am, are) going to the lecture. _____
9. The supervisor and the chief of section (turn, turns) in personnel reports. _____
10. The number of reports being circulated (mean, means) that every manager must read two a day. _____
11. The blueprints for the new machine (appear, appears) to be missing. _____
12. Our competition (sell, sells) mainly to retail outlets rather than wholesalers. _____
13. One of the managers (knows, know) the man to contact in that firm. _____
14. One half of our products (sell, sells) for less than a dollar. _____

15. Each supervisor (talks, talk) to the departing employee to gather helpful information.   _____

16. Several of the workers (has, have) asked for time off.   _____

17. *Effective Secretarial Practices* (contain, contains) good information on handling office routines.   _____

18. The current magazine and today's newspaper (is, are) in my office.   _____

19. Golden Mall Home Furnishings (advertise, advertises) in the evening paper.   _____

20. Mr. Edwards and two of the engineers (seems, seem) to be interested in your plans.   _____

   B.   The following sentences have the main verbs enclosed in parentheses. You are to write the verb in each sentence so that it agrees with the subject(s) in person and number.

Example: Not just everyone (want) to manage a business.   _____*wants*_____

1. American companies (employ) residents of countries in which they have factories.   _____

2. If Dick Clark (accompany) the president to New York, he (need) a briefcase for papers.   _____

3. A salesperson often (measure) the available space for the machine.   _____

4. Mr. Williams (speak) fluently on engineering topics.   _____

5. Each word processor (find) communications a challenge.   _____

6. Handbills and spot announcements (attract) more customers than one mass mailing.   _____

7. One fourth of the workers (be) absent from the meeting.   _____

8. A number of errors (be) found in the figures.   _____

9. What (be) the number of people registered for the convention?   _____

10. The new check-out system (read) coded prices on grocery items.   _____

11. The bookkeepers (plan) to attend the exhibit of office machines because it (promise) to be outstanding.   _____

12. Neither Bert nor the other agents (talk) about the problems.   _____

13. Forty years (be) the lifetime of one of those machines.   _____

14. That machinist always (use) the correct tools for the job.   _____

15. The committee (vote) individually on each issue.   _____

16. The audience (clap) loudly when the music is played well.   _____

17. When the news (contain) financial information, the manager (stop) talking and (listen). _____
18. Mathematics (be) one of the most valuable subjects a person (study) in school. _____
19. The lumber and the nails (arrive) by truck, but the other materials (be) coming by rail. _____
20. Everyone attending the meeting (contribute) fresh ideas to the discussion. _____

C. In the following letter, circle the verb that agrees with the subject in person and number where indicated in the connected copy.

1. Dear Friend:
2.   Please (take, takes) a few minutes to read the enclosed
3. pamphlet. It (summarize, summarizes) the latest thinking on
4. health and nutrition by medical experts in the federal government,
5. universities, and private research centers. Some of the suggestions
6. (is, are) probably familiar to you; others (give, gives) health
7. tips of which most people are unaware.
8.   Impressive progress (is, are) being made on prevention and
9. early treatment rather than on miracle cures or magic immunization.
10. When most of us (think, thinks) of cancer or heart disease, our
11. minds (turn, turns) immediately to images from TV medical shows—
12. radiation, chemotherapy, cobalt, open-heart surgery, even heart
13. transplants. The doctors who prepared this booklet (think, thinks)
14. that it (is, am, are) just as important for us to think of such
15. everyday things as salt, sugar, eggs, and even the humble bathroom
16. scale.
17.   I (believe, believes) you will find this booklet of interest.
18. More important, I (hope, hopes) it will help you and your family
19. enjoy better health and a longer life through simple changes in
20. your daily eating habits.
21.   Sincerely,

D. Circle the verb that agrees with the subject in person and number where indicated in the following connected copy.

1.   All credit unions (offer, offers) attractive savings plans and short-term, low-cost loans.
2. Some also (make, makes) available a variety of other banking services. Credit unions (is, am,
3. are) cooperatives in which members (pool, pools) their money and (earn, earns) interest by
4. making loans to each other. Credit unions (is, am, are) either federal or state chartered.
5. They (function, functions) as democratic organizations with directors who (is, am, are) elected
6. by members. More than 23,000 credit unions (provide, provides) savings and loan services in
7. the United States. Members (total, totals) 27.7 million, and assets (range, ranges) from $28
8. million to $300 million. The larger credit unions (list, lists) from 50,000 to 200,000 members,
9. with assets from $65 million to $300 million.
10.   When someone (join, joins) a credit union, he (buy, buys) shares—about $5 apiece—and
11. (receive, receives) dividends. Usually, the number of shares a person may buy (is, am, are)

12.   unlimited. Dividends paid to members (is, am, are) generally high, compared to other short-
13.   term savings accounts. Often a member (receive, receives) dividends at an annual rate of over
14.   six percent. Many companies (establish, establishes) ways that (enable, enables) one to save
15.   painlessly through payroll deduction. A person (pay, pays) off loans in the same way.
16.   Because laws (require, requires) that credit unions be legally chartered and their books
17.   audited each year, they (is, am, are) considered as safe as any other savings institution. Federal
18.   and state governments (make, makes) insurance of shares mandatory up to $100,000. The
19.   obvious advantages of a credit union (is, am, are) its low-cost loans, good return on savings,
20.   and sympathetic service and counseling.

E.   In the sentences below, indicate whether the subject is singular or plural by writing the verb form that agrees with the subject in the appropriate column.

	Singular	*Plural*
Example: The goods (be) shipped last week.		*were*
1. Purchase orders (be) filed by number and by name.		
2. The data supplied by the field staff (show) that customers (be) clustered in urban areas.		
3. Physics (be) an interesting subject, and it (enlarge) my concept of matter and energy.		
4. Scissors (be) made of steel.		
5. Politics as a topic of conversation often (result) in heated discussions.		
6. The *Dictionary of Linguistics* (contain) both the definitions of traditional grammatical terms and those from the field of historical linguistics.		
7. Each of the two consultants (predict) a slowdown in the securities market, but the president and the treasurer (disagree) with the prediction.		
8. The analysis of our sales potential (mention) several new territories for study.		
9. None of the machines (need) to be repaired, but some (require) oil.		
10. The number to be asked to the meeting (stay) at 25.		

F.   There are hundreds of verbs in our language, and most of us use only a few of them. Try to use as many different verbs as possible in your writing. They are some of the strongest words we can use. The ten verbs in this exercise probably include some you have never made part of your vocabulary. See if you can write an interesting sentence for each one.

1. *recount* _____

_____

2. *re-form* _____

_____

3. *recover* _____

_____

4. *re-mark* _____

_____

5. *recollect* _____

_____

6. *re-collect* _____

_____

7. *relay* _____

_____

8. *re-tire* _____

_____

9. *restore* _____

_____

10. *re-bound* _____

_____

Name _____

Date _____

PRACTICE WRITING

Here is an opportunity to demonstrate your ability to write sentences in which the subject and the verb agree in person and number.

1. Write a sentence containing a plural subject.

   _____

   _____

   _____

2. Write a sentence using a second-person subject.

   _____

   _____

   _____

3. Write a sentence containing two singular subjects joined by *and*.

   _____

   _____

   _____

4. Write a sentence using the verb *be* in third-person, plural, past tense.

   _____

   _____

   _____

5. Write a sentence containing two subjects joined by *or* or *nor*.

_____

_____

_____

_____

6. Write a sentence using an indefinite word, such as *anyone,* as the subject.

_____

_____

_____

7. Write a sentence using the name of a book as the subject.

_____

_____

_____

8. Write a sentence using the name of a company as the subject.

_____

_____

_____

9. Write a sentence using a fraction, such as *one fourth,* as the subject.

_____

_____

_____

10. Write a sentence containing three or more subjects.

_____

_____

_____

3

Verbs express time

Every person or event is bound by time. When you tell someone about a happening, therefore, you should make sure that you indicate as accurately as possible when the event occurred. The English language has a built-in way to indicate time. Through the use of tenses, which change the verb form, you can show *present time, past time,* or *future time.* And you may stress the present, past, or future as *progressive* or *emphatic.* Thus, you can use a variety of ways to get a time message across.

Verbs have six tenses.

Each verb can be used to express action or state of being in six different tenses.

Present:	*dictate*	**Present perfect:**	*have dictated*
Past:	*dictated*	**Past perfect:**	*had dictated*
Future:	*will dictate*	**Future perfect:**	*will have dictated*

Present tense shows action taking place right now.

The *present tense* indicates action or being in progress right now—at the moment. Simple present uses the base or root form of regular verbs and most irregular verbs.

Simple present

I take	we take
you take	you take
he, she, it takes	they take

If you want to show that the action is continuous and moving along, otherwise known as *progressive,* you use the *ing* verb form with the verb *be* as helper. See pages 210–11 for information on the spelling of the *ing* verb form.

Progressive present

I am taking	we are taking
you are taking	you are taking
he, she, it is taking	they are taking

You can make a *negative* progressive statement by using the word *not* in the verb phrase.

Negative progressive present

I am not taking	we are not taking
you are not taking	you are not taking
he, she, it is not taking	they are not taking

You may also make a present action more important by emphasizing it. To do this, you use the emphatic verb *do* as the helper.

Emphatic present

I do take	we do take
you do take	you do take
he, she, it does take	they do take

To make a *negative* emphatic statement, use *not* in the verb phrase—for example, *I do not take, he does not take, we don't take* (*do not* contracted).

Use present tense for statements that are always true or customary.

Two important uses of present tense should be added to your store of knowledge. First, the present tense is used when stating a *general* or *universal truth;* and second, present tense is used to show that an action is *perpetual* or *customary.*

Galileo said that the earth **moves** and that the sun **is** fixed.
She remembered that school days **are** the happiest in life.
A straight line **is** the shortest distance between two points.

Often the general or universal truth is stated in a dependent clause connected to an independent clause containing a past tense verb. In such sentences, you must be careful to express the true statement in *present* tense.

He sailed the boat down the Mississippi River, which **is** the longest navigable river in the United States.

Action begun and ended in the past calls for a past tense verb.

The *past tense* indicates action or being begun in the past and finished in the past. When using a regular verb, form the past tense by adding *d* or *ed* to the present tense—*type, typed; look, looked.* (Past tense for irregular verbs is discussed on pages 205–7.)

Simple past

I typed	we typed
you typed	you typed
he, she, it typed	they typed

If the action in the past was continuous and moving forward and you wish to demonstrate this in your message, you use the *progressive* verb form—*ing* with the past tense of the helping verb *be.*

Progressive past

I was typing	we were typing
you were typing	you were typing
he, she, it was typing	they were typing

To emphasize past action, use *did*, the past tense of the helping verb *do*, with the root form of the verb.

Emphatic past

I did type	we did type
you did type	you did type
he, she, it did type	they did type

Both the progressive and emphatic past verb forms may be made negative by using the word *not* in the verb phrase—for instance, *I was not typing, I did not type.*

Action that will occur sometime in the future takes the future tense.

The *future tense* indicates action or being that will occur in the future. It is formed by use of the auxiliary words *shall/will* and *should/would* with the base or root form of the verb. Progressive action can also be shown in the future tense.

Simple future

I shall talk	we shall talk
you will talk	you will talk
he, she, it will talk	they will talk

Progressive future

I shall be talking	we shall be talking
you will be talking	you will be talking
he, she, it will be talking	they will be talking

Should and would have specific uses.

Should and *would* are used as auxiliaries in *conditional* sentences referring to future time. A conditional sentence tells about an event that is dependent on another event taking place. It is concerned with the "if-then" idea.

If I **should** (or **would**) learn to type, I **should** (or **would**) find a job.

If he **would** go see the desk, he **would** probably decide to buy it.

Usually, you may use *should* and *would* with all three persons. However, in a sentence that indicates *obligation,* e.g., *ought to,* it is best to use *should* with all three persons.

I **should** go see the department manager.

He **should** leave now for the airport.

They **should** lower their voices.

It is also best to use *would* with all three persons when the intent is to show *customary action* or a *condition contrary to fact.*

Customary action:

Every morning he **would** stop at the mail desk before going to his office.

He **would** get the same test results every time he ran the test.

Condition contrary to fact:

If I were the investigator, I **would** find the problem in a hurry.
    (I am *not* the investigator, hence a condition contrary to fact.)

If Mr. Burns were the auditor, he **would** see that reports came out on time.
    (Mr. Burns is *not* the auditor, hence a condition contrary to fact.)

In the latest unabridged dictionary, the definitions for *should* and *would* read as follows:

should   An auxiliary used to express (a) obligation, duty, propriety, necessity: e.g., children **should** get hot lunches; (b) expectation or probability: e.g., since they left Saturday, they **should** be here by Monday; equivalent to ought to and *not* replaceable by **would**; (c) futurity from the standpoint of the past in indirect quotations where **shall** and **will** were used in the direct quotations: e.g., I said I **should** (or **would**) be home by nine.

would   An auxiliary used (a) to express condition: such as, he **would** write if you **would** answer; (b) in indirect discourse to express futurity: such as, he said he **would** bring it; (c) to express a wish: such as, **would** that he were still living; (d) to soften somewhat the force of a statement or request: such as, **would** you do this for me.

Perfect tenses are used to show action begun in the past but completed at some later time or at a stated past time.

Secondary tenses, called *perfect tenses,* may be used to show action *begun* in the past and *completed* at some stated time in the past or *to be completed* in the present or the future.

Present perfect tense is used to show action begun in the past and completed in the present. The helping verb *have* (*has* for third-person singular) is used with the past participle of the verb to form the present perfect tense. (The past participle of regular verbs is the same as the past tense—add *d* or *ed* to the present tense.)

I **have sealed** all the envelopes.
John **has finished** distributing the mail.
The automatic machine **has sawed** all the lumber.

The *past perfect tense* denotes action or being begun in the past and completed at some stated past time or before some other implied time. When it is necessary to use this tense, tie the action to the specific time when it was completed, or tie it to some other event that took place in the past. The helping verb *had* is used with the past participle to form the past perfect tense.

He **had looked** for his pen yesterday before signing the letters.
We **had finished** production on that model before we decided to close down the line.
By the time she quit, she **had worked** for us for five years.

Notice that in each of these illustrations the past action is tied to a specific event or time.

Future perfect tense shows action that will be completed at some definite future time and before some other future action takes place. Future perfect looks back on something from a point in the future. The helping verbs *shall have* and *will have* are used with the past participle to form the future perfect tense.

By the end of the year, we **will have completed** the reorganization.
I **shall have bought** the supplies before the end of the fiscal period.
All these products **will have been sold** before we **shall have begun** production on the new items.

The six tenses allow you to show exact past, present, or future time.

Here is an illustration that shows the relationship of the six tenses to one another in terms of time.

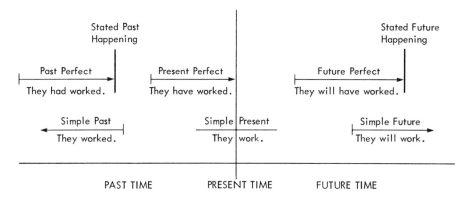

Shall and will and should and would are used interchangeably as auxiliary verbs.

For many years, the use of *shall* and *will* and *should* and *would* to transmit a specific message about *future* action was the mark of a well-educated person. These formal conventions, however, do not reflect present usage in the United States. Today, *shall* and *will* and *should* and *would* are used interchangeably in the future tense with the use of *will* and *would* predominating in all persons.

Tenses of verbs within a sentence should agree.

When writing and speaking, you should be careful to use the verb tense that clearly expresses the time period of your message. If there are several verbs in the sentence, check to see that the time relationship of all verbs is the same. It is incorrect to shift back and forth from one tense to another within the sentence without a good reason. The verb in a *dependent clause* should always be checked to see that it *agrees* in tense with the verb in the *independent clause*. The one exception is a sentence containing a clause that states a universal truth in *present* tense.

Review the spelling of past tense verbs.

The spelling of some verbs is changed in the past tense.

The spelling of the *past tense* of regular verbs centers around the *ed* ending. You usually add *d* or *ed* to regular verbs when changing them from present tense to past tense. Three groups of verbs, however, change their spelling slightly before adding the *ed*. Here are three rules to show you how to form the past tense for them.

1. *Double* the *final* consonant of a *one-syllable verb* if it ends with *one* consonant preceded by *one* vowel.

fit, fitted	ship, shipped
knot, knotted	trim, trimmed
plan, planned	wrap, wrapped

2. *Double* the *final consonant* of a *two-syllable verb* that is *accented* on the *second syllable* if it ends with *one* consonant preceded by *one* vowel.

defer, deferred	omit, omitted
dispel, dispelled	refer, referred
occur, occurred	submit, submitted
equip, equipped	transfer, transferred

3. Change the *y* to *i* and add *ed* in verbs that end with *y* preceded by a consonant.

identify, identified   vary, varied
carry, carried   verify, verified
satisfy, satisfied   nullify, nullified

PART **3**

ASSIGNMENTS

Apply your knowledge of verb tenses

A. Verbs tell us through their form the time that an event took place. They can also tell us whether the time is progressive or emphatic, and they can include a negative aspect by the use of *not*. You merely change the spelling of the base verb or add a helping verb to reflect a time difference in another tense. This exercise will show you how easy it is to change a verb from one tense to another. Follow the directions for each group of five sentences.

Change the verbs in 1–5 from *present tense* to *past tense*.

1. Mrs. Jones plans to empty the drawers in her desk.   _____

2. Some workers want a wastepaper basket by their desk.   _____

3. He is making several copies of the report.   _____

4. Mr. Smith always dictates early in the day.   _____

5. That machine stamps out several hundred pieces an hour.   _____

Change the verbs in 6–10 from *present tense* to *future tense*.

6. The company offers a good salary for that position.   _____

7. The new clerk files the correspondence in the cabinets.   _____

8. Martha finishes assignments on time.   _____

9. The men work in the production department.   _____

10. The engineer in Department Q reads blueprints.   _____

Change the verbs in 11–15 from *past tense* to *present tense*.

11.   The president always signed the letters before leaving the office.   _____

12.   It seemed wise to change our policy about bonuses.   _____

13.   The officials announced the granting of a $100 million loan.   _____

14.   Banks insured accounts up to $100,000.   _____

15.   The ZYZ Company shipped all orders via United Express.   _____

Change the verbs in 16–20 from *future tense* to *past tense*.

16.   The mechanic will fit the tires to the car on Monday.   _____

17.   The gardener will trim the hedges around the parking lots.   _____

18.   He will introduce the speaker at the first session.   _____

19.   John will carry the boxes to the storeroom.   _____

20.   The tools will vary in length by three tenths of an inch.   _____

B.   In Exercise **A** you found that it is easy to change verbs to present, past, and future tenses. In this exercise, let us add the progressive, emphatic, and negative aspects to the three tenses just listed. Follow the directions for each group of five sentences.

Change the verbs in 1–5 from *simple present* to *progressive present*.

1.   Most states regulate interest rates.   _____

2.   Beth Cohen types on a word processing machine.   _____

3.   The oil companies report higher first-quarter profits.   _____

4.   A balanced budget insures a sound fiscal policy.   _____
5.   The directors plan to reinstate the bonus system established last
    year.   _____

Change the verbs in 6–10 from *simple past* to *emphatic past*.

6.   Mrs. Templer telephoned the client last Monday.   _____

7.   The office manager purchased two typewriters and returned one
    for a calculator.   _____
    _____

8.   The shipping clerk packed the machine in a crate for overseas
    shipment.   _____

9.   Our company shipped 12 dozen crates last month.   _____

10.   He turned around when he heard the voice.   _____

Change the verbs in 11–15 from *simple future* to *negative progressive future*.

11.   Mr. Fischer will go to the convention in Detroit.   _____

12.   Our sales will increase within the next three years.   _____

13.   The workers will walk from the factory building to the main gate.   _____

14.   The secretaries will staple enclosures to signed letters.   _____

15.   The agent will park his car in the garage.   _____

Change the verbs in 16–20 from *simple past to negative progressive past*.

16.   That company employed truck drivers, mechanics, and carpenters.   _____

17.   The executives invited customers to attend the reception.   _____

18.   I entered the debits and credits to customers' accounts.   _____
19.   She prepared the production records as of the last day of the month.   _____

20.   Mr. Hinderman duplicated the entire report.   _____

   C.   Write the present perfect, the past perfect, and the future perfect forms of the regular verbs listed in the left-hand column. Use the *person* indicated by the pronouns.

Present tense	*Present perfect*	*Past perfect*	*Future perfect*
it exports	_____	_____	_____
they furnish	_____	_____	_____
she works	_____	_____	_____
I prepare	_____	_____	_____
we compute	_____	_____	_____
you explain	_____	_____	_____

   D.   In this review of verbs, write the tense indicated in parentheses at the end of each sentence for the verb within the sentence. The column at the right has been provided for your answers.

1.   The accountant's explanation (satisfy) the judge. (*past*)   _____

2. Brock & Company (call) and (order) several hundred doors. (*emphatic past*)   _____

3. The advertising campaign on television (create) a large demand for our products. (*progressive future*)   _____

4. He (like) the designs for the new cars. (*negative emphatic past*)   _____

5. The correspondence secretary (finish) corrections on stored material rapidly. (*present*)   _____

6. That company (develop) a better product than ours. (*past*)   _____

7. In the last ten years, we (inform) customers of interest changes before announcing the change to the public. (*past perfect*)   _____

8. If he would study data processing, he (be able) to earn a promotion. (*future*)   _____

9. The engineers (work) on the report for the next three days. (*progressive future*)   _____

10. Cosgrove & Co. (celebrate) 25 years in business before the stockholders' meeting on March 15. (*future perfect*)   _____

11. Several customers (transfer) their accounts to the First National Bank. (*progressive present*)   _____

12. The clerk (distribute) the morning mail. (*present perfect*)   _____

13. Before we leave for the convention, we (complete) the survey. (*future perfect*)   _____

14. It was discovered long ago that the sun (be) the center of our solar system. (*present*)   _____

15. We (cancel) the contract before they offered to lower the price. (*past perfect*)   _____

16. If I were you, I (purchase) an office handbook. (*future*)   _____

17. The workers (assemble) 100 gaskets for the motors. (*present perfect*)   _____

18. Before signing the letters, the supervisor (proofread) them to be sure they were correct. (*past perfect*)   _____

19. Workers (arrive) at the factory by 7:30 a.m. (*future obligation*)   _____

20. If we (control) expenses, we (save) a great deal of money. (*conditional future*)   _____

E.   The past tense of most verbs is formed by adding *d* or *ed* to the present tense. However, there are some verbs that change their spelling when forming the past tense. Review the rules on pages 195–96 for the variations in spelling for regular verbs. Give the past tense for each of the regular and irregular verbs listed below. If you are unsure of the correct form for any irregular verb, be sure to look it up in the dictionary.

| 1 | check | _____ | 3. | bury | _____ |
| 2. | break | _____ | 4. | catch | _____ |

5. occur _____

6. accelerate _____

7. chop _____

8. coincide _____

9. envy _____

10. exempt _____

11. plot _____

12. fly _____

13. grind _____

14. assist _____

15. incite _____

16. infer _____

17. levy _____

18. mention _____

19. negotiate _____

20. pin _____

21. presume _____

22. ship _____

23. certify _____

24. throw _____

25. allot _____

26. carry _____

27. circumvent _____

28. write _____

29. clap _____

30. flee _____

31. flip _____

32. forget _____

33. grow _____

34. submit _____

35. indemnify _____

36. insist _____

37. liquefy _____

38. conduct _____

39. wrap _____

40. blot _____

Name _____

Date _____

PRACTICE WRITING

Your skill in selecting verbs that accurately indicate the time of an action will make both your written and spoken messages clearer and more forceful. As indicated below, compose sentences using verbs in the suggested tenses. You will find that it is quite easy to handle verbs in all the time sequences.

1. *Present* tense _____

_____

_____

2. *Past* tense _____

_____

_____

3. *Future* tense _____

_____

_____

4. *Present perfect* tense _____

_____

_____

5. *Past perfect* tense _____

_____

_____

6. *Future perfect* tense _____

_____

_____

7. Progressive *present* tense _____

    _____

    _____

8. Emphatic *past* tense _____

    _____

    _____

9. Progressive *future* tense _____

    _____

    _____

10. Negative emphatic *present* tense _____

    _____

    _____

Verbs have special features

Verbs are important because they are action words that make messages more colorful, direct, and precise. Every year new verbs are added to our constantly expanding language. Some have short lives, but others are permanent additions, such as *to audition, to televise, to service, to commentate,* and *to defrost.*

In this part, you will study irregular verbs, how to use correctly a few troublesome regular and irregular ones, and the special quality of voice possessed by both regular and irregular verbs.

Irregular verb forms do not follow a particular pattern.

The English language has about 140 irregular verbs in use today. They are called *irregular* because they form the *past tense* and the *past participle* differently from the way regular verbs form them. Regular verbs form the past tense and the past participle by the addition of *d* or *ed* to the present tense. The *present* participle is formed by the addition of *ing* to the present tense.

With irregular verbs, a definite change in spelling occurs from the present tense to the past tense. Also, the past participle, which is usually the same as the past tense, may be spelled differently from the past tense. Notice in the short list of irregular verbs below the changes that occur in spelling.

Present	Past	Past participle (used with helping verbs)
am, are, is	was, were	been
begin	began	begun
break	broke	broken
do, does	did	done
drive	drove	driven
get	got	got, gotten
go, goes	went	went
have, has	had	had

know	knew	known
make	made	made
see	saw	seen
speak	spoke	spoken
take	took	taken
tear	tore	torn
throw	threw	thrown
write	wrote	written

It is important that you become familiar with irregular verbs in order to use and to spell them correctly. Careless errors in their use are noticeable to others. To avoid embarrassment, you should get acquainted with as many of these verbs as possible. Some people feel that the only safe procedure is to memorize those they use frequently and to check the dictionary for those verbs that they suspect might be irregular.

Some verbs need extra study to be used correctly.

There are a few verbs that most people find difficult to use correctly. The only way to master them is to know their meanings and their principal parts. Among the most troublesome irregular verbs in our language are these six: *lie* and *lay*, *sit* and *set*, *rise* and *raise*. In order to use them correctly, you need to know that *lie*, *sit*, and *rise* are *intransitive* verbs and do not have objects. *Lay*, *set*, *raise* are *transitive* verbs and require objects to complete their meaning. You should make a careful study of the meaning of each one so that you will be able to use these verbs correctly.

Principal verb parts

	Definition	Present	Past	Past participle	Present participle
lie	to recline	lie	lay	lain	lying
lay	to place	lay	laid	laid	laying
sit	to rest	sit	sat	sat	sitting
set	to place, to put in readiness, to fix at an amount or in a direction	set	set	set	setting
rise	to get up by its own power	rise	rose	risen	rising
raise	to cause to rise	raise	raised	raised	raising

Lie, sit, and rise are not followed by objects.

Now, notice carefully how these verbs are used in sentences. The *intransitive* verbs—*lie*, *sit*, *rise*—do not need objects to receive the action. The action is complete in itself. The words that follow them merely add interesting facts.

Intransitive lie, sit, rise

Lie—to recline

He **will lie** down in an hour.

The telephone message **lay** on the desk for an hour.

The watch **had lain** on the typewriter stand all night.

Principal Parts of Irregular Verbs

Present	Past	Past participle (used with helping verb)	Present	Past	Past participle (used with helping verb)
am	was	been	hear	heard	heard
arise	arose	arisen	hide	hid	hidden
			hold	held	held
become	became	become			
begin	began	begun	keep	kept	kept
bid	bid	bid	know	knew	known
bind	bound	bound			
blow	blew	blown	lay	laid	laid
break	broke	broken	lead	led	led
bring	brought	brought	leave	left	left
broadcast	broadcast	broadcast	lend	lent	lent
build	built	built	let	let	let
burst	burst	burst	lie	lay	lain
buy	bought	bought	lose	lost	lost
cast	cast	cast	pay	paid	paid
catch	caught	caught	put	put	put
choose	chose	chosen			
come	came	come	rise	rose	risen
cost	cost	cost			
cut	cut	cut	see	saw	seen
			seek	sought	sought
deal	dealt	dealt	shake	shook	shaken
do	did	done	show	showed	shown, showed
draw	drew	drawn	shrink	shrank	shrunk
drink	drank	drunk	sink	sank	sunk
drive	drove	driven	sit	sat	sat
			speak	spoke	spoken
eat	ate	eaten	spend	spent	spent
			split	split	split
fall	fell	fallen	stand	stood	stood
feel	felt	felt	steal	stole	stolen
fight	fought	fought	strike	struck	struck, stricken
find	found	found	strive	strove	striven
fly	flew	flown	swear	swore	sworn
forecast	forecast	forecast			
forget	forgot	forgotten, forgot	take	took	taken
			teach	taught	taught
get	got	got, gotten	tear	tore	torn
give	gave	given	telecast	telecast	telecast
go	went	gone	tell	told	told
grow	grew	grown	throw	threw	thrown
hang	hung	hung	wear	wore	worn
have	had	had	write	wrote	written

Sit—to rest

I *shall sit* in the front row.

Miss Felton *sat* at the switchboard for two hours.

He *has sat* at that desk for many years.

Rise—to get up by its own power

Please *rise* before you speak.

Mr. Humphrey *rose* from his chair in a hurry.

Stock prices *have risen* 20 points in the last three months.

Will you *be rising* at six or seven tomorrow morning?

Objects come after *lay, set,* and *raise* when they are transitive verbs.

In the next group of sentences you will notice that in the majority of messages *lay, set,* and *raise* are transitive verbs followed by objects.

Transitive lay, set, raise

Lay—to place

He *lay* the *book* on the table.

He *laid* the *report* on Mr. Smith's desk yesterday.

She *had laid* her *watch* there when she broke the band.

The workers *are laying* the *bricks* in rows.

Set—to place, to put in readiness, to fix at an amount or in a direction

I *set* the *glass* on the sink.

Mr. Perkins *set* the *timer* on the computer before turning it on.

He *has set* the adding *machine* on that stand after every inventory.

Raise—to cause to rise

Please *raise* the *window* so that we may have fresh air.

Sam *raised* an important *issue* when he mentioned the lack of funds.

The automobile manufacturers *have raised* the *price* of next year's cars.

My gardener *is raising* *strawberries* in tubs.

The regular verbs *affect* and *effect* have specific meanings.

Two other troublesome verbs are the regular ones *affect* and *effect*. Both these words function as verbs, and *effect* may also be used as a noun. No doubt, this double role of *effect* is one reason for much of the confusion. Let's take a look at the meanings of *affect* and *effect* as verbs.

*to affect—*to act upon, to alter or change, to assume, to adopt

*to effect—*to bring about

Affect* is always a verb; *effect* is sometimes used as a verb meaning *to bring about.

The sentences below illustrate the uses of *affect* and *effect* as verbs.

He feels that prior knowledge of the sales volume *would affect* his decision.
(alter or change)

The new policy *will affect* vacation periods.
(alter or act upon)

Lower taxes *will affect* government spending.
(alter or change)

Mr. Preston **affects** a cultured accent when talking to clients.
(adopts)

She **affects** indifference to customers' complaints.
(adopts)

Mr. Shields will be able **to effect** the compromise.
(bring about)

That law **will effect** changes in the State Department.
(bring about)

Effect can be used as a noun.

As mentioned above, *effect* may also be used as a noun. When used as a noun, *effect* means a result, an impression, an intent, or personal property. Read the next sentences carefully to see how you may use *effect* as a noun.

The changes will have a far-reaching *effect*.
(result)

All personal *effects* are to be removed from desks over the weekend.
(personal property)

As soon as the new policy takes *effect,* we will move ahead with advertising plans.
(result)

His speech generated a good *effect* on the audience.
(impression)

The *effect* of his efforts was improved morale.
(intent or result)

Both *affect* and *effect* are used too often in business writing. A more specific word, one that conveys your exact meaning, will result in a clearer message. It may be easy to say, "The progress of the building **has been affected** by the weather." Your choice, however, of a more precise verb—*hindered, delayed, stopped*—will give the hearer or reader a more exact picture of how the weather interfered with the construction of the building.

Verbs show a quality called *voice*.

Within the framework of the several tenses, a *transitive verb* may show a quality called *voice*. There are two voices—*active* and *passive*. In the *active voice,* someone or something—the subject—*acts.*

In active voice, the subject acts.

The *bookkeeper* **added** the column twice.
(**added**—past tense, active voice)

The United Parcel Service **delivers** packages every other day.
(**delivers**—present tense, active voice)

In passive voice, the subject is acted upon.

In the *passive* voice, someone or something—the subject—*is acted upon.*

The *column* **was added** twice by the bookkeeper.
(*column* is acted upon by the bookkeeper; **was added**—past tense, passive voice)

Packages **have been delivered** every other day by United Parcel Service.
(*packages* as the subject is acted upon; **have been delivered**—present perfect tense, passive voice)

Notice that in the *passive* voice, the verbs *be* and *have* are used as helpers. Remember that only transitive verbs that require an object can indicate passive voice. *Intransitive verbs* are always *active,* as *Bob spoke.*

Active voice should be used in the majority of your sentences.

Sentences that have the subject performing the action are much more interesting. Even in business writing—letters, memorandums, reports—communications using the active voice find more interested readers.

When should you use active voice? Try to use it in most of your sentences. Business writing stresses concise, direct, personalized writing. To put these three qualities in your sentences, you will need to use the active voice. It is a simpler and less awkward means of expression, as you will see when you compare these two sentences.

> **Active:** The office *manager* **told** the *workers* to take 15 minutes for a coffee break.
>
> **Passive:** The *workers* **were told** by the office manager to take 15 minutes for a coffee break.

When should you use passive voice? You may use passive voice when you feel an impersonal expression is more appropriate. It may be used (1) to make suggestions, (2) to give instructions and recommendations, (3) to stress the receiver of the action, and (4) to hide or withhold the identity of the doer of the action.

> **Passive:** The *recommendations* for promotion **were sent** to the president by the personnel department.
>
> **Active:** The personnel *department* **sent** the recommendations for promotion to the president.
>
> (In the passive, the word *recommendations* is stressed.)
>
> **Passive:** *Employees* **are asked** to keep their work stations clean.
>
> **Active:** The *company* **asks** employees to keep their work stations clean.
>
> (In the passive, the instructions are impersonal.)
>
> **Passive:** A *question* **was raised** regarding the statistical measurements used in the study.
>
> **Active:** *Mr. Jones* **raised** a question about the statistical measurements used in the study.
>
> (In the passive, Mr. Jones' identity was withheld.)

Too much writing in business is in the passive. People are more familiar with the active *who does what* sequence and can follow a message more easily if they focus first on the doer of the action. Try, therefore, to use the active voice in as many of your sentences as possible.

The spelling of some verbs changes when *ing* is added.

Our language contains a vast number of action verbs. They allow the reader or hearer to visualize exactly what action the subject is performing. You should use as many of them as you can. The following action verbs are used to illustrate the correct spelling of the *ing* verb form. Memorize these four rules for adding *ing* to *regular* verbs.

1. *Double* the *final consonant* when adding *ing* to a *one-syllable verb* that ends with *one* consonant preceded by *one* vowel.

can, canning	plan, planning
fit, fitting	ship, shipping
job, jobbing	wrap, wrapping

2. *Double* the *final consonant* of a *two-syllable verb* that is *accented* on the *last syllable* if it ends with *one* consonant preceded by *one* vowel.

confer, conferring	remit, remitting
equip, equipping	prefer, preferring
allot, allotting	regret, regretting

3. Drop the *e* when adding *ing* to verbs ending with an *e*.

believe, believing	hope, hoping
change, changing	improve, improving
arrange, arranging	receive, receiving

4. Retain the *y* when *ing* is added.

carry, carrying	liquefy, liquefying
identify, identifying	vary, varying
convey, conveying	marry, marrying

Irregular verbs generally follow these same rules; however, a few do not. If in doubt, be sure to consult the dictionary.

PART **4**

ASSIGNMENTS

Apply your knowledge of irregular verbs, voice, and the proper use of *affect* and *effect*.

A.   Irregular verbs are used in the following sentences. You are to write in the right-hand column the correct form of the verb in the tense and voice called for by the message in the sentence. Be sure the verb agrees in person and number with the subject. You may find it necessary to check the spelling of some of these irregular verbs in the dictionary.

1.   We have (drive) three hundred miles today.   _____

2.   Personnel problems should be (deal) with when they occur.   _____

3.   Mr. Smithers (find) two mistakes in the figures.   _____
4.   Martha Edwards (know) about the company from an article in last
     month's *Time* magazine.   _____

5.   The paper around the package (tear) during delivery.   _____

6.   I wish I had (write) that letter last week.   _____

7.   Mr. Burton has (take) the report with him to New York.   _____

8.   What information (do) the insurance company want about the accident? _____

9.   He (lend) his pen to the supervisor, who (forget) to return it promptly. _____

                                                                                      _____

10. The picture that (hang) on the wall behind my desk can be (see) from
     the door.   _____

                                                                                      _____

11. The receptionist (throw) out all the old magazines in the lounge last
     week.   _____

12. My typewriter ribbon has (wear) out.   _____
13. The public-interest program (begin) by our company will be (telecast)
    on KNBC.   _____

14. Our president (have) (speak) to several government officials about the   _____
    need for a new regulation.   _____

15. The union leaders (be) (plan) to ask for health benefits for the workers   _____
    at today's meeting.   _____

16. The key (be) (hide) in the back of the top drawer.   _____
17. The worker (swear) that he (have) (pay) $50 for the tool that he
    bought in Tulsa.   _____

                                                                                                  _____

18. Was the paint can (shake) before it (be) opened?   _____

19. Jack Hill (stand) in line yesterday to collect his paycheck.   _____

20. (Be) you (give) a raise last month?   _____

                                                                                                  _____

B.   This exercise will test your ability to use those troublesome irregular verbs: *lie* and *lay*, *sit* and *set*, *rise* and *raise*. Do you know some of the definitions for these words? Look them up in your dictionary and see how many ways you can use them.

to lie—to recline	*to lay*—to place, to deposit
to sit—to rest	*to set*—to put down, to put in some position, to put in the right place
to rise—to get up	*to raise*—to cause to rise, to lift or move upward

Lay, *set*, and *raise* are usually followed by objects. Choose the correct verb from those in parentheses, and write it in the column.

1. That proposal has (laid, lain) in his incoming tray for three days.   _____

2. Those tools you lost are (lying, laying) on the bench in the corner.   _____

3. They have (risen, raised) questions about the new project.   _____
4. Once we (sit, set) the ground rules, we will (lie, lay) out the course
   for the race.   _____
5. The decision to (rise, raise) prices again was made by the marketing
   department.   _____

6. Plans have been (lain, laid) for next year's convention.   _____

7. A worker should not (lie, lay) down on lunch tables. _____

8. (Lie, Lay) those supplies on the floor, and then (rise, raise) the lower shelf two notches so that the boxes will fit. _____

9. Through hard work and loyalty to the company, Mrs. Jefferson (rose, raised) to a position of responsibility. _____

10. Please (rise, raise) the question in next week's meeting. _____

11. You will find that report (lying, laying) on Mr. Felt's desk. _____

12. (Sit, Set) down at my desk to sign those letters. _____

13. Has the visitor been (sitting, setting) in the reception room for an hour? _____

14. Please (rise, raise) when you wish to speak to a point under discussion. _____

15. (Set, Sit) here while I (set, sit) this matter before you. _____

C. The following connected material might be advertising copy developed to sell a product. Select the correct form of the verbs where needed, and write them in the spaces at the right.

1. Have you ever (risen, raised) the question regarding how _____

2. much you can remember and for how long? Wouldn't you like

3. to (sit, set) your experiences on record so that you can _____

4. recapture them? Home movies (is, are) (rising, raising) in _____

5. popularity partially for that reason. You can gather your

6. family in one room, (sit, set) back in your favorite chair _____

7. with your projector (setting, sitting) beside you, and _____

8. re-create that wonderful vacation you (spend, spent) last year. _____

9. Remember that one particularly beautiful day? You can again

10. watch the sun (rising, raising), see your family (lying, laying) _____

11. on the beach, and see the sun (sitting, setting) behind the _____

12. mountains. You can recapture all this and more with the Bell

13. & Howell camera. There (is, are) no worry in (sitting, setting) _____

14.   the lens—it's automatic. And pick it up—it's so light. The

15.   prices of similar cameras (is, are) (rising, raising), but not   _____

16.   those of Bell & Howell. No wonder sales (has, have) (risen,   _____

17.   raised) to an all-time high. No one can afford to (sit, set)   _____

18.   by and ignore the pleasures this camera can give.

D.   The following sentences test your ability to use *affect* and *effect* correctly. Write your choice in the left-hand column. Next, go back over the sentences and see if you can think of another word or synonym for *affect/effect* that more accurately expresses the message. Write the synonym in the right-hand column.

Synonym

Example: Don't let this difference of opinion (affect,   *affect*   *alter*
    effect) our friendship.

1.   As soon as the plan is implemented, we will (affect,
    effect) some personnel changes.   _____ _____
2.   The reorganization of departments (was affected,
    was effected) over several weeks.   _____ _____

3.   Mr. Jones (affected, effected) a stern manner.   _____ _____
4.   If I am able to (affect, effect) a transfer, you will
    be notified on Monday.   _____ _____
5.   Can the company (affect, effect) a settlement with
    the union?   _____ _____
6.   One (affect, effect) of increased competition will
    be a smaller market for our product.   _____ _____
7.   An increase in the price of our products will
    (affect, effect) sales.   _____ _____
8.   Changes in plant procurement will be (affected,
    effected) as soon as we hear from the bank
    regarding our application for a loan.   _____ _____
9.   Did you notice the (affect, effect) the news of a
    large order had on the workers?   _____ _____
10.   We could all see that Mrs. Parker was (affected,
    effected) by the announcement of her promotion.   _____ _____

E.   This is a review of subject/verb agreement (see Section 4, Part 2). In the following sentences, make the verb agree with the subject in the tense and the voice indicated.

Present tense—Active voice

1.   Managers (delegate) responsibilities to workers and   _____
    (conduct) follow-up procedures to see that jobs are handled
    properly.   _____

2.   One of our older trucks (need) a complete overhaul.   _____

3. Either Nancy or Jane (attend) night school at the local community college. _____

4. Searching the files for lost or misfiled letters (waste) time. _____

5. The president (remember) to compliment managers when they (handle) a difficult situation well. _____

_____

Past tense—Passive voice

6. The recent conference (plan) by Tom Fields and Phyllis Smith. _____

7. Neither Mrs. Porter nor the other supervisors (criticize) for returning late from lunch. _____

8. Most of the machines (repair) last week. _____

9. Each car and each truck (examine) for oil leakage before delivery. _____

10. New employees (tell) the procedures for asking for time off to take care of personal business. _____

Present perfect tense—Active voice

11. Mr. Johnson (dictate) and I (type) the agenda for the board meeting tomorrow. _____

_____

12. Everyone (receive) a copy of the agenda by now. _____

13. All the managers (give) assignments to their assistants for the next three weeks. _____

14. Mr. Hardy and the staff (finish) compiling the annual report. _____

15. The committee (investigate) the complaints from customers. _____

Progressive future tense—Active voice

16. Half of the men (vote) in the coming union election. _____

17. The company (complete) its contract on that project early next spring. _____

18. Hart & Smith Building Contractors (construct) 52 single-family houses in Emeryville soon. _____

19. The authors of *Statistics for College Students* (write) the third edition of their book next year. _____

20. Our company (employ) more workers in the next six months. _____

F.   Fill in the correct tense of the verbs shown in parentheses in the letter below.

1.   Dear Mrs. West:

2.   A business research team recently (conduct) _____

3.   a survey of firms with word processing centers. The main objective

4.   of the study (be) _____ to determine what skills (be) (need)

5.   _____ in secretarial positions in a word processing

6.   system.

7.   Findings (reveal) _____ that a knowledge of grammar

8.   and the ability to proofread (be) (consider) _____

9.   to be very important skills for all secretaries. Administrative

10.   secretaries (place) _____ a high priority on composition

11.   and editing skills. Typewriting skills (show) _____ the

12.   greatest variance in requirements for the positions of administrative

13.   and correspondence secretary. Administrative secretaries (find)

14.   _____ that speed, accuracy, and the ability to correct

15.   errors were less important than (do) _____ the correspondence

16.   secretaries. Both groups (feel) _____ that statistical

17.   typing skills (be) _____ not important. However, correspondence

18.   secretaries (agree) _____ that companies (require) _____ a high-level

19.   transcription skill. Highest ratings (be) (give) _____

20.   to the subject of business attitudes. Respondents (rate) _____

21.   loyalty, cooperation, and a good sense of humor as important attitudes

22.   for secretaries.

23.   Many more areas of skills and attitudes (be) (study) _____

24.   If your firm (conduct) _____ training programs for word

25.   processing personnel, you (find) _____ the complete

26.   study helpful. (Return) _____ the enclosed order blank

27.   promptly, and we (send) _____ you a copy at

28.   no cost to you, except for $1.50 mailing fee.

29.   Sincerely yours,

G.   In the following exercise, you are to add *ing* to the verbs listed below. Some of them are regular verbs and others are irregular verbs. Consult the rules for adding *ing* to regular verbs on pages 210–11, and consult the dictionary if you do not know the correct spelling for the irregular verbs.

1.	spring	___	21.	ignore	___
2.	begin	___	22.	certify	___
3.	identify	___	23.	brake	___
4.	prefer	___	24.	file	___
5.	come	___	25.	explore	___
6.	lie	___	26.	center	___
7.	run	___	27.	incorporate	___
8.	dye	___	28.	correct	___
9.	betray	___	29.	determine	___
10.	use	___	30.	fly	___
11.	forget	___	31.	double	___
12.	cut	___	32.	frolic	___
13.	have	___	33.	reset	___
14.	break	___	34.	pursue	___
15.	employ	___	35.	purify	___
16.	dislike	___	36.	regret	___
17.	duplicate	___	37.	dictate	___
18.	infer	___	38.	put	___
19.	manufacture	___	39.	write	___
20.	transfer	___	40.	plan	___

Name _____

Date _____

—————————————— **PRACTICE WRITING** ——————————————

Here is an opportunity to find out if you can master troublesome verbs. Using the *present, past, future,* or *perfect tenses,* compose your own sentences as instructed below.

1. Use *lie* or *lay* as the principal verb. _____

    _____

    _____

2. Use *sit* or *set* as the principal verbs. _____

    _____

    _____

3. Use *rise* or *raise* as the principal verb. _____

    _____

    _____

4. Use *affect* as the principal verb. _____

    _____

    _____

5. Use *effect* as the principal verb. _____

    _____

    _____

6. Use *effect* as a noun. _____

    _____

    _____

In the remaining part of this writing exercise, compose four sentences that have as the principal verb an *irregular* verb in the *past* or *past perfect* tense. Choose four irregular verbs that are new to you or ones that you have difficulty using correctly.

7. _____. _____

(irregular verb)

_____

_____

8. _____. _____

(irregular verb)

_____

_____

9. _____. _____

(irregular verb)

_____

_____

10. _____. _____

(irregular verb)

_____

_____

Verbs have special forms

Because this course includes more than the study of grammar, this part presents other ways to write more effective sentences. As you have seen in the previous parts of this section, verbs are vital words in every message. Thus, it is important to know how to use all their forms. Verb forms called infinitives, participles, and verbal nouns can be used to make your messages more informative and interesting. They permit ideas to be expressed in many different ways.

Every good writer needs to use a variety of sentences to keep the reader interested throughout the complete message. A sound knowledge of how to use verbals as individual words or in phrases will allow you to keep the reader's attention as you add color to your writing.

Infinitives add the feeling of action to sentences.

Often the verb is preceded by the word *to: to run, to speak, to visit, to commend*. This form of the verb is called *infinitive*. It expresses action or condition without specifically defining person or number. The helpers *be* and *have* are often used in the infinitive to show the exact time of the action.

The supervisor planned **to talk** to the workers during the coffee break.

Give everyone in the organization the opportunity **to be heard** at the next higher level.

Mrs. Garcia is supposed **to have discussed** the problem with her supervisor last week.

The machine appears **to have been broken** several days ago.

The infinitive can be used as a noun, adjective, or adverb.

The infinitive may be used as a noun, adjective, or adverb. Notice in each of the following sentences how the infinitive or the infinitive phrase fulfills the noun, the adjective, or the adverb functions.

1. **Noun functions**

    Subject of a sentence: *To speak truthfully* about your co-workers is honest.

223

Object of a verb: The chairperson asked *to be excused.*

Complement of a verb: Our company policy is *to give customers the benefit of the doubt.*

Object of a preposition (notice here that the *to* is omitted): I can do nothing except (to) *refuse.*

Appositive: Jim's ambition, *to be promoted to auditor,* was never realized.

2. Adjective function

Miss Gary is a secretary *to watch for future promotion.*
(The infinitive phrase *to watch . . .* modifies *secretary*.)

3. Adverb function

Mr. Calkins went *to call on his customers.*
(*To call* modifies the verb **went**.)

They were pleased *to accept our invitation.*
(*To accept* modifies the adjective *pleased*.)

In some cases, the omission of *to* allows a natural flow of words.

In many sentences, the *to* is omitted because the thought flows more smoothly without it.

I watched Mr. Peterson **walk** down the hall.
(**Not:** . . . *to* walk down the hall.)

Did Francis help you **check** the inventory?

Let Jones **drive** the truck to Lewistown.

An infinitive may have a subject and an object.

An infinitive, like all other verb forms, may have a subject and an object.

Jim, our supervisor, expects the department manager **to promote**
o
him next month.
s

The engineer wanted the expediter **to collect** the parts from the
s   o
machine shop.

An infinitive may have an object only.

John found that he would have **to leave** the package with the guard.
o

Mrs. Stahl left early **to find** him.
o

Pronoun subjects and pronoun objects of infinitives take the objective case.

If the subject and the object of an infinitive are pronouns, they must be in the *objective case* (*me, us, you, him, her, it, them*). You can easily find the *subject* of an infinitive by looking for a noun or pronoun immediately *preceding* it. The *object* of an infinitive is the noun or pronoun immediately *following* it.

Mr. Thomas asked *him* to interview *them* before Monday.
(*him*—subject of **to interview**; *them*—object)

Miss Munoz told *us* to visit *her* at the factory in Fort Wayne.
(*us*—subject of **to visit**; *her*—object)

The nominative case is used for the pronoun complement following *to be*.

The only exception to this usage concerns the *to be* infinitive. When *to be* has *no* subject but is followed by a pronoun, the pronoun must be in the *nominative case (I, we, you, he, she, it, they, who)*. In such a sentence, the pronoun is a *complement* and takes the *nominative* case.

The shipping clerk is often thought ***to be*** *he.*

The winners of the contest appeared ***to be*** Jane Turpin, Andy Flaxen, and *I.*

Objective case is used for pronouns that come before and after the *to be* infinitive.

Like all other infinitives, though, if *to be* has a pronoun before it *and* one after it, both pronouns are in the *objective case.*

The treasurer mistook *her* to be *me.*

The infinitive should be used without intervening words.

A split infinitive has a word or words between the *to* and the action word or verb. If at all possible, keep the infinitive as a unit. Do not insert words between the two parts. The only time you may split an infinitive is when you must choose a natural expression over an awkward one. In such instances, the split infinitive is acceptable.

Be sure ***to follow*** directions carefully.
(**Not:** Be sure *to* carefully ***follow*** directions.)

The mechanic was asked ***to check*** the carburetor thoroughly.
(**Not:** The mechanic was asked *to* thoroughly *check* the carburetor.)

Measures *to severely restrict* our activities in that field have been started.
(permissible)

PARTICIPLES MAY BE USED AS ADJECTIVES

A participle is a verbal that functions both as a verb and as an adjective. When used as an adjective, the participle has three forms: present, past, and perfect. The *present participle* is formed by adding *ing* to the simple verb form —*reading, telling, touching, pushing.* The action expressed by the present participle is going on at the same time as the action in the verb in the independent clause.

The present participle indicates action in progress at the same time as the main verb.

The man *striding down the road* shouted to the policeman.

The president, *thinking out loud,* made a prediction.

The machine *running at full speed* turns out 5,000 pieces an hour.

In the preceding sentences, the present participles act as adjectives—*striding* modifies *man; thinking* modifies *president; running* modifies *machine.* They also act as verbs that express action while other action (*shouted, made, turns*) is taking place.

When the present participle functions as an adjective, place it close to the word or words you wish to modify, so that your message is clear.

The man shouted to the policeman, *striding down the road.*
(**Ambiguous:** Who was striding: *policeman* or *man*?)

You should watch the tendency many communicators have to place the present participial phrase at the end of a sentence. When it occurs at the end, the sentence is weakened and becomes ambiguous or confusing. Notice that the following sentence is clearer when it is rewritten without the phrase and with the emphasis on the important point of the message.

Confusing: The production line was shut down for two hours *causing us to fall behind schedule.*

Better: Because the production line was shut down for two hours, we fell behind schedule.

The past participle indicates action before that of the main verb.

The *past participle* is the same as the past tense form of the verb. It may end in *d, n, t,* or *ed—paid, torn, felt, touched.* The past participle used as an adjective may be either one word or part of a participial phrase. The use of the participial phrase often permits a concise or more informative statement. Remember that the past participle expresses time that started *before* that of the main verb.

The stockholders, *reminded of the annual meeting,* mailed in their proxies.
Bored by the speeches, they asked that the meeting be adjourned.

The *reminded* past participial phrase is used as an adjective to modify the noun *stockholders,* and the *bored* phrase is an adjective phrase that describes the pronoun *they.*

The perfect participle indicates action completed before that of the main verb.

The *perfect participle* shows that the action it expresses *was completed* before the action of the main verb took place. Examples of perfect participles are *having fixed, having stopped, having been dropped.*

Mr. Howard, *having completed his study of the situation,* was ready to talk about it when I arrived.
The letters, *having been transcribed,* were not signed until 4:30 p.m.

It is often important in business to show that a task was finished before something else was done or not done. The use of the perfect participle permits this distinction to be made.

VERBAL NOUNS CAN BE USED AS SUBJECTS, OBJECTS, AND COMPLEMENTS

The *ing* form of the verb is often used as a noun.

A verbal noun (or gerund) has the same verb form as the present participle; it also ends with *ing.* The verbal noun, however, is always used as a *noun.* Like a noun, it may be the subject of a sentence, object of a verb or preposition, or a complement. To discover whether the *ing* verb form is a present participle or a verbal noun, check its use in the sentence. If the *ing* form is used as a noun, it is a verbal noun; if used as an adjective, it is a present participle.

As a subject
Tabulating must be completed before the clerks go to lunch.

As an object
He studied *illustrating* in art school.
After *checking,* the teller told Mr. Juarez the balance in his account.

As a complement
A necessary part of bookkeeping is *checking.*

Verbal nouns may have objects.

The verbal noun, like other verb forms, sometimes has its own object. In the sentence below, *statements* is the object of *checking*. The entire phrase *checking bank statements* is the subject of the sentence.

*Checking bank **statements*** is part of a bookkeeper's job.

Remember that when you studied cases of pronouns in Section 3, you learned that pronoun objects of verbs are always in the objective case—*me, him, her, them,* and *whom.* Consequently, the pronoun object of a verbal noun (a verb form) must be in the *objective case.*

After *seeing **him,*** George went on to Mr. Richard's office.
*Finding **her*** in the hall, Sara told her about the phone call.
*Teaching **them*** how to use the computer takes several months.

Verbal nouns may be modified by possessive nouns and pronouns.

Like all nouns, a verbal noun may be modified by another noun or pronoun to show ownership. The modifying pronoun must be in the *possessive case*—*my, mine, our, ours, your, yours, his, her, hers, its, their,* and *theirs;* the noun forms the possessive by the apostrophe and *s* or the apostrophe alone (').

His *asking* for a raise was premature.
Mrs. Simpson appreciated ***Milton's*** *checking* her estimates.

THE USE OF VERBAL PHRASES RESULTS IN MORE INFORMATIVE MESSAGES

You will recall from the discussion in Section 1, Part 2, that infinitive, participial, and verbal noun phrases are groups of words that do not contain subjects and verbs. A closer look at these phrases will help you recognize all of them. As you have seen in this part, these verbals can be nouns, adjectives, or adverbs. They in turn can be modified and can function as verbs in certain ways.

Verbals are modified by adverbs.

Here are sentences that show you how participles, infinitives, and verbal nouns are modified by single adverbs, adverb phrases, and adverb clauses.

By adverbs

Participle: The stenographer *typing **rapidly*** wanted to finish the report by noon.

Infinitive: The supervisor has a problem *to solve **immediately.***

Verbal noun: The doctor warned them *against eating **quickly.***

By adverb phrases

Participle: The letters *lying **on the desk*** are for the credit department.

Infinitive: Instructions were given *to leave **in an hour.***

Verbal noun: *Learning **from others*** is useful.

By adverb clauses

Participial: *Speaking **when he was tired,*** the manager showed his indecision.

Infinitive: The policy *to check an account **when it is unpaid for 30 days*** means that we collect most of the money due.

Verbals have objects and complements.

Verbals have objects and complements just as main verbs in sentences have objects and complements. When you studied pronouns, you learned that it is important to recognize their use as objects and complements so that you would select the correct case for them. Some of the illustrations below have pronoun objects and complements in the case called for by their use in the sentence. Other words used as objects and complements are easy to use correctly.

With nouns and pronouns as objects

Participle: The clerk *delivering* **the mail** is filling in for Doug.

Infinitive: Bob is determined *to find* **a solution** to the problem.

Verbal noun: *Assisting* **them** during the Christmas season is hard work.

With clauses as objects

Participle: Mrs. Graham *realizing* **that data processing is important** signed up for a computer course.

Infinitive: His need *to know* **what changes were** proposed sent him to the telephone.

Verbal noun: *Knowing* **that you are being considered for a promotion** causes you to put forth extra effort.

With nouns and pronouns as indirect objects

Participle: The person *giving* **her** the envelope is the vice president.

Infinitive: The paymaster said that it is important *to take* **Mr. Carlson** his check.

Verbal noun: *Giving* our **employees** a bonus is my ambition.

With noun complements

Participle: *Being a loyal employee,* Jim encouraged his friends to buy Aerofax.

Infinitive: They always wanted *to be* **accountants.**

Verbal noun: *Being an* **auditor** takes many years of training.

With adjective complements

Participle: The employee, *appearing* **unhappy,** asked for another interview.

Infinitive: Their attempts *to seem* **interested** were half-hearted.

Verbal noun: *Being* **patient** seems the best approach.

Use verbal phrases logically.

Be sure introductory verbals modify the subject of the sentence.

When an infinitive or participial phrase introduces a sentence, make sure that the phrase modifies the *subject* of the sentence. If it does not, the phrase is called a *dangling* phrase—loosely connected to the sentence. Dangling modifiers should be tied to the things they describe. Notice in the following sentences how easily modifying phrases can be tied down.

Introductory infinitive phrase

Illogical: To finish before five o'clock, the cards should be stacked in three piles.
(How can cards finish?)

Logical: To finish before five o'clock, *you should stack* the cards in three piles.
(A person can finish.)

Introductory participial phrase

Illogical: Checking the figures, several mistakes were discovered.
(How can mistakes check figures?)

Logical: Checking the figures, *I discovered* several mistakes.
(A person can check figures.)

A prepositional phrase that has a *verbal noun* as its object should also be carefully checked for logical use. When a prepositional phrase containing a verbal noun introduces the sentence, see that it modifies the *subject* of the sentence.

Introductory prepositional phrase with verbal noun object

Illogical: After *listening* to Mrs. Sheets' report, a few changes were made by the manager.
(Changes can't listen.)

Logical: After *listening* to Mrs. Sheets' report, the *manager made* a few changes.
(The manager can listen.)

The important point to remember about logical use is that the phrase in which a verbal occurs should be placed as close as possible to the noun or pronoun that it modifies.

Remember these points about the correct use of verbals.

This discussion of infinitives, participles, and verbal nouns centers on ways to use these verb forms to make your communications more informative and interesting. Here is a list of important points to remember when using them.

1. The infinitive, alone or in a phrase, can be used as a noun, an adjective, or an adverb.
2. The pronoun subject and/or the pronoun object of an infinitive must be in the *objective case,* except for the *to be* infinitive.
3. The *to be* infinitive *having no subject* is followed by a pronoun complement in the *nominative case.*
4. The *to be* infinitive having *both* a pronoun subject and a pronoun complement calls for both pronouns in the *objective case.*
5. An infinitive should be used as a unit but may be split if the resulting expression is more natural.
6. Participles may function as adjectives and should be placed as close as possible to the noun or pronoun they modify.
7. The present participle is the *ing* form of the verb; the past participle ends in *d, n, t,* or *ed;* and the perfect participle uses the helper *have—having fixed.*
8. Verbal nouns end with *ing* and are used in the same way nouns are used; e.g., as subjects, objects, complements.
9. Pronoun objects of verbal nouns are in the *objective case.*
10. Modifiers of verbal nouns are in the *possessive case.*

11. Introductory infinitive and participial phrases and introductory prepositional phrases with verbal noun objects must modify the *subject* of the sentence.

Increase your vocabulary by using synonyms.

As a college student, you are constantly being challenged to increase your vocabulary. One of the easiest ways to add words is to locate synonyms for the words you find yourself using too often. Even you become tired and bored saying or writing those words you overuse. What is a *synonym?* It is a word that means the same or almost the same as another word. The interesting fact about synonyms is that each one has a slightly different shade of meaning. Many of them give you a wide range of shadings so that you can select one that conveys the exact thought that is in your mind. Note the many words that mean almost the same as *old: aged, ancient, antiquated, antique, decrepit, elderly, gray, hoary, immemorial, obsolete, olden, patriarchal, remote, senile, time-honored, time-worn, venerable.* You will find synonyms for words in the dictionary. They are listed near the end of the entry (—*Syn.*), and often the differences in meanings are explained. Suggestions on using the dictionary can be found on pages 353–54.

Make it a practice from now on to check the synonyms for any word you look up in the dictionary. Perhaps you will find there another word that states more exactly the message you are trying to get across. If you use such a synonym immediately, you will find your vocabulary growing by leaps and bounds.

Look up the following verbs in your dictionary and list their synonyms. If the entry says —*Syn. See* _____, be sure to turn to the suggested word and collect its synonyms also. See if you can use the synonyms for these verbs during the rest of this month.

affect _____

_____

make _____

_____

have _____

_____

study _____

_____

get _____

_____

plan _____

_____

write _____

_____

learn _____

_____

effect _____

_____

tell _____

_____

Start a list of synonyms for words you use too often.

_____ _____

_____ _____

_____ _____

_____ _____

_____ _____

_____ _____

_____ _____

PART 5

ASSIGNMENTS

Apply your knowledge of special verb forms

A. Identify the underlined verbals—infinitives, participles, verbal nouns—in the following sentences by placing the appropriate letters—*i* for infinitive, *p* for participle, and *vn* for verbal noun—in the right-hand column.

Example: Typing reports can take several hours.   *vn*

1. Playing golf is good exercise.   _____

2. Are you planning to go to the convention?   _____

3. Please give the writing of this letter your careful attention.   _____

4. Mr. Jones decided to study the situation.   _____

5. Speaking to large audiences requires practice.   _____

6. After adding the figures several times, the bookkeeper finally decided   _____

   to use the calculator.   _____

7. Finding the parking lot full, the visitor parked on the street.   _____

8. To tell the truth, I think you should talk to your supervisor.   _____

9. To ask for a raise takes courage.   _____

10. The accountant, having collected all the figures, proceeded   _____

    to make the balance sheet.   _____

B.   In the following sentences, underline **all** verbal nouns and verbal noun phrases. Then indicate the function of each one by writing *subject, object* (of verb or preposition), or *complement* in the column at the right.

1.   Word processing is another term for handling paperwork.   _____

2.   Filing is an important function in all offices.   _____

3.   You will find the invoices for checking the merchandise in the top drawer.   _____

4.   His careful driving resulted in lower insurance premiums.   _____

5.   A machine tape made checking unnecessary.   _____

6.   Proofreading should be done by two people.   _____

7.   The next step should be training in letter writing.   _____

8.   Spending money wisely should be learned at an early age.   _____

9.   Your feeling about this project should be shared with Fred Baker.   _____

10.   Gathering data for the study is your first assignment.   _____

C.   Identify the infinitives and infinitive phrases in the following sentences by underlining them. Then indicate how they are used in each sentence by writing *subject, object, complement, appositive,* or *modifier* (adjective or adverb) in the column at the right. Refer to pages 227–28 if you need to review the text on these usages.

1.   The president was asked to make a speech at the convention.   _____

2.   My advice to you is to learn to get along with people.   _____

3.   To study engineering is my cousin's goal.   _____

4.   Ask them to learn communication skills.   _____

5.   The quickest way to get to Chicago is to fly.   _____

6.   They are hoping to receive a bonus at the end of the year.   _____

7.   Mrs. Gouch's decision, to rewrite the letter, showed that she recognized the need for an action ending.   _____

8.   To test that machine take it to the laboratory in Building G.   _____

9.   Some workers find it difficult to concentrate with music playing.   _____

10.   Will you try to leave the office by four?   _____

D.   In the following sentences, select the correct pronouns, as *subjects* and *objects of infinitives,* to complete the sentences. Enter your choice in the right-hand column.

1. Did Mr. Wise tell (we, us) to invite (they, them) to the meeting? _____
2. The nominating committee voted to present (they, them) as officers for next year. _____
3. The persons asking for raises were found to be (she, her) and (he, him). _____
4. Does it seem to be (we, us) or (they, them) who will be given that job? _____
5. Before you leave, tell (she, her) to help (he, him) with the tally. _____
6. The supervisor asked (I, me) to find (he, him) a hammer. _____
7. Get (they, them) to check the typewriters in the sales department. _____
8. Find an excuse to tell (he, him) how you feel. _____
9. It seems to be (I, me) who should talk to them. _____
10. The reporter agreed to mention (I, me) in the article about our new product. _____

E.   The verbs in parentheses in the following sentences are to be used as *infinitives*. Some will need helping verbs. Be sure that the tense of the infinitive agrees with the time expressed in the main verb. For those infinitives that have pronoun subjects and objects, select the correct case for the pronoun. Also, remember that the *to* may be left out for a more natural expression and that adverbs that modify infinitives will need your careful attention.

Example: Jim and Bob were asked personally (list) all assets of the client.   *to list personally*

1. Four clerks will help you (check) the stock for the month-end sale. _____
2. The agent is supposed (discuss) the problem with my boss last week. _____
3. The new sales force was found (increase) total sales by 15 percent. _____
4. Mrs. Foster asked Mr. Young (give) (she, her) a copy of the order. _____
5. Insurance is said (regulate) as long ago as 1868. _____
6. I am waiting (call) (she, her) for an interview. _____
7. Mrs. Butler wanted (hire) (he, him) for the Dallas office. _____
8. These documents are (classify) immediately. _____
9. (Plan) a month's work for this department requires everyone's help. _____
10. More stationery will have (order) by July 1. _____

11. It is not known as yet whether the vice president is (be) (he, him) or (she, her).   _____

12. Dr. Baldwin promised immediately (call) when the case is settled.   _____

13. A new procedures manual needs (write).   _____

14. In a timed test, try quickly (answer) all questions.   _____

15. Mr. Bacon told (she, her) (speak) to the customer about the unpaid balance.   _____

16. Bob was able (prepare) the report without any assistance.   _____

17. Banks require checks (endorse) before they can be cashed.   _____

18. They asked (I, me) (be) chairman.   _____

19. A major step in report writing is logically (organize) the findings.   _____

20. Tell Miss Chester (bring) (I, me) immediately the Cooper & Co. file.   _____

F.   Notice in this exercise that you are given sentence *beginnings* that contain participles, verbal nouns, and infinitives. Complete each one by writing an independent clause to accompany the opening phrase. Make sure that the subject you use is the person doing the action expressed by the verbal. If you make the implied actor in the verbal the subject of your sentence, the verbal will be tied to the main clause and will not "dangle."

Example: Knowing that Mr. Porter was waiting for the figures, *I hurriedly collected them and took them to him.*

1. To run efficiently, _____

_____

2. Having been familiar with his ability, _____

_____

3. In talking to the supervisor, _____

_____

4. Being tired and hungry, _____

_____

5. To qualify for a promotion, _____

_____

6. Persuaded that he wanted the facts, _____

_____

7. Completely satisfied, _____

_____

8. Knowing office skills, _____

_____

9. To finish the job on time, _____

_____

10. After answering the telephone, _____

_____

Name _____

Date _____

—————— PRACTICE WRITING ——————

A sentence that contains action and motion is more colorful to a reader. See how many strong verbs you can use as participles, verbal nouns, and infinitives to write interestingly. Follow the directions as given below in writing your ten colorful sentences.

1. Use an infinitive as the subject. _____

_____

_____

2. Use an infinitive as the object of the verb. _____

_____

_____

3. Use a verbal noun as the subject. _____

_____

_____

4. Use a verbal noun as the object of a verb. _____

_____

_____

5. Use a verbal noun as the object of a preposition. _____

_____

_____

6. Use the present participle as an adjective. _____

_____

_____

7. Use the past participle as an adjective. _____

   _____

   _____

8. Use an infinitive as an adjective. _____

   _____

   _____

9. Use a verbal noun with a modifier. _____

   _____

   _____

10. Use an infinitive as an adverb. _____

    _____

    _____

The modifiers

Modifiers are the descriptive words in our language. They are used to develop, restrict, describe, or otherwise enhance, shade, or emphasize the meaning of the main sentence elements—the nouns and the verbs. They add color and interest to our sentences.

Modifiers fall into three general groups: those that modify nouns or noun equivalents, called adjectives; those that modify action or being words (verbs), called adverbs; and those that modify other parts of the sentence or the sentence as a whole.

Phrases and clauses modify nouns and verbs most of the time and are classified as either adjectives or adverbs in such uses. In this section we will look closely at adjectives and adverbs. Some attention will also be directed to prepositions and the phrases that they form.

Adjectives are descriptive words

Adjectives modify nouns and pronouns.

Adjectives are used to modify nouns and pronouns by naming a quality or characteristic of the noun or the pronoun. They help us describe persons, places, things, and ideas, and thereby distinguish one from another.

tall ladder	*short* ladder	*busy* harbor	*deserted* harbor
dull book	*interesting* book	*doubtful* loyalty	*unquestioned* loyalty

These modifying words are formed in several ways but mostly from nouns and verbs. You have already seen in Section 1, Part 2, how participles may be used as adjectives to modify nouns and pronouns. And you have probably noticed that in some instances the base word is completely changed. In the majority of cases, however, the addition of adjective-forming suffixes turns the base word into an adjective. If you are familiar with the following suffixes, you will find it easy to form and to recognize a large number of adjectives.

Adjectives can be formed by the addition of suffixes to nouns and verbs.

-able:	comfortable (comfort)	**-ical:**	biological (biology)
-al:	formal (form)	**-ish:**	foolish (fool)
-an:	European (Europe)	**-ive:**	inventive (invent)
-ese:	Japanese (Japan)	**-ly:**	manly (man; -ly ending occurs more often with adverbs)
-ful:	useful (use)	**-n:**	American (America)
-ian:	Brazilian (Brazil)	**-ous:**	ridiculous (ridicule)
-ible:	digestible (digest)	**-y:**	speedy (speed)

You should think of adjectives as picture-painting words that allow you to make your message more colorful and alive. The larger your vocabulary, the easier it is for you to choose adjectives that paint the best pictures. In business writing and conversation, you will want to avoid the excessive use of adjectives or their use in inappropriate situations. Even in promotional and advertising materials, good judgment must be exercised so that the customer doesn't feel that you are overemphasizing the qualities of your product.

Adjectives usually come before the nouns they describe.

Adjectives are *identified* by their use in sentences. They often appear directly before the nouns they modify, as in the examples given earlier. You can probably identify them in this position quite readily. Another way to identify them is to apply the questions they answer to the nouns they modify. These questions are *which one?*, *what kind?*, and *how many?*. Possessive nouns and pronouns are also used as adjectives because they answer the question *which one?*.

the *brown* house — answers *which one?*
the *oak* table — answers *what kind?*
a *dozen* books — answers *how many?*
his job — answers *which one?*

Two or more adjectives may precede the noun as modifiers, as in the following examples. Notice that these adjectives contribute to one complete thought, and no commas are used between them. For instance, in the first example, *short* describes *sentences* and *two* describes *short sentences*.

two short sentences
many tall buildings
several delicate china cups
large Eastern manufacturing company

Place commas between adjectives that are independent modifiers.

Some multiple adjectives are of equal value, and each one independently modifies the noun or pronoun. The conjunction *and* would often be used between the adjectives; when it is omitted, a comma must appear in its place.

Mr. Phelps is a *warm, understanding* supervisor.
Send for our *specific, detailed* instructions.

Adjectives follow linking verbs.

Another common position for an adjective is after such linking verbs as *be, appear,* and *seem.* In this position the adjective describes the subject of the sentence and is called an adjective complement. It is an adjective used to complete the link between the subject and the verb. You learned about linking verbs in Section 4, Part 1.

The *supply* **seems** adequate.
The *typist* **is** slow.
He **was** angry.

Remember that a noun can also be used as the complement after a linking verb, as in the sentence: *He is my boss.* If the complement names another identity of the subject, it is a noun. If it describes some *quality* of the subject, it is an adjective. Avoid the error of using an adverb (words that usually end in *ly*) in this position. Since the complement describes the subject (a noun or pronoun), an adjective should be used.

Wrong: Your report appears correctly.
Right: Your report appears *correct.*

Verbs that pertain to the senses—*look, smell, taste, feel*—are also used as linking verbs that express no action. These verbs link an adjective in the predicate with the subject it describes.

The annual report looks *interesting.*

The water felt *warm.*

Gasoline smells *pungent.*

However, when a *sense* verb means an action of the body, the verb is followed by an adverb because it describes the action of the verb.

The man looked at us *cautiously.*

Some adjectives come after the noun.

You have probably noticed that some adjectives appear directly after the noun. In the following sentences, the adjective in each case describes the object of the verb.

The speaker made the lecture *interesting.*

Our visitor found the city *congested.*

I considered him *foolish.*

When an adjective is composed of several words or is a prepositional phrase, it may come *after* the noun it modifies.

Phrases— prepositional, infinitive, participial— can be used as adjectives.

A desk *five inches narrower* would fit in that space.
   (several words)

A plan *worthy of consideration* has been submitted.
   (word + prepositional phrase)

We bought a new file cabinet *of steel.*
   (prepositional phrase)

The machine *on the assembly line* needs repair.
   (prepositional phrase)

Infinitive phrases used as adjectives also follow the nouns they modify.

The person *to contact* is Mr. Carson.

There are five rules *to remember.*

Phrases beginning with a present or a past participle usually follow the nouns they modify.

The man *loading the truck* is Jim.

The radio *sold to Mrs. Jones* was defective.

Participial phrases beginning with the present participle are adjectives, but they resemble verbal noun phrases. Since they both begin with the *ing* form of the verb, you can tell these phrases apart only by determining their use in the sentence. If a phrase beginning with the *ing* form of the verb is used as a noun, it is a verbal noun (see page 226). If a phrase beginning with the *ing* form of the verb is used as an adjective, then it is a participial phrase. It is important to make this distinction because nouns or pronouns that modify verbal noun phrases take the possessive form. Look at these two sentences:

Participial phrase
   The workers *opening those boxes* were hired by Mr. Johnson.

Verbal noun phrase
   The workers' *opening those boxes* is unforgivable.

In the first sentence, the subject is *workers,* and the phrase *opening those boxes* merely serves to point out the identity of the workers being discussed. *Opening those boxes* is therefore a participial phrase because it is used as an adjective. In the second sentence, you can see that the phrase *opening those boxes* is the subject because this is the action that is unforgivable. As a subject, it serves as a noun and is known as a verbal noun phrase. The modifying word *workers* must therefore take the possessive form *workers'*.

Dependent clauses may be used as adjectives.

Nouns and pronouns can also be modified by adjective clauses. These clauses are always dependent clauses and may be either restrictive or non-restrictive. You learned about them first in Section 1, Part 1.

The manager *who knows company policies* is better able to manage a department.

The book *that you describe* should help us understand our problem.

Mrs. Huber, *who is the secretary-treasurer of this company*, has an MBA from Stanford.

Proper adjectives are capitalized.

A proper adjective is one that has been derived from a proper noun naming either a person or a place. Proper adjectives should be capitalized.

a *German* scientist   a *European* import
the *Germanic* languages   *Keynesian* economics
an *American* invention   *Mexican* dances

A few such adjectives are not capitalized because they are no longer associated with the proper nouns from which they were derived.

a *herculean* task
pasteurized milk
china cups

Compound adjectives are usually hyphenated.

A compound adjective is formed by combining two or more words into a single descriptive unit. To indicate to the reader that the words are to be considered a unit, you should hyphenate a compound adjective.

Your *down-to-earth* solution was applauded by all.
Tom did a *first-class* job.
He is a *well-informed* sales manager.
We need an *up-to-date* building.

When these same descriptive words follow the nouns they modify, they are *not* considered units and should *not* be hyphenated.

The sales manager is *well informed.*
Our information is *up to date.*
The hotel accommodations were *first class.*

It is important to recognize modifying words that appear to be compound adjectives. In reality, some pairs of words are merely adjectives that in turn are modified by adverbs ending in *ly*. An adverb-adjective combination should *never* be hyphenated.

Please write a properly *worded* order for the new machine.

A highly *paid* executive gives more than eight hours a day to company business.

Compound adjectives containing a number and a noun are used frequently in business. They are hyphenated when they appear before the noun they modify.

The water heater has a *25-gallon* tank.
The workers requested a *35-hour* week.
Please leave a *12-inch* panel.

Notice that the nouns *gallon, hour,* and *inch* are singular when used in compound adjectives. In the following sentences, these same words are used as nouns. When used as nouns, any quantity greater than one makes them plural. The number indicating how many is an adjective modifying the noun; therefore, no hyphen is needed.

The water heater holds 25 gallons.
Please leave a panel 12 inches wide.
We waited over 24 hours for his report.

Fractions are hyphenated when they are used as adjectives but not when they are used as nouns.

Adjective: A *three-fourths* majority is needed to pass the bill.
Noun: *Three fourths* of the employees favor this plan.

If two or more compound adjectives with the same base word are used to modify a noun, the base word may be omitted from the first, second, or subsequent compound adjective; but the hyphen remains. The last word in the compound retains both the hyphen and the base word.

Please buy some *three-* and *thirteen-cent* stamps.
He purchased nails in *4-, 5-, 6-,* and *8-inch* lengths.

Knowing the antonyms for words will increase your vocabulary.

An *antonym* is a word that means the exact opposite of another word. For example, *good* is the opposite of *bad.* For some words you merely add a prefix meaning *not* to the root word in order to form its antonym. Notice how the following positive words have been changed to negative words by the addition of a prefix.

Adding ab to normal   *forms*   abnormal, the antonym.
        ig to noble   —   ignoble
        il to legal   —   illegal
        im to partial   —   impartial
        non to essential   —   nonessential
        un to varnished   —   unvarnished

Besides being able to make up your own antonyms, you should enlarge your vocabulary to include the antonyms that are entirely different words. Make the following short list of antonyms a part of your vocabulary.

strong — weak   static — moving
active — passive   expensive — cheap
worthless — valuable   subtle — obvious
simple — complicated   rough — smooth
interesting — dull   right — wrong
happy — sad   unusual — commonplace
boring — stimulating   functional — ornamental

ASSIGNMENTS

Apply your knowledge of adjectives

A. Adjectives are easy to use. In the following sentences, add adjectives from your own vocabulary that will make the messages colorful and alive.

1. My new car is _____.

2. Look at that _____ building.

3. _____, _____, and _____ flowers grow in our garden.

4. The new employee is an _____ worker.

5. I plan to order _____ pencils, _____ pens, and _____ envelopes.

6. Our new product is _____ and _____.

7. Please send me a _____ and _____ sofa.

8. A _____ employee knows how to get along with people.

9. That secretary is always _____.

10. The _____ desk should be moved to my office.

B. This exercise, containing many sentences with *linking verbs,* calls for you to apply the information you just studied about using adjectives with them. Select a word from the list on the following page to complete each sentence; then write your choice in the space provided.

angrily	complete	efficiently	good	qualified	slowly	tasty
angry	completely	enthusiastic	heavy	qualifiedly	sweet	tastily
careful	different	enthusiastically	heavily	ready	sweetly	tired
carefully	differently	fragrant	pleasant	readily	sympathetic	tiredly
cheerfully	efficient	fragrantly	pleasantly	slow	sympathetically	well

1. Dr. Speroni looks _____ .

2. He was not _____ to our suggestion.

3. Is the secretary _____ to take dictation?

4. Frank is not feeling _____ and will stay home until Monday.

5. The new machine appears too _____ for the foundation of this building.

6. Was the clerk _____ while fitting your shoes?

7. The worker appears _____ about the opportunity to work with computers.

8. Our new automobile is quite _____ .

9. The roses smell _____ after a rain.

10. John is _____ for the position but is too _____ to do a good job.

C. Some of the sentences in this exercise contain *compound adjectives*. Add hyphens to these compound adjectives, and place a check opposite the sentences in which you find them.

1. Test flight crews are paid well.   _____

2. Adopt our six part action program now.   _____

3. We have an ever growing base of personal savings.   _____

4. We have allotted $25,000 for the repair of our two, three, and five ton trucks.   _____

5. Workers who are highly skilled should have no trouble securing jobs.   _____

6. Please send us a 12 foot high, 4 foot wide, and ¼ inch thick walnut panel.   _____

7. Our city constructed a 5,000 gallon water tank.   _____

8. Did you say that there will be a 17 month delay in shipment?   _____

9. The finance professor conducted a three day series on investments. _____

10. Up to date information about that project is available in the library.   _____

11. A second hand desk and chair should be located for the factory office.   _____

12. Ms. Sternberg composed a properly worded memorandum.   _____

13. There will be a one hour and fifteen minute delay in departure.   _____

14. Reports that are up to the minute are an asset to managers.   _____

15. We should order another 12 inch lathe.   _____

16. A well known person will speak at the conference on Tuesday.   _____

17. A highly recommended consultant has agreed to study the production problem.   _____

18. Take those high quality, low intensity, blue green lamps to shipping.   _____

19. The subject was "How someone can get rich by investing five or ten thousand dollars."   _____

20. Purchase a first class air ticket when any trip is over three hours' flying time.   _____

D. Many proper nouns have adjective forms. Change the following proper nouns to adjectives. If in doubt, consult the dictionary.

1. Africa   _____   nations

2. Alaska   _____   salmon

3. Canada   _____   bacon

4. Columbia   _____   art

5. France   _____   politics

6. Great Britain   _____   sport cars

7. Hawaii   _____   pineapple

8. Australia   _____   opals

9. Texas   _____   petroleum

10. Ireland   _____   tweed

11. Israel   _____   agriculture

12. Italy   _____   designers

13. Japan   _____   pearls

14. Mexico _____ weaving

15. Netherlands _____ tulips

16. North Carolina _____ tobacco

17. South America _____ alliance

18. Spain _____ citrus fruits

19. Sweden _____ furniture

20. Switzerland _____ banking

E. Write an *antonym* for each of the following adjectives.

1. economical _____
2. nonessential _____
3. binding _____
4. unbelievable _____
5. comfortable _____

6. white _____
7. bright _____
8. necessary _____
9. antique _____
10. practical _____

Name _____

Date _____

─────────────── **PRACTICE WRITING** ───────────────

To develop your own skill in using adjectives correctly, compose original sentences as directed below.

1. Use a proper adjective in a sentence. _____

_____

_____

2. Use a hyphenated compound adjective in a sentence. _____

_____

_____

3. Use a prepositional phrase as an adjective. _____

_____

_____

4. Use an infinitive phrase as an adjective. _____

_____

_____

5. Use a participial phrase as an adjective. _____

_____

_____

6. Use an adjective with a linking verb. _____

_____

_____

PART **2**

Adjectives have special qualities

Adjectives describe, make it possible to compare, and make definite the meaning of the nouns or pronouns they modify. Thus, the reader or hearer gets a better picture of the person, thing, or characteristic named by the noun or the pronoun. As you learned in Part 1, adjectives add color and force to writing. They also suggest qualities of the objects modified.

Adjectives have three degrees of comparison.

Adjectives have several qualities, called *degrees,* to allow us to compare the nouns they modify. The *positive* degree is used to describe one thing. The *comparative* degree is used to compare two things. The *superlative* degree is used to compare three or more things.

Positive degree (no comparison)
We have a *new* building.

Comparative degree (comparing two things)
We have a *newer* building than the Jones Corp.

Superlative degree (comparing three or more things)
We have the *newest* building on the block.

Comparative and superlative degrees can be formed easily from the positive degree.

Almost all adjectives of one syllable, and some containing two syllables, form the *comparative degree* by adding *r* or *er* to the positive degree. The *superlative degree* of most adjectives of one syllable, and a few of two syllables, is formed by adding *st* or *est.* In others, the comparative and the superlative are formed by changing *y* to *i* and adding *er* or *est.*

Positive		Comparative		Superlative	
high	sincere	higher	sincerer	highest	sincerest
small	cool	smaller	cooler	smallest	coolest
pretty	cold	prettier	colder	prettiest	coldest

Most adjectives of more than one syllable form the *comparative degree* by the addition of the word *more* or the word *less* in front of the adjective. They form the *superlative degree* by adding *most* or *least* before the adjective.

253

Positive	Comparative	Superlative
faithful	*more* faithful	*most* faithful
energetic	*more* energetic	*most* energetic
popular	*less* popular	*least* popular
grateful	*less* grateful	*least* grateful

Some adjectives have irregular forms.   A few adjectives form degrees in an irregular manner. The most common irregular adjectives are shown below.

Positive	Comparative	Superlative
bad, ill	worse	worst
far	farther, further	farthest, furthest
good, well	better	best
late	later, latter	latest, last
little	less, lesser	least
many, much	more	most
old	older, elder	oldest, eldest

Farther/further.   Both these words are used as the comparative degree of *far*. *Farther* is, however, the preferred word in referring to measurable distance; *further* is the preferred word in referring to degree or quantity.

> It is *farther* to the airport than it is to the subway.
> Please use the west entrance until *further* notice.
> *Further* communication is unnecessary.

Later/latter.   *Later* is used to refer to *time; latter* means *near the end* or the *second of two items. Later* is pronounced with a *long a* (lāter); *latter* is pronounced with a *short a* (lătter).

> See if you can get a reservation on a *later* plane.
> The mail is *later* today than usual.
> Mr. Jones can see you the *latter* part of this week.
> We considered acreage in both Boston and Hartford but decided on the *latter* site.

Latest/last.   *Latest* means most recent; *last* means that which comes after all others.

> John has the *latest* issue of *Fortune*.
> This is the *last* copy he will receive before his subscription expires.

Less/fewer.   *Less* and *least* are used to describe nouns that emphasize *amount* or *quantity; fewer* and *fewest* are used to describe nouns that emphasize *number*.

> There is *less* candy in that box.
> There are *fewer* pieces of candy in that box.
> We will select the process that takes the *least* time.
> Bill worked the *fewest* hours on Thursday.

Older, oldest/elder, eldest.   *Older* and *oldest* are used to describe both people and things. *Elder* and *eldest* are used only with people, especially members of the same family.

James is the *older* of the two men.
This company is the *oldest* in the business.
Bill is the *eldest* of Mr. Friedman's three sons.
   (*Oldest* son may also be used.)

Quick review

Let's take time now to see if you can select the correct form of the comparative adjective for the particular situation in each of the following sentences. Circle the correct adjective from those you find in parentheses.

1. Both letters are well written, but I think this one is the (best, better).
2. The rain this year is (heavy, heavier, heaviest) than last year.
3. Several of the reports provide workable recommendations, but Harry Butler's is the (more, most) practical.
4. Do you think it is (farther, further) to Miami than Chicago?
5. This carton holds (less, fewer) books than the one we used last year.
6. Lester is one of the (more, most) faithful employees we have.
7. Is Mary (less, least) popular than Joan and Susan?
8. Of all the women in the department, Agatha is the (less, least) energetic.
9. The (older, elder, oldest) car in the parking lot is a Buick.
10. Of the three sweaters you tried on, this one is the (pretty, prettier, prettiest).

(Answers in reverse order: prettiest, oldest, least, less, most, fewer, farther, most, heavier, better)

Some adjectives cannot be compared.

Some adjectives cannot logically be compared because they already express the highest possible degree. Examples of such words are *accurate, complete, continual, correct, dead, empty, ideal, perfect, round,* and *unique.* If Bill's computations are *correct,* can Jim's be *more correct?* We can compare Bill's and Jim's computations, however, by saying that Jim's are *more nearly correct* than Bill's. To compare two things, we add *more nearly* to words of this type. To compare three or more things, we add *most nearly.*

Of the two reports submitted, yours was *more nearly* complete.
Of all the reports submitted, yours was the *most nearly* complete.

In the section on nouns, you found that a noun can serve to modify another noun. Nouns used as modifiers are similar to adjectives in that they help to distinguish one noun from another (*shoe* salesman, *tire* salesman). They are unlike adjectives, however, in that they cannot form comparative degrees. Note the differences in the modifiers in these examples.

Adjective	Noun
beautiful parlor	*beauty* parlor
refreshing committee	*refreshments* committee
skinny specialist	*skin* specialist

We could talk about a *more beautiful parlor* or a *skinnier specialist,* but we wouldn't say a *more beauty parlor* or a *more skin specialist.* To compare words modified by nouns, we must add the comparative form of an adjective in front of the two nouns.

Adjective	Noun	Noun
most expensive	beauty	parlor
most famous	skin	specialist
best	finance	committee

Quick review

You need to be able to recognize adjectives that already express the highest degree of comparison. Also, you need to remember that noun modifiers never form the comparative degree. In the following sentences, see if you can choose the correct form of the adjectives by drawing a circle around your choice.

1. The windows in our building are (more, most, more nearly, most nearly) spotless than those in the building next door.
2. Of all the calculations submitted, yours is the (more, most, more nearly, most nearly) right.
3. The (better, best) tire shop in town is Tires On Wheels, Inc.
4. My in-basket is the (emptier, emptiest, most nearly empty, more empty) one in this office.
5. Which worker is the (more, most, more nearly, most nearly) efficient, Jones or Pelham?

(Answers in reverse order: more nearly, most nearly empty, best, most nearly, more nearly)

Avoid these common errors in using comparative forms.

Anyone who wants to use adjectives correctly must be alert to these common errors that many people make when using comparative forms.

1. If an adjective is already in the comparative (*r* or *er* ending) or the superlative (*est* or *st* ending) degree, you *cannot* add the words *more* or *most.* A *double comparison* should be shunned as much as a double negative.

That desk is *larger* than this one.
   (**Not:** *more larger)*
He has the *finest* car on the block.
   (**Not:** *most finest*)

2. When comparing a thing to *other members* of the same group, use the comparative degree and a word such as *other* or *else.*

Correct: Miss Jones is a *faster* typist than any *other* person in her division.

Wrong: Miss Jones is a faster typist than any person in her division.

Correct: James receives a *larger* salary than anyone *else* in the office.

Wrong: James receives a larger salary than anyone in the office.

3. When an item is *included in the group* being compared, use the superlative degree.

Miss Jones is the *fastest* typist in her division.

Other words accompany nouns.   Another group of words that accompany nouns are the pointing or determining words. This group includes *a, an, the, that, this, these, those, each, every, both, only, some, either, neither,* and other words like them. Since words of this type point out the nouns that they accompany, they are sometimes called pointing words but are known more commonly as *determiners.* These words are similar to adjectives in function and position, but they are quite different in their influence or meaning. In the following sentences, the determiner *the* and the adjective *large* do occupy the same position in the sentence.

We like *the* offices.
We like *large* offices.

But determiners cannot, for example, be used in the complement position.

Our offices are *large.*
(**But not:** Our offices are *the.*)

As a person who speaks English, you already know where to use most of these words in a sentence. You know, for instance, that they always come before adjectives when both words accompany a noun.

We looked at *those* large offices.
(**Not:** We looked at large those offices.)

Emphasized in the paragraphs that follow are things to remember when using some of the most common determiners.

1. *The* is sometimes called a *definite article* and is used to point out some particular person or thing. *A* and *an* are called *indefinite articles* and are used to designate any one member of a class or group.

The records are kept on file.
(indicates specific records)
A doctor must be on hand.
(indicates any doctor)
An efficient secretary is on time.
(indicates any efficient secretary)

2. *A* is used before words beginning with (*a*) a consonant sound, (*b*) the letter *h* when pronounced, and (*c*) the long *u* sound.

a desk	*a* union	*a* one-week trial
a heavy desk	*a* unique idea	*a* UCLA graduate

3. *An* is used before words beginning with a vowel sound (except the long *u* sound). Remember that the sound of the word is important, not the spelling.

an operator	*an* average score
an honest man	*an* eight-hour wait
an unusual task	*an* f.o.b. order

Note that *a* or *an* should not be used after such expressions as *kind of, sort of, type of.*

Correct: What *type of problem* is this?

Weak: What type of a problem is this?

4. *This* and *that* are singular and modify singular nouns.

Did you work for *that* company?
 (one company)

This kind of food is healthful.
 (one kind of food)

These and *those* are plural and modify plural nouns.

Those mistakes are costly.   Send the letters to *these* companies.
 (more than one mistake)   (more than one company)

Note that *them* should never be used in place of *these* or *those*. *Them* is a pronoun.

Correct: He delivered *those* boxes.

Wrong: He delivered *them* boxes.

5. *Either/neither* and *each/every* may be used as adjectives or pronouns. When they are used with nouns, they are adjectives. But when they are used alone, they are pronouns.

Either plan will provide full coverage.

Neither plan has been considered.

Each clerk is to file her own copies.

Every clerk will report at 8 a.m. tomorrow.

In the above sentences, the words *either/neither* and *each/every* are used as adjectives. In these next sentences, *either* and *each* are used as pronouns.

He will choose *either* of the clerks for promotion.

Give *each* of them a copy.

Either is used with *or; neither* is used with *nor*.

The new manager will be *either* John *or* Harold.

Neither Mr. Witt *nor* Mr. Moore will be present.

6. *Each other* refers to two persons or things.

English and speech are closely related to *each other*.

Mary and Linda saw *each other* at the party.

One another refers to more than two persons or things.

Many phases of management depend upon *one another*.

Mary, Linda, and June help *one another* in the office.

7. *Only* should be placed close to the noun or noun and adjective that it modifies.

Accurate: Mr. Smith joined our staff *only* last week.

Misleading: Mr. Smith *only* joined our staff last week.

Accurate: I have *only* one secretary.

Misleading: I *only* have one secretary.

8.   When two or more adjectives modify the same noun, the *determiner* is used before the *first* adjective only.

A beautiful and charming hostess greeted us.
   (one hostess)
We ordered *a* brown, beige, and white carpet.
   (one carpet)
The large and roomy trailer was well designed.
   (one trailer)

But if the adjectives modify different nouns (one expressed and one implied), the determiner is used *before each* adjective.

The expensive and *the* inexpensive gloves arrived today.
   (two kinds of gloves)
We ordered *a* brown, *a* beige, and *a* white carpet.
   (three carpets)

9.   When two nouns joined by *and* refer to a *single* person or thing, use only *one* determiner.

This adding machine and calculator is the newest model.
This programmer and systems analyst is an important person.
The secretary and treasurer of the company is ill.

But if two nouns joined by *and* refer to two different persons or things, the determiner is *repeated* before each noun.

This adding machine and *this* calculator are the newest models.
The programmer and *the* systems analyst are on the second floor.
The secretary and *the* treasurer of the company are ill.

10.   When the two nouns are closely associated and considered to be a unit, only *one* determiner need be used.

We gave him *a* rod and reel.

ASSIGNMENTS

Apply your knowledge of adjective qualities

A. Select the correct word or words from those in parentheses that complete the following sentences. Write your choice in the right-hand column.

1. Our profits are (higher, highest) this year than last. _____
2. Lending policies of banking institutions are usually quite (strict, strictly). _____

3. July 10 was the (hotter, hottest) day of the summer. _____

4. You will receive (farther, further) instruction in the mail. _____
5. Rainfall this year is the (heaviest, heavier, more heavier, most heaviest) in five years. _____
6. My friends are convinced this is the (less effective, least effective) method we have ever tried. _____
7. Joe is the (fatter, fattest) of the two men, but he is the (more active, most active). _____

8. Sally was the (more helpful, most helpful) supervisor I ever had. _____

9. My new home is (farther, further) from our office than the old one was. _____

10. Of all the models, this refrigerator will keep your food (colder, coldest). _____
11. Jim has worked in the accounting department longer than (anyone, anyone else) in the company. _____
12. We sold (less, fewer) memberships this year, as (less, fewer) people attended the conference. _____

13. We will postpone the meeting until (later, latter) in the week. _____
14. John's diagram is (more perfect, most perfect, more nearly perfect, most nearly perfect) than mine. _____

15. Business is slower this month than (any, any other) month this year.   _____

16. If you accept the (later, latter) of the two suggestions, please tell us.   _____

17. My supervisor is (more patient, patienter) than yours.   _____
18. The employee selling the (more, most) merchandise will be given a bonus.   _____

19. There are (less, fewer) stockholders now than there were two years ago.   _____

20. Is the president expected the (later, latter) part of August?   _____

B. For each sentence below, determine the correct comparative degree of the adjective in parentheses, and write it in the space provided.

1. Today's task is (difficult) than yesterday's.   _____

2. Jean is the (good) organizer of the two.   _____

3. No one knows whether coal, oil, or natural gas is the (scarce).   _____

4. Jim and Bob are both smart, but I think Jim is (intelligent).   _____

5. All the buildings were inexpensive, but his building cost the (little).   _____

6. Our bank is paying the (high) interest rate allowed.   _____

7. All our trucks are in poor condition, but #42 is the (bad).   _____

8. Los Angeles is (large) than Boston.   _____

9. Promotions are (easy) to make this year than last year.   _____

10. My desk is the (far) from the water cooler.   _____

11. Our Chicago office is the (modern) of all our offices.   _____

12. Bill Smith is the (enthusiastic) person in the sales department.   _____

13. He is the (known) machinist in the shop.   _____

14. John's report was (accurate) than Jerry's.   _____

15. These three motors are the (efficient) on the market.   _____

16. Fred is (famous) for his writing than any of the other professors.   _____

17. His solution to the problem is (creative), but John's is (unique).   _____

18. Select replacements that are the (troublefree).   _____

19. The president is (considerate) than the administrative assistant.   _____

20. Find the (economical) computer system that will handle our accounting needs.   _____

    C. From your own vocabulary, choose nouns and adjectives to modify the following words.

	Noun modifier	*Adjective*
Example:	*neighborhood* store	*small* store
1.	_____ worker	_____ worker
2.	_____ tools	_____ tools
3.	_____ secretary	_____ secretary
4.	_____ desk	_____ desk
5.	_____ truck	_____ truck

    D. Select the correct pointing or determining words from those in parentheses, and write your choice in the right-hand column.

1. Buy (a, an) orange and brown rug for the office.   _____

2. For safety's sake, you should not wear (that, those) kind of shoes.   _____

3. All employees will be given (a, an) one-month vacation.   _____

4. Preservatives are (a, an) ingredient often found in bakery goods.   _____

5. The history of business is (a, an) interesting subject.   _____

6. You must wear (a, an) clean uniform and (a, an) net cap to work every day.   _____

7. Do you understand why the boss chose (that, those) media?   _____

8. (These, This) persons (is, are) the best promoters of our products.   _____

9. Our sales are at (a, an) all-time high.   _____

10. Please hand me (that, those) scissors.   _____

11. Marian and Wilma are efficient whenever they help (each other, one another).   _____

12. We would like (a, an) honest opinion from each employee.   _____

13. Engineers, accountants, and salespeople depend on (each other, one another) to accomplish a common objective.   _____

14. The four shop apprentices help (each other, one another).   _____

15. We selected (this, these) criteria for judging (a, an) employee for promotion.   _____

16. Harry should have (a, an) x-ray taken of his foot.   _____

17. You should consider this (a, an) unique offer.   _____

18. Fred does not understand (this, these) type of equipment.   _____

19. I know (a, an) reliable plumber who will do the job.   _____

20. When you return, put (them, those) keys back in the drawer.   _____

E. Provide the missing words for these sentences, and underline the sentence elements they connect.

1. Neither Jim _____ Jack could solve the problem.

2. Ask either the supervisor _____ the section head to attend the meeting.

3. _____ proficiency nor efficiency can be accomplished without effort.

4. We must either decide today _____ meet again tomorrow.

5. Some insurance policies cover neither earthquake _____ cyclone damage.

F. In the sentences that follow, you will find some determiners used incorrectly and some that are omitted. Particularly, you may find the word *only* in the wrong position. Write in the sentence the words you add; cross out those used incorrectly; and indicate by an arrow the change in position of *only*. If the sentence is correct as it stands, place a *C* in the column at the right.

1. Tack each picture and poster on the bulletin boards in the production department.   _____

2. Ask both the manager, the supervisor, and the employee to come to my office.   _____

3. A secretary and clerk are necessary employees in this office.   _____

4. The interpreter and printer is an extensively used machine.   _____

5. The president and the chairman is here for the meeting.   _____

6. I thought that Bob was the person attending night classes only.   _____

7. Please buy an new typewriter for every department.   _____

8. We need some blue, yellow, and white paper.   _____

9. We are sending this letter to every public and private school in California. _____

10. I have invited both the vice president and the secretary to attend the meeting. _____

11. We only printed a thousand copies of that booklet. _____

12. Either an 11-inch or 14-inch paper cutter is a good buy. _____

13. The attorney and the ex-congressman, Mr. James Clark, spoke to the employees. _____

14. A black and white magnetic tape is used with this model. _____

15. John only worked four days this week. _____

16. You will receive the blue and the red chair by Thursday. _____

17. The plastic and the metal brace was unpacked this afternoon. _____

18. Mr. Fricker and Miss Nolan will attend the conference only in Washington. _____

19. Bill was our only representative at the conference. _____

20. I am sending you this factual and this interesting paper with my compliments. _____

Name _____

Date _____

PRACTICE WRITING

In this assignment, write sentences using two or more adjectives (not including determiners) to describe the words given below. Use as many adjectives in your sentences as you can, being careful to use them appropriately and with some restraint. Circle all adjectives and enter the total at the bottom of the page.

1. *building* _____

_____

_____

2. *company* _____

_____

_____

3. *supervisor* _____

_____

_____

4. *machine* _____

_____

_____

5. *report* _____

_____

_____

Total adjectives _____

PART 3

Adverbs add color and intensity to the words they modify

Adverbs, like adjectives, are descriptive words that add color and intensity to the action of a sentence. They stimulate and maintain interest in what we say or write. They help the hearer or reader visualize more precisely the idea being communicated.

WHAT IS AN ADVERB?

An *adverb* describes, interprets, or limits any verb form, an adjective, or another adverb. All adverbs, whether *single words, phrases,* or *clauses,* answer the questions *how?, when?, where?, to what degree?,* and *what quality?.*

We will go *immediately* to the bank.

When you go to the bank, pick *up* our last month's statement.

The workers are going *to see their union representative.*

The secretaries decided *in haste* to ask for a longer lunch break.

Most adverbs are formed by adding *ly* to adjectives and participles.

A single-word adverb is usually formed by adding *ly* to adjectives and participles.

Adjectives	Adverbs	Participles	Adverbs
courteous	courteously	convincing	convincingly
definite	definitely	seeming	seemingly
financial	financially	according	accordingly
glad	gladly		
direct	directly		
immediate	immediately		

There are four exceptions to the simple addition of *ly* to an adjective when forming the adverb.

Some adverbs are formed by a change in spelling before the *ly* is added.

1. Adjectives that end with *e* preceded by *l*: drop the *e* and add *y* to form the adverb.

Adjectives	Adverbs
considerable	considerably
possible	possibly
reasonable	reasonably

2. In the following adjectives, which end in *e*, drop the *e* and add *ly* to form the adverb.

Adjectives	Adverbs
due	duly
true	truly
whole	wholly

3. Adjectives ending with *y* preceded by a consonant: change the *y* to *i* and add *ly* to form the adverb.

Adjectives	Adverbs
ready	readily
satisfactory	satisfactorily
unnecessary	unnecessarily

Not all adverbs end with *ly*.

4. Some words that are adverbs do not end in *ly*.

a. Words that are often used as adverbs are *almost, always, ever, fast, here, never, not, now, often, only, seldom, sometime, soon, then, there, today, tomorrow, too, very,* and *yesterday*. Many other words, including nouns, may occasionally be used as adverbs, as illustrated in the sentences below.

The new employees started this *morning.*
The package was delivered last *Thursday.*
The receptionist went *home.*

b. A few words have two adverbial forms. For instance, it is acceptable in some sentences to use *slow* for *slowly, loud* for *loudly.* The usual *ly* ending is always correct, however, and often preferred.

Drive *slow.*   Play *fair.*   Speak *loud.*

c. Adverbs that are identical to prepositions do not have the *ly* ending: *above, across, away, behind, below, down, in, off, over, up,* to name a few.

The disgruntled customer went *away.*
The clerk *often* looked *up.*

d. Words such as *fast, hard, late, far, first, well,* and *loud* may be used as either adverbs or adjectives. Words like *too, how, perhaps,* and *soon* are always adverbs. Check how a word is used to determine its part of speech.

Douglas works *harder* than the other salesman.
    (*harder* used as an adverb to modify **works**)
Of the two salesmen Douglas is the *harder* worker.
    (*harder* used as an adjective to modify *worker*)
Please count the parts *faster.*
    (*faster* used as an adverb to modify the verb **count**)

Mr. Humphrey gave a *faster* answer than Mr. Jones.
(faster used as an adjective to modify the noun answer)

e.   A conjunctive adverb may serve as a connector to show the relationship of one idea to another. The commonly used conjunctive adverbs are the following:

accordingly	likewise	otherwise
consequently	moreover	then
hence	nevertheless	therefore
however	notwithstanding	thus

Note: When a conjunctive adverb is used as a connector between two independent clauses, a *semicolon* is placed before it.

The meeting adjourned at 1:30 p.m.; *consequently,* the officers missed the luncheon.

He expects to support the recommendation; *however,* he plans to study the situation first.

Conjunctive adverbs may also be used as simple adverbs to modify adjectives, or they may be used parenthetically.

The personnel manager plans to counsel Mr. Smithers *however* long it might take.
     (simple adverb *however* modifies the adjective *long*)
The budget, *however,* will not be discussed at the meeting.
     (parenthetical)
You should, *therefore,* speak to Mr. Phillips about the matter.
     (parenthetical)

WHAT MAY AN ADVERB DO?

Adverbs may modify verbs, adjectives, and other adverbs.

An adverb may modify a *verb,*

By placing the data in the computer, we *quickly* found the answer.

an *adjective,*

She is an *exceedingly* competent stenographer.

and another *adverb.*

He finished assembling the parts *very rapidly.*

As explained in the discussion of adjectives, to achieve clarity a modifier should be placed as close as possible to the word it modifies. Changing the position of an adverb can change the meaning of a sentence.

Clearly Mr. McAdams is able to read it.
Mr. McAdams is able to read it *clearly.*

Place an adverb that modifies a verb in the position that accurately conveys your message. When the adverb modifies an adjective or another adverb, however, place it as close as possible to that word.

Adverbs may compare.

Adverbs permit three degrees of comparison. The rules for the comparative and superlative forms of the adverb are the same as those for adjectives.

Positive	Comparative	Superlative
efficiently	more efficiently	most efficiently
clearly	more clearly	most clearly
well	better	best
thoughtfully	less thoughtfully	least thoughtfully
hard	harder	hardest
soon	sooner	soonest

The following sentences illustrate the use of adverbs in the comparative and the superlative degrees.

John types *more efficiently* than he used to.

Of the three bookkeepers, Mr. Emparo *most clearly* explains the profit and loss statement.

Some adverbs cannot be compared because they already express the exact condition, for instance *entirely, perfectly, completely,* and *never.*

Adverbs may be troublesome.

Scarcely, only, hardly, but, and *never* are negative in meaning; consequently, be careful to use them alone to avoid a *double* negative.

She mentioned that she *scarcely* had time to finish.
(**Not:** . . . that she hadn't scarcely time to finish.)

Fred has *never* before operated the lathe.
(**Not:** . . . has not never or hasn't never . . .)

Good is an adjective; *well,* an adverb. When *well* refers to health, it is classified as an adjective.

           adj   adv
Henry is a *good* packer, but Norman handles all tasks *well.*

                  adj
She did not feel *well* and left early.

Very is an adverb that modifies only an adjective or another adverb. Never use *real* (an adjective) when you mean *very* or need an adverb.

He drove *very* rapidly through traffic.

A mimeograph machine is *very* heavy.

He is *very* conscientious.

Very loses its power to intensify an adjective or another adverb if used too often, so use it sparingly.

Sometime is an adverb that refers to a time not specified or definitely known.

The company may set up a bonus program *sometime.*
(*Sometime* modifies the verb **set**.)

Sometimes means *now* and *then* or *not always.*

Sometimes the employees go bowling after work.
(*Sometimes* modifies the verb **go**.)

Some time (two words) should be used when talking about an indefinite period, usually past or present.

Some time ago I asked for a new typewriter.
(*Some time* modifies the verb **asked**.)

Also, the noun *time* may be modified by the adjective *some* as in the following sentence.

He expects to put in *some time* on the problem tomorrow.
(time object of preposition *in)*

Somewhat used as an adverb means *in some degree.* Do not use *kind of* or *sort of* when the adverb *somewhat* should be used.

We were *somewhat* bored.
(**Not:** We were kind of bored.)

Test your skill in forming and spelling adverbs.

Your spelling review for this section is to learn (memorize, if necessary) the four rules for forming adverbs. (See pages 268–69.) Do this review before you complete the assignments.

Some people have trouble spelling adverbs because they are uncertain of the adjective form of the word. Here are a few troublesome words. For each word below, decide first if it may be used as an adjective in its present form. If it cannot be, change it to an adjective; then write the adverb form. If the word is already an adjective, merely change it to an adverb.

1. public _____
2. incidental _____
3. unusual _____
4. accident _____
5. basic _____
6. occasion _____
7. apparent _____
8. mutual _____
9. respectable _____
10. radical _____
11. adverse _____
12. casual _____
13. logical _____
14. agreeable _____
15. condition _____
16. desire _____
17. favor _____

18.   capable   _____

19.   terrible   _____

20.   necessary   _____

Practice spelling both the adjective and the adverb forms of these words, so that you will have confidence in your ability to use them correctly.

Apply your knowledge of adverbs

A. The following sentences contain underlined adverbs. Write the word that the adverb modifies on the line following the sentence.

*Word modified
by the adverb*

Example: Our work has been <u>noticeably</u> lighter during the past month. ___*lighter*___

1. The <u>unusually</u> large crate of supplies arrived by truck. _____

2. His leaving <u>immediately</u> for the airport will assure his catching the plane. _____

3. We are <u>extremely</u> sorry to hear of your loss. _____

4. I am calling <u>to let you know that your order has been received.</u> _____

5. This desk is priced <u>considerably below the retail price.</u> _____

_____

6. The supervisor greeted them <u>cordially.</u> _____

7. The new delivery trucks run <u>quietly</u> and <u>smoothly.</u> _____

_____

8. Mr. Schmidt agreed to meet me <u>promptly.</u> _____

9. <u>Quickly</u> walking to the door, Mr. Quincy opened it and entered. _____

10. <u>Sometimes</u> we send flowers to fellow workers in the hospital. _____

11. Before you go to St. Louis, telephone the hotel for a reservation.   _____

12. We will discount those machines if they are not sold by next month.   _____

13. Slowly the ambulance door closed behind me.   _____
14. This widely known management book has been read by many of
our staff members.   _____

15. The orders came entirely from friends.   _____

16. Place the box under the table.   _____
17. More than one hundred million people own stock in corporations,
directly or indirectly.   _____

18. The brochure was attractively designed.   _____

19. The room has been specially arranged for the conference.   _____
20. He almost missed that question because he
did not read the letter carefully.   _____

_____

B.   Adverbs are usually formed by adding *ly* to the adjective or participle. There are also a few exceptions with which you should be familiar. Write the adverb for each of the adjectives and participles listed below. In numbers 1, 2, 6, and 9, write the adverbs in the comparative degree; and in numbers 11, 16, 18, and 19, write them in the superlative degree. (See pages 269–70.)

1. able   _____   11. effective   _____

2. like   _____   12. true   _____

3. functional   _____   13. uneasy   _____

4. possible   _____   14. general   _____

5. heated   _____   15. bad   _____

6. satisfactory   _____   16. favorable   _____

7. active   _____   17. month   _____

8. faithful   _____   18. becoming   _____

9. excessive   _____   19. essential   _____

10. arbitrary   _____   20. animated   _____

C.   Select the correct word in parentheses and circle it.

1. He functions (good, well) as department chairman.

2. (Some time, Sometime, Sometimes) will be spent on developing the new product.

3. Mr. Winters brought the supervisors (altogether, all together).

4. He now must walk (farther, further) to get to work than he did last month.

5. Miss Terry types statistical tables (more accurate, more accurately) than Miss Brown does.

6. The visitor was (almost, mostly) two hours late.

7. The steel desk is (real, very) heavy.

8. Please type the paper (more exactly, exactly) to specifications.

9. Is there any (real, very) reason why he should be promoted?

10. The doctor was here (scarcely, not scarcely) an hour ago.

11. I told him to pay me (direct, directly).

12. We (could, couldn't) hardly believe the outcome.

13. How are you feeling today? Very (good, well), thank you.

14. The office looks (good, well) after being painted.

15. Do you like the new catalog? Yes, it is very (good, well).

D.   Adverbs may function as *connectors* between independent clauses or between dependent and independent clauses. Because of this function, sentences require punctuation to show the relationship of the clauses to each other. Punctuate the following sentences according to the rules discussed and illustrated in this and previous sections.

1. If I am elected president I shall act quickly to complete the new building.

2. The meeting however attracted many participants.

3. These figures appear correct nevertheless you should check them again.

4. The auditors are coming tomorrow consequently the bank will be closed.

5. If you will ask Helen for a copy you will subsequently receive one from the library.

6. When a new customer places a large order we frequently ask for payment in advance.

7. Our company's contribution to the fund drive therefore will be increased.

8. When you complete that report please go to the bank.

9. Although we were tired we worked until the job was finished.

10. Businesses are finding it difficult to move merchandise hence they are holding more sales than usual.

11. The workers complained bitterly obviously they were disappointed.

12. I will collect the money however difficult it may be.

13. Next week I shall be in San Francisco however we should arrange to keep in touch by telephone.

14. Although she knew it would cause problems she agreed to accept their plan.

15. The checks should be mailed today therefore please type envelopes for them.

Name _____

Date _____

PRACTICE WRITING

In this exercise you have an opportunity to compose interesting sentences containing adverbs. Follow the instructions given below.

1. Use an adverb to modify a verb. _____

_____

2. Use an adverb to modify an adjective. _____

_____

3. Use an adverb to modify another adverb. _____

_____

4. Use an adverb that does not end in *ly* or *ily*. _____

_____

5. Use a conjunctive adverb as a connector. _____

_____

6. Use an adverb in either comparative or superlative degree. _____

_____

_____

7. Use a negative adverb. _____

_____

8. Use an adverbial noun. _____

_____

9. Use an introductory adverb phrase. _____

_____

10. Use an introductory adverb clause. _____

_____

PART **4**

Prepositions serve as connectors between words

The function of the preposition is to serve as a connector between words. The preposition shows the relationship of its noun or pronoun object to some other word in the sentence. The word group it forms is called a *prepositional phrase*. This word group is composed of the preposition, the object, and modifiers of the object. You first learned about prepositional phrases in the section on sentences, and you also studied them in the section on modifiers. As you learned there, prepositional phrases function as adjectives and as adverbs.

The object of a preposition is always a noun, a pronoun, or a clause that functions as a noun. As you remember from the section on pronouns, all pronoun objects must be in the *objective case (me, us; you; him, her, it, them; whom)*. Noun or pronoun objects may be modified by adjectives or possessive pronouns. The prepositional phrase itself can modify almost any word in the sentence. In other words, it may be either an adjective or an adverb phrase.

Read the following sentence:

Most people are aware *of* the importance *of* business *in* our whole economic structure.

This sentence contains three prepositional phrases. The relationship of these three phrases to other words in the sentence is indicated by the following diagram. As you can see, *aware* is an adjective complement modifying *people*.

Most people are aware

of the importance *(adverb phrase)*

of business *(adjective phrase)*

in our whole economic structure. *(adjective phrase)*

Pronoun objects of prepositions are in the objective case.

Here are some examples of *objective case* pronouns as objects of prepositions.

Please give the money *to* John and *me*.

277

Send the letter *to me.*
Did you receive the telegram *from them?*
The file *behind her* is open.
Whom did you hear *from?*
Whom are the reports really *for?*

Objects of prepositions may be noun clauses.

The object of a preposition may also be a dependent clause used as a noun. In the following sentence, the *whoever/whomever* clause, which is the object of the preposition *to,* needs to be rearranged before you know which case to use.

Please give the report to (*whoever/whomever* you wish).

Rearranged, the noun clause reads, *you wish whoever/whomever.* You can see that the verb **wish** takes an object and that the objective case *whomever* is the correct choice.

Please give the report *to whomever you wish.*

Note that in the first sentence given below the correct choice is *whoever* because it is the subject of the clause (nominative case).

Send it *to whoever asks for it.*

In the following sentence, on the other hand, the choice is *whomever* because it is the object of the verb *choose.*

You may assign the job *to whomever you choose.*

Prepositions show relationships.

In the following illustrations, notice how prepositions show a logical connection to the words that the phrases modify.

The letter was *in* the drawer.
                 on the desk.
                 behind the file.
                 at the printer.
                 beneath the blotter.
                 near the pen.

Study these relationships by which prepositions connect words and ideas. When you wish to show *position, direction,* or *time,* choose the preposition that indicates the precise relationship you want.

Position		**Direction**	
in	in the drawer	**to**	to the store
on	on the table	**from**	from the man
by	by her side	**toward**	toward the car
under	under the tree	**down**	down the street
above	above the water	**up**	up the stairs
beside	beside the radio	**at**	at the window
across	across the street	**through**	through the doorway
against	against the wall		
inside	inside the house		
near	near the door		

Time		Miscellaneous	
before	before Tuesday	**of**	of importance
after	after the show	**for**	for me
during	during lunch	**about**	about securities
until	until noon	**with**	with illustrations
within	within ten days	**except**	except Ed and Jim
since	since 1978		

Prepositions can be word groups.

Some prepositions are made up of two or more words—the whole unit is the preposition. A few of these prepositions are listed below with examples of their usage.

Preposition	Phrase
according to	according to plan
apart from	apart from the others
as far as	as far as possible
as to	as to costs
by way of	by way of Chicago
instead of	instead of the original
in accordance with	in accordance with our agreement
in addition to	in addition to the report
in lieu of	in lieu of a balance sheet
in place of	in place of Mr. Jones
in regard to	in regard to expense accounts
in spite of	in spite of minor difficulties
on account of	on account of rising costs
with regard to	with regard to circumstances

Prepositions can be left out.

Often a better sentence results when you omit the preposition, as illustrated in the sentence below.

Weak: Where is the typewriter *at?*

Better: Where is the typewriter?

At is merely tacked on and has no object to make up a prepositional phrase.

In other sentences, the flow of words is smoother when the noun or pronoun is placed before the object as an *indirect object*. The indirect object could be used as the object of a preposition, but notice below how the sentence is improved when the preposition *to* is omitted.

Correct: The secretary gave the report to *him.*

Better: The secretary gave *him* the report.

Prepositions at ends of sentences should be avoided, if possible.

Modern usage occasionally allows a sentence to end with a preposition. You may place it at the end of a sentence to lend emphasis and fluency. Many people, however, prefer that the sentence end in a word other than a preposition. Overuse of this construction calls attention to a grammar usage that is in transition. You should try, therefore, to reword a sentence that ends in a preposition.

Weak: *Whom* are you coming to the party *with?*

Better: *With whom* are you coming to the party?

> **Weak:**   He was a man that everyone had trouble *with*.
> **Better:**   He was a man *with whom* everyone had trouble.

End sentences with a preposition only when you wish to emphasize or avoid an awkward expression. Remember that sentences ending with a noun or verb are more effective than those ending with structure words.

> What are you calling me *about?*
> What were you thinking *of?*
> Show me what this file is *for.*
> Be careful which car you get *behind.*
> What letter was his folder filed *under?*

Prepositions should be logically joined to other sentence elements.

The meaning you wish to express will determine your choice of preposition. Some prepositions are commonly misused and confuse the logical joining of the other sentence elements. Some of the troublesome ones are discussed below.

From is used after *different* or *differently*.

> The plan worked *differently from* our expectations.
> The new machine has parts that are *different from* those in the previous model.

All of and *both of* must be followed by a pronoun.

> *All of them* will be paid on Friday.
> *Both of them* are to be returned.

At indicates position; *to* indicates motion or direction toward something.

> The officers were *at* the convention all day.
> The officers went *to* the meeting this morning.

Between is used with *two; among* with *three or more*.

> He divided his work *between* John and me.
> The samples were distributed *among* the staff.

Beside means *by the side of* or *next to; besides* means *in addition to*.

> The desk was placed *beside* the file.
> Is anyone planning to attend *besides* you?

In is used for place or position; *into,* for movement from one place to another.

> The letter is *in* the desk drawer.
> Please put the letter *into* the desk drawer.

Of, off. Never use *of* when you mean *have.* Never use *off* when you mean *from.* Never use *off of.*

> She *could have been* more careful with erasures.
>   (**Not:** . . . could of been . . .)
> He borrowed the book *from* his friend.
>   (**Not:** . . . off of . . .)
> His dictionary fell *off* the shelf.
>   (**Not:** . . . off of . . .)

To is the preposition. *Too* is used as an adverb to mean *also* or *more than enough. Two* is the numeral 2.

> Please go *to* the store and buy *two* reams of paper.
> The supervisor, *too,* felt Mary typed *too* many carbons.

Accept is a verb that means *to receive; except* is a preposition that means *to exclude.*

> Please *accept* my thanks.
> They were all going to the meeting *except* Mr. Brown.

Like is a preposition.

> Please make a model *like* this one.
> It looks *like* rain.

Per is used only before Latin nouns or weights and measures.

> What is our cost *per* capita?
> The ore assayed at $30 *per* ton.
> The interest was 5% *per* annum.

Note: Avoid the use of *per* before English words other than accepted scientific terms.

See Appendix 3, page 424, for a list of words used with specific prepositions.

Remember these points about prepositions.

Prepositions are fairly easy to use, but you should review these points in order to become a skilled communicator.

1. Prepositions are connectors that join an object and its modifiers into a phrase that, in turn, modifies some word in the sentence. These phrases add interesting, descriptive, and specific information to the message.
2. The object of a preposition is always a noun, a pronoun, or a clause used as a noun.
3. The pronoun object must always be in the objective case.
4. The preposition chosen should indicate the exact relationship wanted—position, direction, or time.
5. Some prepositions are made up of two or more words, such as *according to, in addition to,* and *on account of.* Try to use them to show an important relationship.
6. Prepositions may end sentences for emphasis or to avoid awkward expressions. At other times, reword the sentence to place the prepositional phrase within the sentence.

Continue to add words to your usable vocabulary.

In Appendix 1, pages 418–20, you will find 500 words that are used in business. If you could add all these words to your usable vocabulary, you would possess an asset that will assure you success in business. When speaking of a usable vocabulary, we mean one that contains words you can define, spell, and use correctly.

Spend time from now on reviewing the words in Appendix 1. Look up definitions, practice pronunciation, learn the spelling, and use the words in conversation and written work. Here are 20 words picked at random for you to review right now. Assignment E, page 285, is a worksheet on which you can write the definition, pronunciation, and spelling of each word.

1. abundance
2. acknowledgment
3. advertisement
4. analyzing
5. appointment
6. behavior
7. believable
8. bulletin
9. cancellation
10. chargeable
11. collateral
12. commodities
13. conscientious
14. correspondence
15. deductible
16. delinquent
17. guarantee
18. maintenance
19. permissible
20. reimbursement

PART 4

ASSIGNMENTS

Apply your knowledge of prepositions in sentences

A. Underscore the correct word or words shown in parentheses.

1. (Beside, Besides) being a good teacher, the new professor has a pleasing personality.
2. The salary increase for cost of living may be as much as $50 (a, per) month.
3. The carpenter fell (off, off of) the roof.
4. The president's office is (beside, besides) the vice president's.
5. (Among, Between) my fellow workers, few are outstanding.
6. Will this proposal be worked out differently (than, from) the preceding one?
7. (To, Too, Two) a great extent, your job satisfaction will depend (on, upon) your fellow workers.
8. The new manager looks (like, as) the former one (except, accept) that she wears more stylish clothes.
9. Many contracts are made verbally (between, among) employer and employee.
10. (To, Too, Two) (who, whom) you address your remarks depends upon the nature of your complaint.
11. Do you expect the new president to be much different (from, than) the old one?
12. From the standpoint of good judgment (all, all of them) were responsible.
13. All the trustees are eligible to vote (accept, except) Mr. Johnson.
14. The office manager was (at, to) the board of directors meeting this morning.
15. (All, All of) you should plan to be here in the morning.
16. The visitor borrowed a pen (off of, from) the receptionist.
17. (All of, All) the books are to be sold at auction.
18. The sofa is (at, into) the shop for repair.
19. I saw the clerk go (in, into) the stockroom.
20. Did you see a picture (as, like) this one for sale?

B. The following copy contains 17 prepositions. Identify them by underlining each one.

1. The use of company or subsidiary funds or assets for any unlawful or improper purpose is
2. strictly prohibited. The company's policy is to be in compliance with all laws and regulations
3. that are applicable to its business—at all governmental levels in the United States and in

4. foreign countries. In some instances the laws and regulations may be ambiguous. In all cases,
5. however, management has access to legal advice throughout the company's operations, and
6. management should seek such legal advice as is necessary for compliance with the company's
7. policy of observance of all laws and of all regulations.

   C.   In the following sentences, underline the correct pronoun (from those in parentheses) that is the object of the preposition preceding it.

1. The committee will have to choose between (he, him) and (she, her) for the position.
2. We should wait a reasonable time for (they, them) to accept our offer.
3. Did you receive a check from (they, them)?
4. To (who, whom) did you make the long-distance call?
5. My assistant is the person upon (who, whom) I must depend.
6. The accountant sat between John Shelton and (I, me) at the meeting.
7. Several hundred people will be there besides (we, us).
8. You are indebted to (who, whom)?
9. Everyone attended the union meeting except you and (I, me).
10. There will always be problems for (she, her) to solve.
11. The telegram was sent by H. H. Leonards, Inc., and (they, them).
12. It is all right with (I, me) if you leave early.
13. The samples were distributed among (we, us) by (she, her).
14. They differ on (who, whom) should be chosen for the job.
15. We have been corresponding with (them, they) for a long time.
16. Mr. Jones is an authority in (it, its).
17. What did he demand from (we, us) in payment?
18. He seemed to be against (he, him) for the position.
19. The car came toward (I, me) at high speed.
20. They sat near (we, us) at the convention.

   D.   Some words are used with a particular preposition. The following practice will test your ability to select the correct preposition to convey your exact meaning. Check your answers with the list of words in Appendix 3, page 424.

1. The annual report was adequate _____ the company's needs.

2. The officers agree in principle _____ the demands of the president.

3. Most companies will demand payment _____ customers in 30 days.

4. My friend was annoyed _____ the interruptions.

5. Mr. Fisher set the policy and it applies _____ all offices.

6. He assures us each will comply _____ the policy.

7. Recently received information indicates money was paid _____ large amounts.

8. In all respects the police orders will be followed _____ full cooperation.

9. Please advise him _____ his rights.

10. Mr. Orr agrees _____ our decision to hire another engineer.

11. The employees are encouraged _____ participate in the program.

12. Each employee should discuss the policy _____ the supervisor.

13. You must comply _____ the company's sick leave regulations.

14. Were the members influenced _____ the decision of the president?

15. You are accountable _____ your employer for office supplies.

16. What did he demand _____ them in return?

17. The new employee will be transferred _____ the sales department next Tuesday.

18. The amount will be excluded _____ the monthly sales figures.

19. Did you furnish us _____ your previous employment record?

20. There is a discrepancy _____ your figures.

   E. This exercise will assist you to add to your usable vocabulary the 20 words from Appendix 1 that are listed on page 282. Take time to look each one up in the dictionary, even though you know what the word means in a general sense. You may find several definitions that will allow you to use the word more precisely.

	Definition	*Pronunciation*	*Spelling*
abundance	_____	_____	_____
	_____		
	_____		
acknowledgment	_____	_____	_____
	_____		
	_____		
advertisement	_____	_____	_____
	_____		
	_____		
analyzing	_____	_____	_____
	_____		
	_____		

	Definition	*Pronunciation*	*Spelling*
appointment			
behavior			
believable			
bulletin			
cancellation			
chargeable			
collateral			
commodities			

	Definition	Pronunciation	Spelling
conscientious	_____	_____	_____
	_____		
	_____		
correspondence	_____	_____	_____
	_____		
	_____		
deductible	_____	_____	_____
	_____		
	_____		
delinquent	_____	_____	_____
	_____		
	_____		
guarantee	_____	_____	_____
	_____		
	_____		
maintenance	_____	_____	_____
	_____		
	_____		
permissible	_____	_____	_____
	_____		
	_____		
reimbursement	_____	_____	_____
	_____		
	_____		

Name _____

Date _____

————— PRACTICE WRITING —————

You have probably noticed that you use at least one preposition in most sentences you write. Because these words are needed so often, develop skill to show precise relationships in composing the following sentences.

1. Use a preposition to show direction. _____

_____

2. Use a preposition to show position. _____

_____

3. Use a preposition to indicate time. _____

_____

4. Use a word-group preposition. _____

_____

5. Use *in spite of* in a sentence. _____

_____

6. Use *in addition to* in a sentence. _____

_____

7. Use *all of* in a sentence. _____

_____

8. Use *like* as a preposition in a sentence. _____

_____

9. Use *toward* in a sentence. _____

_____

10. Use *among* in a sentence. _____

_____

Punctuation of sentences

Punctuation is important for clarity.

Punctuation is more than a mechanical device. It is an important part of written composition because it adds expression and meaning to your writing. You have learned, in your study of the sentence, how punctuation makes your writing clearer to the intended reader. While there are generally accepted guidelines that govern the use of the various marks of punctuation, your common sense in the use of punctuation is also important.

The use of punctuation in writing is a development of the past three or four hundred years, although writing is thousands of years old. Punctuation came into use in the Middle Ages as priests and preachers marked their manuscripts for pause and emphasis to be used as they delivered their sermons. Their marks, combinations of squiggles and dots, were cast into type by the early printers and eventually became our commas, semicolons, periods, and other marks.

Rules fit most applications; but at times punctuation is a matter of personal taste, style, or understanding. Think of punctuation as an aid to clear and orderly sentence structure. On the other hand, poorly constructed sentences will not be made clearer by any number of punctuation marks. If you understand the sentence patterns studied in Section 1, you should be able to punctuate correctly.

Knowledge of the role of punctuation in effective writing will increase as you study the material in this section. Periods, exclamation points, and question marks are presented in Part 1. The internal marks of punctuation in sentences—commas, semicolons, colons, and dashes—are discussed in Parts 2 and 3. Miscellaneous marks—parentheses, quotation marks, the apostrophe, ellipses, and italics—are presented in Part 4.

Periods, exclamation points, and question marks have many uses

Periods are used at the end of certain sentences.

All statements, ordinary commands, requests, and indirect questions end with a period.

With statements

Your shipment will be made Friday.

The program will be ready tomorrow.

With commands

Bring the letters to my office.

Send the customer a check.

With requests

May I have your attention.

Please lend me your pen.

With indirect questions

The manager asked the clerk if the letter had been mailed.

My friend asked me whether you were going with us.

Occasionally, a fragment—usually an answer to a question—is used in business writing, such as advertisements or announcements. Most fragments end with a period, but question marks or exclamation marks may be appropriate.

Yes, tomorrow.	Where?
Frankly, no. (or !)	Help!
In my office.	For me? (or .)

Periods are used with abbreviations.

Periods follow most abbreviations. In Section 8 there is a detailed discussion of abbreviations and their punctuation and capitalization. Appendix 2 has several lists of commonly used abbreviations.

a.m., p.m.	addl.	Co.
Jan.	recd.	Corp.
Nov.	misc.	c.o.d.'s

Letters designating government agencies or any well-known organization usually do not require punctuation. The letters, however, are capitalized. No periods are used with the capitalized two-letter state abbreviations authorized for use with ZIP codes.

SEC	UCLA	NY
NBC	AFT	KS

The following sentences have abbreviations that require periods. Notice that the period in an abbreviation at the end of a sentence is also the end-of-sentence mark.

Mr. Alan Crump, Sr., was awarded an honorary degree.

Dr. Albert Katz performs surgeries on the heart.

We will meet at 12:45 p.m.

Please ship the order f.o.b.

Periods are used with figures and sums of money.

See Section 8 for a more detailed discussion of the use of periods with numbers.

A *12.5* percent increase in production is expected in the second quarter.

One millimeter is equal to *0.001* meter.

Our newest toy costs *$12.50* wholesale.

Periods are used in enumerations.

The number or letter in an enumeration is usually followed by a period. The first word of each item in an enumeration is capitalized, but no period is placed after the item unless it is a complete sentence.

<table>
<tr><td colspan="2" align="center">Lists</td><td colspan="2" align="center">Outlines</td></tr>
<tr><td colspan="2">Please send me the following:</td><td>I.</td><td></td></tr>
<tr><td>1.</td><td>A copy of the by-laws</td><td>A.</td><td></td></tr>
<tr><td>2.</td><td>A list of members</td><td></td><td>1.</td></tr>
<tr><td>3.</td><td>The year's calendar of events</td><td></td><td>2.</td></tr>
<tr><td colspan="2"></td><td></td><td>a.</td></tr>
<tr><td colspan="2">Here are my suggestions:</td><td></td><td>b.</td></tr>
<tr><td>1.</td><td>Collect all facts</td><td></td><td>(1)</td></tr>
<tr><td>2.</td><td>Isolate the important ones</td><td></td><td>(2)</td></tr>
<tr><td>3.</td><td>Interview each member of the staff for additional information</td><td>B.</td><td>1.
2.</td></tr>
<tr><td colspan="2"></td><td>II.</td><td></td></tr>
<tr><td colspan="2"></td><td>A.</td><td></td></tr>
</table>

Exclamation points follow words and sentences that show strong emotion.

The exclamation point (!) is used to express strong emotion, urgent commands, and various degrees of surprise. It may be placed at any position in a sentence and does not require other punctuation. *For mild exclamations,* use a comma or a period.

Mild: Oh, what a house.

Stronger: Oh! What a house!

Question form: How can you lose!

Who knows, it may turn out well!

Emotion: The building's on fire!

Congress declared war!

Ejaculations: Call a doctor!

It can't be true!

Remarkable! Stop!

Question marks follow words and sentences that ask questions requiring an answer.

The question mark (**?**) is usually an end-of-sentence punctuation mark. It should not be used in addition to a period except following an abbreviation at the end of a sentence. Familiarize yourself with the use of question marks in these situations.

Direct questions

Where are you going?

Who is the personnel director?

Indirect questions.   Omit the question mark when the sentence does not require an answer.

He asked if you could go.

But who knows what he will do next.

This question would be more emphatic if the question mark were used.

But who knows what he will do next?

Quoted questions.   If a quotation is a question, place the question mark inside the quotation marks.

The employer asked, "Why aren't you working?"

Following the period after an abbreviation at the end of a sentence.

Are you sending the coat c.o.d.?

To indicate doubt (in parentheses).

The artist was born in 1850 (**?**) in Venice.

For a series of questions within a sentence.

Are the principal teams of participants made up of boys? of girls? of both?

ASSIGNMENTS

Apply your knowledge of periods, exclamation points, and question marks

A. Supply periods, question marks, and exclamation marks where required in the following sentences.

1. Alan Singleton is my neighbor
2. He asked me whether you were coming for lunch
3. Give the report to your supervisor
4. My What a game
5. Where are you going
6. Henry Jones, Jr is my friend
7. Call the police I've been robbed
8. Will you send it cod
9. Is she going to become our new manager
10. Please bring me the latest annual report
11. When will the SEC look into the matter
12. Richard D Irwin, Inc is the publisher of this book
13. All MDs should know about nutrition
14. The committee will meet at 10 am tomorrow
15. Run for your lives It's a fire
16. Are the runners from California Utah Oregon or all three
17. Where is your jacket
18. Stop tormenting your brother
19. May we have your check today
20. Tell your friend to meet me at 2:30 pm

B. In this exercise write each word or abbreviation in the sentence that should be followed by end-of-sentence punctuation and place the punctuation after the word.

Example: Are the workers out to lunch   _lunch ?_

1. Help I'm hurt   _____

2.   Is your accountant a CPA   _____

3.   She asked whether she should call the typewriter repair company   _____

4.   How many times must I tell you   _____

5.   We sent the report today   _____

6.   Will you please give Virginia the memorandum   _____

7.   Drop what you are doing, immediately   _____

8.   Who repaired your car   _____

9.   The garden needs attention   _____

10. I asked, "Why aren't you going to school"   _____

11. Are the workers ready to go   _____

12. "Help" he shouted, "The fire is out of control"   _____

13. He inquired whether he should get the motor fixed   _____

14. Did you ask Harold O. Jones, Jr   _____

15. Mrs. Fisher seems to know all the routines, doesn't she   _____

16. He asked how many of us wanted to work overtime   _____

17. "Don't be late," yelled the manager   _____

18. The machine cost more than $500.50   _____

19. Is your appointment for 2:45 pm   _____

20. The best colors are these: blue, tan, and green   _____

C.   Set up the following material in outline form.

I, A, 1, a, b, 2, a, b, c, B, 1, 2, a, b, 3, a, b, c, II, A, 1, 2, 3, a, (1), (2), b, (1), (2), 4, B, 1, 2, III, A, 1, a, b, (1), (a), (b), (2), (3), 2, B.

Commas help make messages clear

Punctuation is more than a mechanical problem. You must consider the meaning you wish to convey when punctuating sentences. Emphasizing and highlighting your meaning are important parts of the thinking you must do when you write. Basic rules are important, but creativity in writing requires more than following rules of punctuation blindly.

Internal marks used in sentences are the following: commas, semicolons, colons, and dashes. Let us look first at the comma, the most frequently used internal mark of punctuation.

Use commas in compound sentences.

A compound sentence is made up of two or more independent clauses joined by one of the coordinate conjunctions *and, but, or, nor, so,* and *for.* Use a comma to separate these independent clauses, unless they are short clauses.

> The vice president will be in to see us today, but she will not stay for lunch.

Note that there is a subject and verb in each clause in the compound sentence above and that the clauses are joined by the conjunction *but.* A comma is generally used before the conjunction because it makes the sentence easier to read.

In the first sentence given below, the subject is omitted in the second clause. The omitted subject is understood to be *Mr. Jones* or *he.* This construction avoids the repetition of the subject. Therefore, no comma is used before the conjunction. If, however, the subject *he* is used, a comma is needed.

> Mr. Jones, the president, expects high-quality work and plans to check each employee carefully.

> Mr. Jones expects high-quality work, and *he* plans to check each employee carefully.

Compound sentences may be misread if the comma is omitted. If such sentences are short, however, the commas are generally omitted as the reader can find the way without them.

You spoke and I answered.
   (short—use no comma)
Our team looked rather slow yesterday, but our opponent was slower.
   (long—use a comma)

A sentence with a compound verb may be mistaken for a compound sentence. In the following sentence there is no subject after the conjunction. It is, therefore, not a compound sentence and no comma is necessary.

Her fellow workers *liked* her and *praised* her friendly manner.

The sentence may easily be changed to a compound sentence by the addition of a subject after the conjunction *and*. A comma is then necessary.

Her fellow workers liked her, and they praised her friendly manner.

In compound sentences where the verb in both independent clauses is the same, the second verb may be replaced by a comma indicating its omission. This construction adds variety to business writing.

The robes are $62 a dozen; the gowns, $43 a dozen.

Use commas after introductory expressions.

Sentences are often introduced by adverbial modifiers—words, phrases, or clauses. Such expressions may give writing greater variety or emphasis. You must decide whether or not to use a comma in situations similar to those given below. Keep in mind your main objective—to make meaning clear.

Introductory words.   Use a comma after an introductory adverb if you wish to give it emphasis or attract more attention. The comma helps the reader grasp the meaning of the adverb.

Lately, I've been working overtime.
Finally, we reached home.

Use a comma after an introductory expression used as a connector, such as *therefore, however, accordingly, of course,* and *after all.*

After all, I am a senior accountant.
Accordingly, I shall see you as planned.
Of course, we will go to the business show.

Short introductory phrases.   Again, the degree of emphasis desired gives you the clue. Use a comma after introductory phrases to gain more attention.

Emphasis: For a president, John Jones was exceedingly friendly.

Less emphasis: For a president John Jones was exceedingly friendly.

Introductory phrases that state time or place are usually not followed by commas.

On Wednesday the teaching assistants will meet with the dean.
At Los Angeles the Angels will play the Dodgers in the Southern California series.

Always use a comma after an introductory phrase *if* the sentence could be misread without it. If the introductory phrase contains a verb, it is usually set off by a comma.

Unclear: To help the accountant provided some information.

The sentence above, without a comma, could be misread.

Clear: To help, the accountant provided some information.

Long introductory phrases.   A comma is usually essential after a long introductory phrase to help the reader grasp the full meaning of the main statement.

For a man with two jobs, he was unusually efficient.

Introductory dependent clauses.   Use a comma after an introductory dependent clause that precedes the main clause. If the dependent clause appears at the end of the sentence, a comma is usually unnecessary.

When the new evidence was introduced, the judge reversed his decision.

The judge reversed his decision *when the new evidence was introduced.*

If you are a good person, you will drop the case.

You will drop the case *if you are a good person.*

Use commas in a series.   Commas are used in sentences to separate a series (three or more) of words, phrases, or clauses that follow one after another in parallel form.

A series of words.

Jones, Schmidt, and *Bergstrom* are accountants.

If you write "Jones and Bergstrom are accountants," no commas are necessary because there are only two in the series.

The treasurer was *thoughtful, constructive,* and *encouraging* about my proposal.

He considered it *practical, thorough,* and *detailed* enough for his use.

A series of phrases.

The coal dust was *on our desks, in our clothes,* and *in our hair.*

If you write "The coal dust was on our desks and in our clothes," no comma is necessary because there are only two phrases.

The value of the employee to the employer was exhibited *by devotion to duty, by loyalty to the firm,* and *by outstanding poise and tactfulness.*

Painting the frame, polishing the glass, and *hanging the picture* were his tasks for the morning.

Mrs. Smith *went to the bank, wrote out a deposit slip,* and *stepped to the teller's window.*

If you write "Mrs. Smith went to the bank and made out a deposit slip," no comma is necessary because there are only two phrases.

The work that you do, the payment that you receive, and *the satisfaction that you feel for your job* are important to you.

The agency *writes the copy, plans the campaign,* and *selects the media for our promotion.*

A series of clauses.

Who has it, how soon can we get it, and *what will it cost us* are three good questions.

Take the sample to the laboratory *where it will be inspected for defects, where it will be photographed,* and *where a strength test will be applied.*

Coordinate adjectives.   Coordinate adjectives modify the same noun and, if not connected by a conjunction, should be separated by commas. Try using the conjunction *and* in place of the comma to determine whether the adjectives are equal modifiers.

Preparing financial statements is an exacting, tiring job.

Preparing financial statements is an exacting *and* tiring job.

She is a reliable, efficient, creative assistant.

She is a reliable *and* efficient *and* creative assistant.

Some adjectives are used so commonly with certain nouns they are considered part of the noun, for example:

spring rain   stucco house   platinum ring   compact car

Commas are not used between two adjectives, therefore, if the second adjective is considered part of the noun it modifies.

He presented his wife with a beautiful *platinum ring.*

They lived in an attractive *stucco house.*

The noun *ring* is modified by *beautiful* and *platinum.* The noun *house* is modified by *attractive* and *stucco.* In each case, the first adjective refines the description provided by a second adjective commonly associated with the noun. If the two adjectives can be reversed or if *and* can be inserted between them, a comma is necessary.

Interrupting expressions are enclosed in commas.   If a word, phrase, or clause interrupts the main thought in a sentence, it should be enclosed in commas. Such expressions do not change the meaning of a sentence but emphasize or enhance it.

Parenthetical expressions.   These include: *on the other hand, however, nevertheless, for example, of course, by the way, after all, therefore, perhaps,* and *generally speaking.*

The office manager, *after all,* was responsible for the payroll.

Jones, *however,* was not the general manager.

If the interruption is slight, the comma is omitted.

Perhaps he will come.

Of course I will help.

Single words as sentence openers.   *Yes, no, why, oh,* or *well* used at the beginning of a sentence should be followed by a comma.

No, I have not finished the report.

Well, you may receive permission from the supervisor.

Expressions in apposition.   An appositive is generally not essential to the meaning of a sentence and, therefore, should be set off by commas. It is a noun or pronoun, with helpers, that follows and explains another noun or pronoun.

Arthur Farris, the *sales manager,* sent me a brochure.

My brother, a *man from Milwaukee,* is an enthusiastic baseball fan.

Nouns in direct address.   Direct address is an interruption not essential to the meaning of the sentence; therefore, it is set off by commas.

Be sure, *Anne,* to check the personnel file.

Our office, *fellow workers,* is going to be redecorated.

Dates and addresses.   Use commas to separate the parts of dates: after the day of the week when followed by the month and after the date in figures, and before and after the year when preceded by the day of the month.

On *Tuesday, May 15,* we will take inventory.

Pearl Harbor was attacked on *December 7, 1941,* early in the morning.

Use a comma to separate the parts of addresses: to set off the name of the street, city, and state when used together.

The *Santa Monica City College,* 1815 Pearl Street, Santa Monica, California, is a two-year college.

Learn to use commas with restrictive and nonrestrictive *clauses.*

A *restrictive clause* restricts or limits the meaning of the word it modifies. Such clauses *should not* be set off with commas.

Accounting students *who do poor work* are not likely to become professionals.

The clause *who do poor work* restricts or limits the students to which the statement refers. The sentence *would not* be true if you omitted the restrictive clause. The clause is essential to the meaning of the sentence, so you do not set it off with commas.

The business department should not publish a list of the names of students *that has not been carefully checked with the records.*

Would you place a comma after students? No! The intention of the writer is to caution the business department to check carefully any list of students before publishing it. Remember, a restrictive clause is *not* set off with commas. A *nonrestrictive* clause, on the other hand, may be omitted without destroying the basic meaning of the sentence. It is less important to the meaning of the sentence, therefore, than a restrictive clause. It is similar to a parenthetical expression, appositive, or direct address and is set off with commas.

The office manager, *who graduated from Cornell,* is a good correspondent.

The clause could be omitted because it is *not essential* to the basic meaning of the sentence.

Note that nonrestrictive clauses are set off with two commas unless they occur at the beginning or end of a sentence.

The average age of the city college faculty is 33 years, *which is low.*

As I entered the meeting hall, I was greeted by friends.

Some clauses may be either restrictive *or* nonrestrictive, depending on what you intend to say.

Restrictive: Business students *who are trained in operations management* may be hired as systems analysts.
(This statement means that all business students are not qualified as systems analysts. Only those who take operations management are qualified.)

Nonrestrictive: Business students, *who are trained in operations management,* may be hired as systems analysts.
(This statement means that all business students are trained in operations management and, therefore, are qualified as systems analysts.)

Restrictive: Middle managers *who do only their job and nothing more* will not advance in the firm.
(Only those managers who do nothing beyond their jobs will be denied advancement.)

Nonrestrictive: Middle managers, *who comprise an important segment of all firms,* are people with many pressures.
(All middle managers are subject to pressures. The nonrestrictive clause may be omitted without changing this meaning.)

Restrictive: I'll buy the horse *if you will board him.*

Nonrestrictive: Take your vacation now, *unless you'd rather go later.*

Restrictive: John will join us *unless he is caught in the traffic.*

Nonrestrictive: We should leave for our appointment now, *since it is nearly eleven o'clock.*

Learn to use commas with restrictive and nonrestrictive *phrases.*

A participial phrase can also be restrictive or nonrestrictive and the same comma usage you learned for clauses applies to phrases.

Restrictive: All secretaries *leaving the building* were handed notices of the impending strike.

Nonrestrictive: The president, *making no comment,* left the room.

Apply your knowledge of the use of commas

A. In the space at the right of each sentence, write the word and the comma that should follow. If no comma is needed, place a check in the space. If a comma is optional, write the word and the comma that may follow.

1. Henry is a good student and his teachers urge him to attend college. _____

2. My neighbors are on vacation but they will be home soon. _____
3. The dean expects all students to attend meetings and takes roll to be sure they do so. _____

4. In December the first installment is due on real estate taxes. _____

5. Of course I want to go with you. _____

6. When you have prepared carefully for a test you are likely to do well. _____

7. For a person with many responsibilities she had a great sense of humor. _____

8. You will always complete outside assignments if you are a good student. _____

9. On Sunday the first game will be played. _____
10. As long as the details were properly explained we accepted the new bonus plan. _____

11. Sheila wrote the paper and I reviewed it. _____
12. The board of governors elected him president and gave him complete authority. _____

13. If you are looking for security save your money. _____

14. Occasionally the failure of unions and management to reach agreement is the result of poor communication.   _____

15. At one time commercial banks gave everyone free checking accounts.   _____

16. At last the interest was paid.   _____

17. My new assistant is reviewing the proposal but he will be finished soon.   _____

18. You will stop bothering me if you are a good person.   _____

19. To assist the lawyer provided some information.   _____

20. The principal stated the rules but did not explain them.   _____

B.   Place commas where necessary in the following sentences.

1. Of course the insurance policy has not expired.
2. Social Security payments to a wife or dependent husband may end if a divorce is granted.
3. When a child entitled to benefits reaches age 18 payments are stopped unless the child is disabled.
4. As you get older you will begin to think of the time when you will no longer be able to earn an income.
5. Ordinary life insurance gives protection primarily to beneficiaries in the event the insured dies; and secondarily it builds up cash surrender values for the insured.
6. An "annuity" is any fixed periodic payment (weekly monthly quarterly or yearly) for a given period of time or for life.
7. Annuities are possible because a group of people get together to share risks usually through an insurance company.
8. As individuals they probably could not all live on their savings after retirement because they might outlive these savings.
9. As members of a group however each can pay some savings to an insurance company and in exchange will receive a promise of payment for life after retirement.
10. Of course payments to the insured depend on how much savings was turned over to the insurance company.
11. Annuities are sold both to individuals and to groups.
12. Naturally buying annuities on the installment plan is easier than paying in a lump sum.
13. Younger people prefer installment purchase of a deferred annuity whereas older people are more likely to prefer a single premium.
14. If you think about it you'll realize why this is so.
15. Inasmuch as the straight life annuity might pay income for only a few months it is not favored by some people.
16. A straight life annuity is advisable for the person who wishes to receive the largest possible income while alive.
17. Insurance programs should be reviewed often for we live in a changing world.
18. For a poor man with little education he had planned his insurance program with care and insight.
19. In January her earnings for self-employment were high.
20. If you are employed your contribution to Social Security is deducted from your wages each payday.

C. Place commas where necessary in the following sentences.

1. Ask a friend to help you plan your retirement and I'm sure he or she will do so.
2. Relatives may also be helpful if they take an interest.
3. Sooner or later every family or individual sets out to save.
4. A family finance class can be most helpful but individual study is also necessary.
5. Most students find the topics taught in family finance useful and they are likely to be intensely interested.
6. If family finance education has any purpose it is to help individuals manage their financial affairs.
7. First the class will pay attention to basic expenditures because they consume the largest share of total income.
8. Today financial success depends on what you save not what you earn.
9. Occasionally magazine articles throw helpful light on financial topics of interest to young people.
10. Habits of thrift which mean careful use of your resources are important to everyone.
11. The community college is a good place to learn about family finance but not all of them offer specific courses.
12. Business teachers know about family finance and will be glad to give you advice.
13. They are likely to give considerable help for they are interested in the welfare of students.
14. In many instances people make financial decisions based on hunch and not on careful planning.
15. If you prepare yourself to manage your own financial affairs life will be much more pleasant.

D. After each of the following set of two sentences, write the letter *a* or *b* for the sentence punctuated correctly.

Example: (a) Mary is a good student, but she is more interested in sports.
(b) Mary is a good student, but is more interested in sports. _____*a*_____

1. (a) We had only ten minutes to catch the bus, and every minute counted.
   (b) We had only ten minutes to catch the bus and every minute counted. _____
2. (a) Robert wrote the paper and I reviewed it.
   (b) Robert wrote the paper, and I reviewed it. _____
3. (a) At last I received the appointment.
   (b) At last, I received the appointment. _____
4. (a) If you leave now, you should be home before it is dark.
   (b) If you leave now you should be home before it is dark. _____
5. (a) The child was very quiet but he was not asleep.
   (b) The child was very quiet, but he was not asleep. _____
6. (a) The players were warned that a storm was coming, so they moved into the clubhouse.
   (b) The players were warned that a storm was coming so they moved into the clubhouse. _____
7. (a) When speaking, we use pauses and gestures to get emphasis.
   (b) When speaking we use pauses and gestures to get emphasis. _____
8. (a) Commas might have been used in the quoted passage but they would have weakened its humorous force.
   (b) Commas might have been used in the quoted passage, but they would have weakened its humorous force. _____
9. (a) For well-known writers, punctuation is a rhetorical rather than a mechanical concern.
   (b) For well-known writers punctuation is a rhetorical rather than a mechanical concern. _____

10. (*a*)   Both you and your teacher suffer when you write carelessly, and neither can win.
    (*b*)   Both you and your teacher suffer when you write carelessly and neither can win.   _____
11. (*a*)   The student asked the teacher, "Is my report ready?"
    (*b*)   The student asked the teacher, "Is my report ready"?   _____
12. (*a*)   Of course I want to go to the play.
    (*b*)   Of course, I want to go to the play.   _____
13. (*a*)   Before you apply for a job learn as much as you can about the company.
    (*b*)   Before you apply for a job, learn as much as you can about the company.   _____
14. (*a*)   On Friday we want to have a party.
    (*b*)   On Friday, we want to have a party.   _____
15. (*a*)   Given the circumstances he did an excellent job.
    (*b*)   Given the circumstances, he did an excellent job.   _____

E.   After each of the following sets of two sentences, write *a* or *b* to indicate the sentence that is punctuated correctly. Also, write *a* or *b* in the space at the right to answer questions about these sentences.

Example: (a) Many friends and relatives came to the wedding.
            (b) Many friends relatives, and neighbors came to the wedding.   *a*

1.   In the above example, which sentence contains a series of nouns?   _____
2.   (*a*)   Throughout the world there are many scientists, artists, and inventors who receive little recognition.
    (*b*)   Throughout the world there are many scientists artists and inventors who receive little recognition.   _____
3.   (*a*)   Mr. Harrison who graduated from the University of Illinois once worked for an accounting firm.
    (*b*)   Mr. Harrison, who graduated from the University of Illinois, once worked for an accounting firm.   _____
4.   Why did you choose your answer to number 3?
    (*a*)   It contains a restrictive clause.
    (*b*)   It contains a nonrestrictive clause.   _____
5.   (*a*)   The druggist, by the way, is my best friend.
    (*b*)   The druggist by the way is my best friend.   _____
6.   Select a reason for your answer to number 5.
    (*a*)   It contains an interrupting expression.
    (*b*)   It contains a nonrestrictive clause.   _____
7.   (*a*)   My best friend a man from Tampa, Florida will meet me next month in Atlanta, Georgia.
    (*b*)   My best friend, a man from Tampa, Florida, will meet me next month in Atlanta, Georgia.   _____
8.   (*a*)   The dean urged all faculty members to keep their office hours, to meet their classes promptly, and to file their reports on time.
    (*b*)   The dean urged all faculty members to keep their office hours to meet their classes promptly and to file their reports on time.   _____
9.   (*a*)   The offices of the Southern California chapter of the Arthritis Foundation are located at 4311 Wilshire Boulevard Los Angeles California.
    (*b*)   The offices of the Southern California chapter of the Arthritis Foundation are located at 4311 Wilshire Boulevard, Los Angeles, California.   _____

10. (*a*) June 15, 1982, has been set for the opening of summer session.
    (*b*) June 15 1982 has been set for the opening of summer session. _____
11. (*a*) Studying law may be a boring exacting job.
    (*b*) Studying law may be a boring, exacting job. _____
12. (*a*) Many years have passed since I purchased my house, and many changes have taken place in the neighborhood.
    (*b*) Many years have passed since I purchased my house and many changes have taken place in the neighborhood. _____
13. (*a*) We had to wait for the teacher, was talking to another student.
    (*b*) We had to wait, for the teacher was talking to another student. _____
14. (*a*) I was at the Peachtree Plaza Hotel, Atlanta, Georgia, from May 13, 1981, until May 16, 1981.
    (*b*) I was at the Peachtree Plaza Hotel Atlanta Georgia from May 13, 1981 until May 16, 1981. _____
15. (*a*) The firefighters especially their chief were praised for their prompt efficient action.
    (*b*) The firefighters, especially their chief, were praised for their prompt, efficient action. _____

F. Place commas where needed in the following sentences.

1. When the credit manager hired her he said "Shirley I need a secretary who is not afraid to work."
2. Well she proved to be outstanding in talking to customers on the telephone.
3. She learned that the usual credit investigation is made by phoning the applicant's landlord employer bank and trade references.
4. The average consumer credit applicant is a mature family person who has been making an honest steady living.
5. On the other hand there is a type of applicant not in the majority who works off and on and who consequently pays bills late.
6. Some people however fail to understand that credit is not free.
7. Stores generally speaking that grant credit incur a cost they must absorb or pass along to the customer.
8. Pawnbrokers were probably the first agency to make cash loans to the customer in this country.
9. Years ago the merchant the physician and the pawnbroker were the principal agencies of consumer credit.
10. Individuals who are college graduates frequently become teachers.
11. Such individuals from the retailer's point of view are good credit risks.
12. Secretaries who have exceptional competence on the telephone are in demand by credit bureaus.
13. Yearly cost of a bank loan depending upon the particular bank will range from 3 to 15 percent less than for retail installment credit.
14. Anyway the lesson to be learned is to shop around for credit.
15. If you do not do so your purchases may be costly.

G. Place commas where needed in the following paragraph.

Jones Richards and Boothby will handle promotion of the congressman's campaign for election. They will write advertising copy formulate campaigns and select the media. Recently they have expanded the advertising by directing appeals to the northwest southwest parts of the southeast and the central areas of the district. By this move we should increase our votes in these areas but the election is not assured. If we increase the voter turnout however we will have accomplished our goal. Our congressman an effective dynamic leader has great plans for the future. Mr. Fogo the campaign manager has often talked about the dynamism of the candidate. Last week he said "Our country fellow campaign workers greatly needs our candidate." He also said that if elected the candidate will do something about employees who are doing inefficient work and that very likely those employees would be replaced. He will attempt to put his policies to work as soon as possible after the election on Tuesday November 4. These announcements came from party headquarters in the Bay View Women's Club 3458 Johnson Road Pacific Palisades Washington.

Name _____

Date _____

—————————————— **PRACTICE WRITING** ——————————————

When composing your own sentences, you will have to consider where marks of punctuation are needed. Often, these marks are automatically placed as you write because you know where they belong. At other times you will finish writing the sentence and then reread it to see if punctuation is needed. Occasionally, you may refer to a grammar text, such as this one, to check recommended usage. To give you practice in placing punctuation marks as you write, compose original sentences as suggested below. Check your work to see that all commas are placed correctly.

1. Write a sentence using two or more adjectives to modify a noun.

    _____

    _____

    _____

2. Write a sentence using an expression in apposition.

    _____

    _____

    _____

3. Write a sentence using a nonrestrictive clause.

    _____

    _____

    _____

4. Write a sentence with a series of phrases.

    _____

    _____

    _____

5. Write a sentence with a parenthetical expression and a series of nouns.

_____

_____

_____

6. Write a sentence with a proper noun in direct address.

_____

_____

_____

7. Write a sentence that includes a date and a complete address.

_____

_____

_____

8. Write a sentence that begins with a long introductory phrase or clause.

_____

_____

_____

PART **3**

Semicolons, colons, and dashes may be used in several ways

Semicolons are important aids to clarity.

A semicolon (;) is used to connect the main clauses of a compound sentence when a conjunction is *not* used. *And, or,* and *but* are the most commonly used conjunctions although others used to join main clauses are *nor, for, yet,* and *so.* Thus, either a conjunction alone or a semicolon with a conjunction is necessary to hold main clauses together. Think of the semicolon as more like a period than like a comma.

This home study course shows you how to write clearly; it helps you learn how to spot errors.

Organizational structure is constantly changing; it should change as objectives and other factors change.

Collection letters are among the most challenging; their effectiveness is measured by the amount of money they bring in.

If other commas are used in a compound sentence, the main clauses are separated by a semicolon even though a conjunction has been used between the main clauses.

All supermarkets have yards of refrigerated cabinets for frozen foods; and some even have mechanized check-out counters, belt conveyors, and intercommunication systems.

Self-service is more and more prevalent in hardware, clothing, and drug stores; and some wholesalers now have open warehouses based on self-service.

A semicolon may be used before a word(s) that introduces a list in a sentence. The word is followed by a comma.

There are a number of financial institutions willing to help; for example, banks, savings and loans, credit unions, and insurance companies.

The dash (—) is also appropriate to introduce such words. (See page 313.) Some authorities find the dash more desirable as punctuation when the following words are used to introduce a list.

311

for example   namely   for instance   such as   that is

Physical features are important in an office—for example, lighting, furniture, decoration, air conditioning.

A semicolon is also used to separate items in a series when one or more of the items has inside punctuation.

Please ask Mrs. Jones to send copies to Frank R. Smith, Chicago, Illinois; Janet Fleming, Scranton, Pennsylvania; and Hugh Allerton, Miami, Florida.

Learn the important uses of colons.   A colon is a stop to warn the reader that something important is coming. It may be used in a number of situations to link the main thought with some explanatory remark. While the colon indicates a major stop in written prose, it is not used for end-of-sentence punctuation. On the other hand, a complete thought may be expressed after the colon. The use of a colon, however, is generally indicated by lead-in words in the first part of the statement. A good principle to keep in mind is that *a colon follows a grammatically complete statement*. The most important uses of the colon are the following:

To follow a lead-in statement.   Words such as *these, there are, following*, and *as follows* lead naturally to the use of the colon.

There are three men on the committee: Phil Jones, Wilbur Johnson, and Marvin Green.

The jobs you should have completed are *these*: file the letters, straighten the desk, and cut the stencils.

Usually, if some such lead-in is not used, the colon should be omitted.

Chain stores depend for success on moderately priced merchandise and effectively operated merchandise-control systems.
    (It would be incorrect to place a colon after *on* because the thought preceding *on* is not complete.)

In the next sentence, the lead-in words, *the following*, make the use of the colon logical and give the ideas greater emphasis.

Chain stores depend for success on the following business practices: moderately priced merchandise and effectively operated merchandise-control systems.

Before listed items.   A statement introducing a list of items is followed by a colon. The list may follow in sentence form, or it may follow in outline forms.

The improvements needed in our office are these: increased secretarial assistance, better duplicating service, prompt mail delivery, and daily janitorial service.

Administrators are responsible for the following activities:
    budgeting   purchasing
    employing   supervising

To introduce quotations.   A complete grammatical statement should precede a quotation.

The office manager gave the new employees the following advice: "Take an interest in your job if you expect to become an important part of this office."

Routine uses of the colon.   There are two uses of the colon in everyday practice.

1.   Between figures written to express hours and minutes.

7:30 a.m.   3:00 p.m.   10:45 a.m.

2.   Following the salutation in business letters.   (A more modern practice, however, is to omit the colon after the salutation and also the comma after the complimentary close in business letters.)

Dear Mr. Wilson: or   Dear Mr. Wilson
Dear John: or   Dear John

Use dashes for abrupt interruptions.

A dash (—) should not be considered a general punctuation mark to be used at random for any and all purposes. It is used to add force to your writing, as a stronger mark than a comma—it interrupts more abruptly.

Dashes may be used in the following ways.

To add force.

The vice president was the only one authorized to write checks—and he was not available.

To set off a series of appositives without confusing them with the nouns they explain.

Clear: Several members of the chancellor's staff—the administrative assistant, the budget analyst, and a secretary—attended the personnel committee meeting.

Confusing: Several members of the chancellor's staff, the administrative assistant, the budget analyst, and a secretary, attended the personnel committee meeting.

To indicate a sharp interruption or a sudden turn in the flow of thought.

The office manager was here with—what was the name of the man to whom we sold our old desks?

For two years—and two were plenty—we used an old war-surplus typewriter.

Before the words *for example, namely, such as, that is, e.g.,* and *i.e.,* when a complete thought precedes the expression.

A secretary needs many unusual qualities—for example, a sense of urgency, a spirit of dedication, a high level of technical skill.

There are a number of things you can do to improve this office—such as, improving the lighting, changing the layout, and carpeting the floor.

PART **3**

ASSIGNMENTS

Apply your knowledge of semicolons, colons, dashes, and commas

A. Place colons, semicolons, dashes, or commas where needed in the following sentences.

1. Our department is constantly changing its work methods it will never be out of date.
2. Our former manager believed he was always right it helped his pride to think so.
3. His opinion was not the same as that of the members of the company's executive committee the vice president the secretary the treasurer or the president who asked him to leave the company.
4. One might judge from these statements that the following traits might be helpful to any manager modesty open-mindedness and the ability to listen.
5. On the other hand if you were the manager you would need a great deal of confidence determination would also be an important quality.
6. A good office manager should understand the following office routines data processing duplicating mail regulations letter costs typing practices and many other services.
7. Business managers according to Dean Fielden say "People just can't write!"
8. He also asked for your response to the following observation "You simply can't write."
9. The manager unless insensitive to current thinking must pay attention to statements such as the following "It has become important for business to undertake social responsibility on a major scale."
10. There are many complex problems in business management and some of these include labor relations legal regulations selling and buying.

B. Place commas, semicolons, colons, and dashes where needed in the following sentences.

1. A good department head needs some very important qualities for example will power initiative optimism and self-confidence.
2. There are many complex forms of business entities and some of these include informal agreements trusts mergers amalgamations and holding companies.
3. Collection letters are a challenge to the letter writer their effectiveness is measured not only by the amount of money they bring in but also by the extent to which they do so without offending the customer.
4. Three essentials of effective business writing are the following clearness correctness conciseness.
5. Key mail personnel must know the postal costs and requirements so that the proper amounts of postage no more and no less are affixed.

315

6. In general first-class mail includes correspondence securities and documents second-class mail newspapers magazines and other periodicals third-class mail unsealed printed matter and form letters fourth-class mail packages and parcels.

7. When you talk on the telephone the impression you make must rely entirely on your voice its tone clearness and pleasantness your selection of words and your manner of speaking.

8. Domestic long-distance telephone rates are determined by the method and time of the call such as station to station person to person 8 to 5 weekdays or weekends and holidays and special rates for other than those hours.

9. A prominent business leader made the following statement "The profit motive provides incentive for businessmen to help solve the economic problems of the disadvantaged."

10. The fundamental functions of the manager controlling organizing and putting into action are essentially, activities to implement plans.

C. Place colons, semicolons, dashes, and commas where needed in the following copy.

1. Our instructor an outstanding teacher explained what he expected from the class at the same
2. time he told us what we could expect from him. Some students missed half of the professor's
3. first lecture they came late. The text for the course covered the following on communication
4. theory organization memoranda and reports. We were excited about the subject even though
5. it seemed difficult but it became easier in succeeding class periods. From 900 a.m. to 1100
6. a.m. daily the class met without a break. The class activities were very interesting and in-
7. cluded the following group study individual skills inventory test various writing and speaking
8. problems and discussions of semantics. The instructor made the following statement "An
9. interesting seminar is only possible when students read and think before coming to class."
10. He stated further "A productive class depends upon student-oriented subjects and individually
11. motivated participation." Some members of the class thought we should limit our discussions
12. to the communications problems of managers for example upward downward and horizontal.
13. Not all of us could agree on what to do but that is fairly typical of group activity.

D. Place colons, semicolons, dashes, and commas where needed in the following copy.

The instructor told us to remember the following "This book is not a dictionary formula book or cookbook to be followed blindly. Largely your success in the long run will depend upon your attitude proper attitude is your most important asset. If your attitude toward your intended reader is good ask yourself Is my style interesting clear and inconspicuous? To be effective then your style should be to your reader interesting enough to be read clear when read and inconspicuous. Even perfectly good words phrases clauses or sentences may misfire if you don't think about meaning and context. There are many other points to emphasize of course in clear writing so it's up to you to study how to achieve conciseness consideration and courtesy."

Name _____

Date _____

PRACTICE WRITING

A. Compose two sentences each to illustrate the use of the marks of punctuation listed below.

1. Semicolon _____

_____

_____

_____

_____

2. Colon _____

_____

_____

_____

_____

3. Dash _____

_____

_____

_____

_____

4. Comma _____

_____

_____

_____

_____

B.   Here is an opportunity to demonstrate that you can write effectively. Follow the directions as given.

1.   Write a sentence to demonstrate the use of the semicolon to connect the main clauses of a compound sentence when a conjunction is *not* used.

_____

_____

_____

2.   Write a sentence to demonstrate the use of the *colon* to follow a lead-in statement.

_____

_____

_____

3.   Write a sentence to demonstrate the use of *dashes* to set off a sharp interruption or sudden turn of thought.

_____

_____

_____

4.   Write a sentence to demonstrate the use of the *semicolon* in a compound sentence even though a conjunction has been used between the main clauses.

_____

_____

_____

5.   Write a sentence using *commas* to set off an interrupting expression.

_____

_____

_____

6. Write a sentence to demonstrate the use of the *colon* before listed items.

    _____

    _____

    _____

7. Write a sentence to demonstrate the use of the *semicolon* before a word that introduces a list.

    _____

    _____

    _____

8. Write a sentence to demonstrate the use of the *comma* to separate a series of words.

    _____

    _____

    _____

9. Write a sentence to demonstrate the use of the *colon* to introduce a quotation.

    _____

    _____

    _____

10. Write a sentence to demonstrate the use of *dashes* before the words *for example.*

    _____

    _____

    _____

PART **4**

Miscellaneous marks of punctuation have special uses

Parentheses de-emphasize the material they enclose.

Parentheses, as marks of punctuation within sentences, are used in a variety of situations. Business writers are not likely to use parentheses frequently, as parenthetical expressions are also enclosed by other means—commas and dashes. Material enclosed with dashes and commas usually contributes something to the main thought of the sentence. Words enclosed by parentheses make no contribution to the main thought of the sentence even though information is provided. De-emphasis is more effective with parentheses than with other marks of punctuation. Some common situations indicating the use of parentheses are given below.

To enclose parenthetical word groups not of special importance.

My lawyer *(who smokes too much)* is meeting me this afternoon.

After a hard day of work *(Really, she does work hard.),* she is still cheerful.

Note the punctuation in the two sentences above. In the first, commas are not necessary in the sentence or in the enclosed element. In the second, because the parenthetical element comes at the end of a clause, the punctuation is placed outside the second parenthesis. Notice also that the enclosed element in the second sentence requires punctuation. All marks of punctuation may be used within parentheses. The first word in a parenthetic element within a sentence is not capitalized unless it is a proper noun or begins a quotation. If a complete sentence is enclosed in parentheses, it is capitalized and takes the appropriate end punctuation, including a period.

After several successes *(and what successes!),* the company continued to prosper.

(Note the comma after the right parenthesis and the exclamation point within the parentheses.)

As enclosures for letters or numbers that precede a series in a sentence.

Social Security provides three different kinds of benefits: *(1)* retirement, *(2)* survivors, and *(3)* disability.

321

You should know that an ellipsis is used to indicate an omission of words: *(1)* at the beginning of a sentence, *(2)* within a sentence, and *(3)* at the end of a sentence.

In legal papers to enclose a figure following a spelled-out number.

I hereby agree to purchase the house at 143 Albright Street, Los Angeles, California, for the sum of eighty thousand dollars *($80,000).*

The publisher may destroy Author's finished typewritten manuscript if Author does not request in writing its return within thirty *(30)* days after it has been published.

To enclose reference information such as page numbers and publication references.

The *United States Postal Guide (which can be obtained from the Superintendent of Documents, Washington, D.C. 20402)* is especially recommended.

A person who presents evidence of ability to write good letters, memos, and reports becomes a favored applicant for nearly any job. *(See p. 4, Communication through Letters and Reports.)*

Quotation marks enclose material quoted directly.

If you repeat the exact words of another person, you are making a *direct* quotation. If you report those remarks in your own words, you are making an *indirect* quotation.

Direct: Anne Bohn said, "I think business students are most cooperative."

Indirect: Anne Bohn said that she thinks business students are most cooperative.

In the first statement, the *exact* words of Ms. Bohn are used and quotation marks enclose them. Quotation marks are not necessary in the second illustration because we have reported her statement indirectly. The word *that* is often used to make the change from a direct to an indirect quotation.

You must capitalize the first word of a direct quotation. Use a comma to separate a direct quotation from the words that introduce it.

Ellen Rubin said, "I am the assistant dean of the school."

When commas and periods are adjacent to quotation marks, they appear *before* the marks. If we turn the previous sentence around, the same rule applies.

"I am the assistant dean of the school," said Mrs. Rubin.

To achieve variety in reporting dialogue, you may wish to break a quotation by inserting *he said* or some similar phrase. Note in the following illustration that a break requires the use of two sets of quotation marks.

"I am the assistant dean," said Mrs. Rubin, "so I see many students every day."

The two parts in quotation marks constitute one sentence. Consequently, you do not capitalize the first word of the second part unless it should be capitalized for another reason—for example, if it were the pronoun *I*.

There are numerous ways to give direct sentence quotations variety, but you should have little difficulty punctuating them properly if you remember these simple guidelines:

1.   If you quote material of more than one sentence, only one set of quotation marks is needed at the beginning and end of the entire direct quotation. Long quotations are often set off in a separate paragraph and indented on both sides. No quotation marks are used for such long quotations.

2.   If the direct quotation is a question, use the question mark in place of another appropriate punctuation mark and place it inside the quotation mark.

Frank asked, "Are you the assistant dean, Mrs. Rubin?"

"Mrs. Rubin, are you the assistant dean?" questioned Frank.

3.   In the question that contains a direct quotation, place the question marks outside the quotation mark. The whole sentence is a question, not the quotation.

Did you hear Mrs. Rubin say, "It is time to file your study list"?

4.   A question may include a quoted question; in this case, you place the question mark inside the quotation mark.

Did you hear Frank ask, "Mrs. Rubin, are you the assistant dean?"

The exclamation point in quotations is handled in the same way as the question mark.

"We won!" exclaimed Bonnie.

What a tremendous fear is aroused in people by the cry "Fire!"

An apostrophe may show ownership, a contraction, or a special plural.

Forming possessives.   An apostrophe, correctly used in writing, shows ownership.

Henry's book was stolen.

Note that the noun *Henry* tells who possesses the book, but without the *apostrophe s* (*'s*) the sentence does not make sense.

The word that shows ownership (*Henry's*) is in the possessive case. It follows, then, that to form the possessive case of a *singular noun,* you add *apostrophe s* (*'s*). No change in spelling is necessary.

If a *plural noun* ends in *s,* the possessive case is formed by adding an *apostrophe only.*

students' books	gardeners' tools
teachers' guides	programmers' outlines

Most plural nouns end in *s;* but if they *do not,* the possessive case is formed by adding *apostrophe s* (*'s*). The most common plural nouns that do not end in *s* are *men, women, children,* and *people.*

men's program	children's zoo
women's jobs	people's platform

Be certain that you use the apostrophe with the word that shows ownership. Also, spell correctly the noun for which you wish to write the possessive and then add the apostrophe.

Singular possessive	Plural possessive
country's	countries'
industry's	industries'
municipality's	municipalities'
child's	children's

Frequently, the thing possessed is not named in the sentence. Nevertheless, the possessive noun must be correctly written.

Your typewriter behaves in the same way that Kathy's does.

The noun *typewriter* is understood to name what Kathy owns.

Writing contractions. You are familiar with contractions. They are made up of two words run together that leave out letters to form a shortcut. You use these shortcuts in your daily speech without thinking very much about the process. In writing, however, clarity is achieved by knowing precisely how to show what was cut out to create the contraction.

did not = didn't   I have = I've
we will = we'll   you are = you're

The apostrophe is used to indicate the letter or letters omitted to form a shortcut. It is placed at the point where the letters are missing.

do not—don't   is not—isn't   it is—it's

In these contractions little time or effort is gained in writing them. They do, however, make for shorter speech forms and are frequently used in writing, especially in informal, conversational prose.

To assure yourself of accuracy in your writing, remember these guidelines for writing contractions.

1. Do not change letters in the original word. *Won't* for *will not* is an exception.

We *haven't* heard from them in a long time.

2. Distinguish between possessive pronouns and contractions that are pronounced the same.

your and *you're*
its and *it's*
whose and *who's*

Your salary is paid monthly.
   (*Your* shows ownership.)
You're going to earn a monthly salary.
   (*You're* is the contraction for *you are*.)
You will like *its* color.
   (*Its* shows ownership.)
I think *it's* beautiful.
   (*It's* is the contraction for *it is*.)

Special plurals. Plural nouns that do not show ownership are usually written without apostrophes. There are some special cases, however, where the apostrophe is used to form the ordinary plural. Use the apostrophe and *s* (*'s*) to write plurals for *words, numbers, signs,* or *letters* to which you refer. They will be easier to read and understand.

The accountant uses too many *see's* in his discussion of reports.

There are five *+'s* and two *−'s* in the financial statement.

Write your *3's* and *8's* more clearly.

How many *I's* are there in the word totally?

Ellipses indicate words omitted from quoted passages.

An ellipsis (a series of three spaced periods . . .) is used in writing, typewriting, or printing to indicate the omission of words or letters from the beginning, the middle, or the end of a sentence. It is used more often in quoted material than in an author's own prose. The person quoting believes the meaning of the passage can be expressed without using all the words of the original author. The usual punctuation (including the period) is used at the end of a sentence even though an ellipsis also appears.

Ellipsis marks are required in quoted or other material also.

Omission of the beginning of a sentence.

". . . interest centers upon the budget of the office manager."

Omission within a sentence.

"This method is very effective if . . . properly organized and operated."

Omission of the end of a sentence.

"Supervision and control mean studying costs at all times. . . ."

Italics identify titles and key words.

Italics are type faces that slant upward and toward the right. Such type is used to set off important words and phrases to make written communications more readily understood. The same emphasis is obtained in typewritten or handwritten material by underlining. Some of the more common uses of italics (underscoring) are shown here.

Titles of magazines, books, and newspapers. Only titles of separately published works are shown in italics. Thus, an article in a magazine or a chapter from a book would not be shown in this manner. Such items are enclosed in quotation marks.

The *California Management Review* is a magazine for professional managers. It publishes articles such as "Policies of the Successful Manager."

(Note that the name of the magazine is written in italics, but the title of an article from the magazine is enclosed in quotation marks.)

The Wall Street Journal is a newspaper for those interested in securities markets.

(Note that *the* is in italics and capitalized only when it is part of the name.)

Communication and Culture is a book of readings on human communication.

(Note that the word *and* is not capitalized, but it is in italics.)

Letters, words, phrases, and numbers used as terms.

How many *l's* and *t's* are there in the word allotted?

Write your *3's* and *8's* more clearly.

The word *scissors* is often misspelled.

He repeats the phrase *you know* at the end of almost every sentence.

Names of planes, trains, ships, works of art.

We rode in *The Super Chief* train to Chicago.

A cruise on the *Princess* will be restful.

We flew to Mexico City on the *Golden Aztec*.

Rembrandt's *Night Watch* is in the Rijksmuseum in Amsterdam.

Foreign words and phrases not included in common English usage. Dictionaries identify such words by either labeling them French, German, Spanish, and so on, or by a sign of some kind. If you have occasion to use such words or phrases, consult a recently published dictionary for guidance.

lycée
  (French secondary school preparing students for a university)
Liederkranz
  (a group of songs, a men's singing society, a soft strong cheese)
de facto
  (actual, in fact)
double entendre
  (a word or phrase with two meanings, especially when one of
  these has some indecorous connotation)

Most of the foreign words you are likely to use have been included in common English usage. Frequent use of foreign terms not included in common usage may make it difficult for your reader to understand you without consulting a dictionary.

Special emphasis on a word in direct quotation.

She said, "I mean *no*."

"Give me that pencil, *now!*" he exclaimed.

Special emphasis in business writing. Too frequent use of italics (or underscoring in typewritten messages) makes the emphasis less effective.

PART 4

ASSIGNMENTS

Apply your knowledge of miscellaneous marks of punctuation

A. Place commas, quotation marks, dashes, parentheses, and apostrophes where needed in the following sentences.

1. The instructor said Adapt your words and ideas to your reader.
2. If you dont do so according to experts it would be much like communicating in a foreign language.
3. I dont see the need for that the student said since its the readers job to understand.
4. The instructor pointed out that he believes you should begin by visualizing your readers.
5. No two readers can be alike he said for no two have the same knowledge experience bias or emotions.
6. Johns paper and several others as well wasnt acceptable as his word selection was poor.
7. Did you hear the student ask Why are short words better than long ones?
8. Did the instructor ask whether you have had work experience Mary?
9. Marys instructor told her Business writers dont use everyday language enough.
10. He also made the statement that there is really nothing wrong with hard words but you shouldn't use them too often.
11. Obviously dont write so simply you insult your readers intelligence.
12. People who read business letters according to Malcolm Forbes are as human as thee and me.
13. He also said A good business letter can get you a job interview.
14. As you write remember Tony Randalls advice Words can make us laugh cry go to war fall in love.
15. Edward T. Thompson Editor in Chief *Readers Digest* said If you are afraid to write dont be.
16. He also said Its not easy but its easier than you might imagine.
17. Letters that are pleasant and unobtrusive undistracting in appearance, are more effective.
18. Unvaried sentence pattern type length or rhythm causes a readers mind to wander.
19. Typewritten work can be measured in the following units 1 pages 2 standard-length lines 3 key strokes 4 square inches of typed material or 5 tapes from which material is transcribed.
20. The United States Postal Guide has detailed directions on how to write figures abbreviations and numerous other items.

B. Place parentheses, italics, and any other needed marks of punctuation in the sentences on the following page. Indicate italics by underlines.

327

1. Raymond Lesikars book Business Communication Theory and Application contains a chapter on The Role of Communication in the Business Organization.
2. The layout of this page is a too fat b too skinny c too low d too high or e off center as marked.
3. Use the five Ws as a check for completeness who what where when and why.
4. The opening could be improved by making it 1 on the subject 2 logical or 3 interesting.
5. I heard him say Bill your writing has improved steadily.
6. The Jaycees are sponsoring Salute to Business Writing a fair honoring business students in the area.
7. An article by John P. Wiley Jr. Racing a Shadow of the Moon Across the Skies appeared in the April 1980 Smithsonian.
8. The Golden Odyssey is a cruise ship of the Royal Cruise Line.
9. The New York Times is read not only in New York but also in such cities as Washington Chicago and Los Angeles.
10. Be sure to put in both commas or dashes or parentheses around a parenthetical expression in the middle of a sentence.

C.   Put in punctuation and emphasis where needed in the following paragraph.

Make your writing clear quick and easy to read. Use commas between independent clauses connected by *and but or* or *nor* semicolons between independent clauses with other connectives or no connecting words. Use commas for dependent clauses and verbals or long phrases at the beginnings of sentences for nonrestrictive ones elsewhere and for simple series and semicolons for complex series like the one in this sentence.

D.   Write the correct form of the word given in parentheses in the blank space in the sentence.

1. The _____ obligation is to create goodwill. (*writer,* singular, possessive)

2. Is there an _____ manual to accompany our text? (*instructor,* plural, possessive)

3. If you want your writing to build goodwill, you _____ ignore tone. (*cannot,* contraction)

4. The _____ training course emphasized courtesy in writing. (*employee,* plural, possessive)

5. _____ anger and petulance were indications of his unwillingness to accept responsibility for successful human relations. (*Henry,* singular, possessive)

6. _____ be insensitive to your _____ needs. (*Do not,* contraction; *reader,* singular, possessive)

7. I sent the _____ responses to the supervisor. (*man,* plural, possessive)

8. _____ you be more effective with a subdued tone? (*Will not,* contraction)

9. The _____ instructions were to point out benefits to the reader in your writing. (*manager,* singular, possessive)

10. _____ greatest need is for good writing. (*Industry,* plural, possessive)

Name _____

Date _____

PRACTICE WRITING

Write a short paragraph of a conversation between a salesperson and a customer. Pick a retail outlet that sells clothing. Be sure to use the actual words of both the salesperson and the customer. Careful punctuation of the sentences will be necessary. Use contractions for a natural effect.

_____

_____

_____

_____

_____

_____

_____

_____

_____

_____

_____

_____

_____

_____

_____

_____

_____

_____

_____

_____

_____

REVIEW

Apply your knowledge of the punctuation of sentences

To prepare for the unit examination on punctuation, you should complete the following assignments.

A. Insert the correct punctuation marks in the following sentences.

1. Any person group company or government department or agency whose purpose is to produce or sell products or services is a business

2. If businesses like individuals are to succeed they must be responsive to life around them

3. The primary task of business of course must be to produce and sell products and services that people want and can buy

4. Businessmen have a sincere although somewhat belated recognition that they cannot ignore any part of their environment

5. For the businessman or businesswoman population growth presents both opportunities and problems

6. There were 64 million people employed or looking for jobs in 1950 86 million in 1970 and 1985 forecasts indicate the work force will be 110.7 million

7. A program for reducing office accidents consists of educating employees to potential danger spots checking on machines equipment and environment and following up to ensure that employees are observing good safety practices.

8. Where individuals work together they must to varying degrees learn the language of business

9. Organizational structure is constantly changing and it should change as objectives personnel general conditions methods and other factors change

10. Unfortunately I said the real world will not promote free competition everywhere even in a society such as ours that considers free competition one of its ideals

11. The managers view is that an effective business letter however makes a friend or keeps one

12. People learn their attitudes and beliefs from their families friends teachers and coworkers they also learn from political leaders

13. Peter Drucker said years ago The purpose of business is to create a customer.

14. Business must live within its environment social economic technological political and legal.

15. A moments reflection will make us see that most of business buying selling borrowing money hiring people or getting materials depends upon a system of agreements and understandings

331

16. William Haney in Communication and Organizational Behavior asks the following question ... how can I develop trust under todays pressures and complexities

17. Sometimes in order to clear the air its helpful to pause for a moment when you feel your ideas and position being challenged reflect on the situation and express your concern to the speaker

18. Without question communication is important to business organizations important because business wants its communication to be well done

19. Lack of conscious effort courtesy or consideration may and most likely will drive customers away

20. You may easily offend a customer by such statements as It is unlikely your garment is defective but we will take it back and give you a new one

B.   Insert the correct punctuation marks in the following passage, including the reference.

The social and cultural influences affecting business include peoples attitudes desires degrees of intelligence and education beliefs problems and customs. Other important factors are the size and location of the population peoples occupations and their incomes. These affect business operations because they influence customers workers managers and investors. The major traditional American beliefs in private property competition and finding better ways of doing things have provided a climate for business growth and success for many years. In more recent times increased emphasis has been put on human rights especially the right of all people to a better life without discrimination because of sex race religion or age. (Kuntz Harold and Robert M Fulmer A Practical Introduction to Business. Homewood, Illinois: Richard D Irwin Inc 1976)

Writing effectively

Learning to write effectively is important to your future success in business. There is growing agreement among businesses today that the ability to put information to use is critical.

Business firms depend on the accurate transfer of ideas from one individual to another. They expect a prospective employee, therefore, to have mastered the ability to communicate. Writers agree that writing is hard, that one must write and rewrite, that study of techniques improves skill, and that practice is essential. This section includes several techniques to improve your skill in composing sentences. You will have an opportunity in the practice material to strengthen that skill as you apply the techniques.

Improve your writing techniques

A sentence should have unity: contain one complete thought. An effective sentence conveys a clear, concise message with accuracy and force. Authorities say that a good sentence has *unity, coherence,* and *emphasis.* Unity in sentence construction means that a sentence is a unit, containing one complete thought. Every element within it contributes to that one thought. When you think of another idea, start a new sentence. By limiting a sentence to one idea, you help your reader get a clear message. Read the following sentence. How many ideas does it contain?

> In celebration of its 50th year, the company gave the employees a holiday, who are planning a trip to Catalina.

By combining three ideas—50th-year celebration, company holiday, and employees' trip to Catalina—the writer confuses the reader. Two of the ideas appear to be important, and each of these should be placed in a separate sentence. One idea, the 50th-year celebration, seems less important and can rightly be written as a phrase. The three ideas as now written are clearer and possess unity.

> In celebration of its 50th year, the company gave the employees a holiday. Several of the employees are planning a trip to Catalina.

To maintain unity in a sentence, check to see that you do these things:

1. Express a complete thought. Phrases or clauses that are not sentences, but stand alone as if they were, are called sentence fragments. Fragments distract the reader, who finds it difficult to understand the point you are trying to make.

Sentence:	We agreed that I was to work this Saturday.
Fragment:	Mr. Case to work the following Saturday.
Rewritten for unity:	We agreed that I was to work this Saturday and that Mr. Case would work the following Saturday.

334

The next fragment should be rewritten as a complete sentence and also must be clarified as to intended meaning. When a decision may be expected appears to be of primary importance. Notice how the time of the forthcoming decision is clearly stated in each of the two rewritten sentences.

Fragment: Even though I expect to talk to him next week and will let him know our decision.

Rewritten: Even though I expect to talk to him next week, I will let him know our decision today.

Or: I expect to talk to him next week and will let him know of our decision then.

2. Join two closely related thoughts in a compound sentence by using correct punctuation and/or a conjunction.   Remember that a comma and a conjunction or a semicolon separate two complete thoughts. Many errors occur when a writer uses a conjunctive adverb (*i.e., however, consequently, hence*) as the sentence connector.

Run-together or comma splice: The rough draft was completed today, the report is due in two weeks.

Correct: The rough draft was completed today, but the report is due in two weeks.

Run-together or comma splice: The rough draft was completed today, however, the report is due in two weeks.

Correct: The rough draft was completed today; however, the report is due in two weeks.

3. Place the important idea in the independent clause and subordinate minor related ideas by means of a dependent clause or a phrase.

Mr. Roberts purchased a new adding machine and he had it shipped to the Tulsa office for their old machine was too slow and it needed to be repaired.

The sentence above is an example of a run-on sentence that fails to highlight the main idea for the reader. To clarify the meaning, the writer should isolate the main idea to be expressed from the minor points that would interest the reader. The main idea of the sentence might be the following:

Mr. Roberts purchased a new adding machine.

Minor points are these:

had new machine shipped

to Tulsa office

to replace old machine

which is too slow and in need of repairs

Minor ideas can be subordinated by using dependent clauses, appositives, verbal phrases, and prepositional phrases.

Subordination: Because the adding machine at the Tulsa office is too slow and needs repairs, Mr. Roberts purchased a new machine to be shipped to them.

Or: Mr. Roberts, aware that the adding machine at the Tulsa office is slow and needs repairs, purchased a new one to be shipped to them.

Or: Mr. Roberts, realizing that the adding machine at the Tulsa office is slow and needs repairs, shipped them a new one.

Apply *unity* to the following sentences:

1. Examining the machines once a week. Several were found in need of oil.

_____

_____

_____

_____

2. Bob has been hired for the job and he will take over Fred's place in records but he will be moved to the sales department as soon as an opening occurs.

_____

_____

_____

_____

3. Send for a sample of the new metal, however we have almost decided to use copper.

_____

_____

_____

_____

4. You will be in Chicago in March and you should stop in at the Furniture Mart.

_____

_____

_____

_____

5. Although he knew that was probably the right information. He asked to check further.

_____

_____

_____

_____

A sentence should have coherence: be clear and specific.

Coherence in sentence construction depends on the proper arrangement of words in the sentence so that there is no misunderstanding as to the intended meaning. As you write each sentence, determine exactly what you want to say. You should then experiment with the placement of words, phrases, and clauses to find the arrangement that is closest to your precise meaning. By using correct wording, your sentences will be free of ambiguous, misleading, or illogical ideas. To insure *coherence* in your sentences, you should do the following:

1. Make all pronoun references clear. Be sure that your reader knows what noun a pronoun replaces.

  a. Watch that your pronoun refers to only one antecedent.

Weak: Mr. Percy told the manager that *his* check was lost.
  (Whose check is lost, Mr. Percy's or the manager's?)

Clear: Mr. Percy, whose check was lost, told the manager.

  b. Be sure that your pronoun refers to a noun that has been expressed.

Weak: When I arrived late, he called me into his office.

Clear: When I arrived late, *my employer* called me into his office.

Weak: *They* don't hire many keypunch operators in this city.

Clear: *The companies in this city* don't hire many keypunch operators.

2. Place modifiers close to the words to which they refer. A *dangling modifier* is a word, phrase, or clause that expresses an illogical or ridiculous idea because it has been separated from the word on which its meaning depends. Here are a few examples of dangling modifiers.

Participial phrase:	*Having finished school,* it was important to find a job.
Verbal noun phrase:	*After reading the suggestions,* the office was rearranged.
Infinitive phrase:	*To be a good typist,* accuracy is necessary.
Prepositional phrase:	*After filing the letters,* the memorandums should be filed.
Elliptical clause:	*When at home,* work piled on my desk is forgotten. (In an *elliptical clause,* the subject and verb are omitted.)

Watch for dangling modifiers and rewrite the sentence so that the phrase clearly modifies the correct word. Usually you may leave the modifier as it is and rewrite the rest of the sentence. Another way to correct the sentence is to expand the dangling phrase into a complete dependent clause. Each of the sentences containing dangling modifiers has been rewritten. Notice how they have been corrected.

Participial phrase:	Having finished school, *I knew I must find a job.*
Or:	Having finished school, *I found it important to find a job.*
Verbal noun phrase:	After reading the suggestions, *he rearranged the office.*
Infinitive phrase:	To be a good typist, *you must type accurately.*
Prepositional phrase:	After filing the letters, *you should file the memorandums.*
Elliptical clause:	When at home, *I forget the work piled on my desk.* (An *elliptical clause* takes the same subject as the independent clause.)

A *misplaced modifier* can be corrected easily by moving the word, phrase, or clause used as the modifier to its proper place in the sentence. Modifiers of the verb or the complete sentence are usually easy to move about.

Verb modifier:	*Rapidly* the elevator sped to the 41st floor.
	The elevator *rapidly* sped to the 41st floor.
	The elevator sped *rapidly* to the 41st floor.
	The elevator sped to the 41st floor *rapidly.*
Sentence modifier:	*Nevertheless,* the vote of the members was conclusive.
	The vote of the members, *nevertheless,* was conclusive.
	The vote of the members was conclusive, *nevertheless.*

Some words, however, call for exact placement. For instance, *only, nearly, alone,* or *almost* are some of the words that change the meaning of the sentence when moved about. Notice in the following sentences how placement of *only* gives four different meanings.

Only he worked overtime on that task.
He worked *only* overtime on that task.
He worked overtime *only* on that task.
He worked overtime on that task *only.*

In these sentences the placement of *nearly* changes the meaning.

Nearly half the orders were filled by noon.
Half the orders were *nearly* filled by noon.
Half the orders were filled by *nearly* noon.

Misplaced phrases and clauses cause confusion. Notice that confusion also results when the modifier appears to modify two or more words or is separated from the word it modifies.

Ambiguous:	The salesman exceeded his quota *who handles the southwest territory.*
Clear:	The salesman *who handles the southwest territory* exceeded his quota.
Ambiguous:	Mr. Jenks discussed the problem with Mr. Taylor after which he telephoned the customer. (Who telephoned, Mr. Jenks or Mr. Taylor?)
Clear:	Mr. Jenks, *who discussed the problem with Mr. Taylor,* then telephoned the customer.
Or:	Mr. Jenks discussed the problem with Mr. Taylor, *who then telephoned the customer.*

Remember to (*a*) place a phrase or a clause as close as possible to the word it modifies, (*b*) place a relative or adjective clause *immediately after* the word it modifies, and (*c*) keep the subject as close to the verb as possible.

3. Use parallel construction to express two or more related or similar ideas.

Not:	The meeting was called *to elect new members, for making plans,* and *because we needed to get acquainted.*
But:	The meeting was called **to elect** new members, **to make** plans, and **to get acquainted.**

Make sure items in a series and compound items, such as subjects, objects, and complements, are parallel.

Not:	Neither the sales force wanted a larger quota nor the production department.
But:	Neither the sales force nor the production department wanted a larger quota.
Not:	Please send me two reams of paper, six rulers, and whatever is your best glue.
But:	Please send me two reams of paper, six rulers, and your best glue.

4. Include all words necessary when making a comparison.

Not:	The new sports model is faster than any sports car on the road.
But:	The new sports model is faster than any *other* sports car on the road.

It is illogical to say that a sports car is faster than itself. It is only faster than *other* sports cars. You may say, however, *The new sports model is the **fastest** sports car on the road.*

5. Use *a* or *the* with each of two or more persons or things.

He met *the* auditor and attorney at the courthouse.
    (one person)
He met *the* auditor and *the* attorney at the courthouse.
    (two persons)

6. Repeat a preposition if it helps to clarify the meaning of the sentence.

Please give the tapes *to* the office manager and bookkeeper.
    (one or two persons?)

Please give the tapes *to* the office manager and *to* the bookkeeper. (two persons)

7.   Maintain consistent sentence structure.   Avoid shifts in person, number, tense, and voice.

Shifts in person, number, and tense:	Those employees who wanted his vacation in July should tell their supervisor by the 10th. You should submit your request in writing.
Better:	Those employees who want their vacations in July should tell their supervisors by the 10th. They should submit their requests in writing.

Apply *coherence* to the following sentences.

1.   Jim told the supervisor that it was broken and he would have to fix it.

_____

_____

2.   Please give her a copy before she tells him that he forgot to send it to her.

_____

_____

3.   After figuring the cost, a work sheet should be prepared.

_____

_____

4.   When at work, the golf course is in the back of my mind.

_____

_____

5.   Mr. Howard was promoted to vice president last month, after much deliberation by the board.

_____

_____

_____

6. That hand soap is better than any soap on the market.

_____

_____

_____

7. He sent for the section leader and supervisor.

_____

_____

_____

8. He is going on his vacation after he finished the project.

_____

_____

_____

9. Because we need the facts and to give to the board of directors, the accountant should be asked to compile it.

_____

_____

_____

10. Whom did you ask to tell her that she will not be in until ten?

_____

_____

_____

A sentence should have emphasis: possess action and force.

Your sentences may be absolutely correct and yet be dull to the reader. An important ingredient in a good sentence is *emphasis.* Emphasis puts force into your writing. You can be emphatic by using simple, direct language and by keeping your sentences free of unnecessary words. The reader wants to discover your message easily and will appreciate a direct, forceful opening. For example, parenthetical expressions should be placed in the middle of the sentence.

Your proposal, *it seems,* is based on sound reasoning.

We want you to be the first to know, *since we value your business,* that our new product will fit your need better than ever.

Invert the natural order of a sentence for emphasis.

The way you end a sentence can add emphasis, too. Place important words at the end of a sentence by inverting the natural order. As you learned earlier, the natural order of a sentence is the subject with its modifiers and then the verb with its modifiers. Sentences that change this order add emphasis, such as the following sentence, which begins with an introductory adverb clause.

When we receive your answer, we will ship your order by air freight.

Notice that the above sentence written with the adverb clause separated from the verb it modifies is more emphatic than if it were written in the natural order.

We will ship your order by air freight when we receive your answer.

Do not depend only on *complex* sentences in inverted order to provide emphasis. You must construct strong *simple* sentences that are concise and forceful, as well. You will need *compound* sentences to link two closely related ideas, and you will need *complex* sentences to tie minor ideas to major ideas. Variety in sentence structure makes writing more interesting. In each type of sentence you can gain emphasis through choice of words, placement of ideas, elimination of unnecessary words, and use of the active voice of verbs.

The active voice has the subject performing the action.

The active voice of a verb is the most forceful verb form, because the *subject* of the sentence *acts*. Notice the emphasis in the following sentences that use the active voice.

Active: *The committee reported* that changes would be made in the organization.

Mr. Porter announced a new health program.

The passive voice has the subject acted upon.

The passive is much less direct and forceful.

Passive: It *was reported* by the committee that changes would be made in the organization.

That changes would be made in the organization *was reported by* the committee.

Passive voice is useful when you wish to spotlight an idea by making it the subject of the sentence.

Passive: A new *health program was announced by* Mr. Porter.

You can avoid mentioning the person responsible for an action or the source of certain information by using the passive. Notice that these sentences in the passive voice hide the identity of the person making the announcement.

Passive: A new health program *was announced.*

It *was announced* that a new health program *was accepted.*

Apply *emphasis* to the following sentences.

1. We will ship you the equipment when you send your check for one half the amount due.

   _____

   _____

   _____

2. I think he plans to distribute the merit ratings before noon.

   _____

   _____

   _____

3. Your account is overdue according to our records.

   _____

   _____

   _____

4. It was learned by the secretary that the electric typewriters would arrive on Monday.

   _____

   _____

   _____

5. A new bonus plan is being used by Kaiser Steel.

   _____

   _____

   _____

Careful application of these techniques to assure *unity, coherence,* and *emphasis* in your sentences will make your writing effective. Keep these principles in mind: **WRITE, CRITICIZE, REWRITE.**

Do not try to be completely perfect on the first draft. Experienced writers get their flow of ideas on paper rapidly, then go back and severely criticize their writing. Finally, they rewrite for polished sentence structure. Follow their example. You will be proud of the results of your efforts when you find that you can create an effective message.

Learn to express yourself in a natural way.

Some people seem to think that certain expressions should be used in business writing. Such people have an old-fashioned view of writing in today's business world. A conversational flow of words as you talk to the reader is the manner in which business writing is done today.

Here is a list of trite, hackneyed, old-fashioned expressions that you should avoid. There are suggestions after each that will supply other words to use.

according to our records	Everyone knows you get information from your records. Be specific.
at the present writing, **at this time,** **at this writing**	Use *now*.
at all times	Say *always*.
at your earliest convenience, **at your convenience,** **at an early date**	Be specific: *by tomorrow, by March 15.*
attached find, **attached hereto**	Say *attached is* or *here is*. It will be found if attached.
due to the fact that	Use *because* or *since* and eliminate four words.
enclosed herewith, **enclosed please find**	Use *enclosed is, we are enclosing,* or *we enclose.*
for the purpose of	Wordy. Say it more concisely.

> **Not:** The supervisor called the meeting *for the purpose of* discussing the new agreement.
>
> **Better:** The supervisor called the meeting *to discuss* the new agreement.

for your information	Omit. Everything you say is for the reader's information.
herein, hereto, herewith	These words are too formal and often redundant. Omit.
hoping to receive, **hoping to hear**	Never close a letter with a participial phrase. It is clumsy, impersonal, shows lack of confidence, and is out of date.
in accordance with	Use *by*.
in a position to	Use *can*.
inasmuch as	Use *since*.
in lieu of	Use *instead*.
inquired as to	Use *asked*.
in regard to	Use *about*.
in the amount of	Use *for*.
in the event that	Use *if*.
in the near future	Be specific: *tomorrow? next week?*

of the above date, **recent date**	Mention the date, if important.
please be advised that, **this is to advise you,** **this is to inform you**	Omit. Begin with the subject you want to discuss with the reader.
referring to, replying to, **regarding your, and** **similar participial phrases**	Avoid as you would the plague.
thank you in advance, **thanking you in advance**	Avoid because you imply that your request will be granted.
under separate cover	Be specific: *by express, by parcel post, by mail.*
your letter received **your letter of August 9,** **your letter of recent date**	Begin your message immediately. Obviously, you received the letter or you wouldn't be writing.

ASSIGNMENTS

Apply your knowledge of effective sentences

A. All the sentences below can be classified as ineffective sentences. Some are sentence fragments; some lack unity; some are incoherent and ambiguous; and some lack emphasis. Read each sentence carefully to locate the important idea that needs to be expressed. Next type or write your sentence so that it has unity, coherence, and emphasis. You may find it necessary, for instance, to make one sentence out of two or two sentences out of one, or to change simple sentences to complex or compound.

1. Signs are clearly posted in the halls, and there are always some visitors who lose their way.

2. John did not finish the project and reprimanding him didn't get it finished on time.

3. The time of departure approached. He became more and more excited about attending the seminar.

4. Mrs. Harrison is an excellent accountant and was born in Michigan, graduating from Michigan State University.

_____

_____

_____

_____

5. When shipment is made and you have your new stereo in your home.

_____

_____

_____

6. The new secretary was three years younger than the secretary she replaced but she transcribed her notes much faster and accurately.

_____

_____

_____

7. The computer is an asset in any office, turning out reports rapidly from stored information.

_____

_____

_____

8. Mrs. Edwards hired an accountant and clerk and paid him $850 per month while she offered the other new employee $575.

_____

_____

_____

9. Our new product will be offered to the public on January 15, it was developed by our talented designers. It has been advertised in *Fortune* magazine.

_____

_____

_____

10. Mrs. Perkins, the office manager, told him that she was quitting at the end of the week and she didn't know where she would find someone to take her place.

_____

_____

_____

11. Looking for a qualified machinist, several employment agencies were called by Mr. Stephens.

_____

_____

_____

12. Before leaving for the day, the lights should be turned off.

_____

_____

13. However, the change in procedure should not be made until the figures for the month are in.

_____

_____

_____

14. The personnel department surveyed all the employees before they saw the additional requests of the union.

_____

_____

_____

15. The savings and loan association which is one of the oldest in the city and which developed several desirable savings plans offers to the local savers prepaid certificate accounts or minimum term accounts.

_____

_____

_____

_____

B. Because the principles discussed in this section are so important to anyone who wants to become an effective writer, here are a few exercises that will test your understanding of the writing principles discussed in the text.

1. Define in your own words the following terms:

unity _____

_____

subordinate minor ideas _____

_____

coherence _____

_____

dangling modifier _____

_____

parallel construction _____

_____

emphasis _____

_____

active voice _____

_____

passive voice _____

_____

2. Fill in the word that completes the sentence.

    (*a*) Two or more related ideas should be written in _____ construction.

    (*b*) When making a/an _____, include all necessary words.

    (*c*) You should avoid shifts in _____, _____,

    _____, and _____.

    (*d*) Pronoun references should be _____.

    (*e*) When you express a complete thought, your sentence has _____.

(*f*)   Independent clauses joined in a compound sentence should be _____

_____.

(*g*)   The important idea should be placed in an _____ clause.

(*h*)   Minor related ideas should be placed in a/an _____ clause.

(*i*)   When your sentence is clear and all the words are in the right places, it has

_____.

(*j*)   When your sentence includes action and force, it has _____.

(*k*)   A good business writer should learn to use three types of sentences—

_____, _____, and _____.

(*l*)   The special placement of words at the beginning, the middle, or the end of a sentence can

achieve _____.

Name _____

Date _____

————————————————————— **PRACTICE WRITING** —————————————————————

Here is an opportunity to apply the effective writing principles you have just studied. In the writing assignments below, see that your sentences have unity, coherence, and emphasis.

A. Write a memorandum to a co-worker, asking for information about a job you've just been assigned. You will need to know how to do the job, what tools are needed and where to get them, and who to go to when you need help. You may also want to know how many pieces it is possible to turn out in a day. If you think of something else you would like to know, include it, too. Make your message clear, specific, and forceful.

_____

_____

_____

_____

_____

_____

_____

B. Write a letter to a company ordering several articles you need. Be sure to give complete information as to quantity, color, size, price, and so forth. Include when and where you want the items delivered.

_____

_____

_____

_____

_____

_____

_____

_____

Increase your knowledge of words

The dictionary is a valuable tool for everyone.

The dictionary is the most valuable tool you can use to develop your communication skills. Its main purpose is to record current usage. A modern dictionary tells us the meaning the "average" person is likely to understand. It also reminds us of common meanings that we may not know or tend to forget. When you know the many sections of a dictionary and can use them rapidly and correctly, you will have found valuable companions to accompany you into the business world.

Be sure to read carefully the introductory pages and explanatory notes in the dictionary you are using. These sections usually include an explanation of the content, a guide to pronunciation, and a list of abbreviations used in the book.

The appendixes of most dictionaries include a list of abbreviations used in writing and printing; arbitrary signs and symbols for such subjects as astronomy, chemistry, mathematics, medicine, money, and commerce; biographical names with their pronunciations; a pronouncing gazetteer containing information about countries of the world; a pronouncing vocabulary of common English given names; a vocabulary of rhymes; rules for spelling, punctuation, compounds, capitals, use of italic type, and setup of a bibliography; information on preparing copy for the press plus proofreaders' marks; and a list of colleges and universities in the United States.

Thus you can see that a *good* dictionary also functions to some extent as an English handbook. The following abridged dictionaries are recommended:

Webster's New World Dictionary (College Edition)
Webster's New Collegiate Dictionary
The American Heritage Dictionary of the English Language
Funk and Wagnalls' Standard College Dictionary
Random House College Dictionary

Dictionary entries include spelling, pronunciation, definitions, and other information.

Words are listed alphabetically with the preferred spelling first in **heavy** or **boldface** type. Other accepted spellings follow in heavy type. Foreign words or phrases (*avant-garde*), abbreviations (*c.o.d.*), irregular plurals (*data*), derived forms (*mistrust*), and proper names (*Chiang Kai-shek, Gaspé Peninsula*) are included in the alphabetical listing. Centered periods are used to divide the entry into syllables unless there is a hyphen instead (**ac·com·mo·da·tion, ob·jec·tive, self·re·li·ance, self·re·spect·ing**). The syllabic divisions indicate the proper places for hyphenating at the end of a line. Capitals and apostrophes are also indicated in the entry (**Parkinson's disease**). For compounds, the heavy type entry indicates whether the compound should be hyphenated (**top·heavy**), spelled as two words (**top secret**, *n*), or spelled as one word (**top·most**).

After the boldface entry, the pronunciation of the word is given in parentheses; for example, **live·li·hood** ('līv-lē,hůd), *n*. Immediately following the pronunciation, the part of speech is given (noun, *n.;* pronoun, *pron.;* transitive verb, *v.t.;* intransitive verb, *v.i.;* adjective, *adj.;* conjunction, *conj.;* adverb, *adv.;* preposition, *prep.*). Transitive uses of verbs (those that can take an object) are customarily given before intransitive ones.

Some words can be used as two or even three parts of speech; these are listed in the same entry. Next the various irregular forms of a word are given; for example, nouns with irregular plurals, adjectives with irregular comparatives and superlatives, and irregular verbs. Credit for the origin of a word and its derivations are usually shown after the meaning is given. More space in every dictionary is devoted to the meaning of words than to any other type of information.

Correct spelling and correct pronunciation make it possible to use a word properly.

By acquiring the habit of checking the dictionary for the correct spelling of words that are difficult for you, you will add to the number of words you use easily. Before long, you will have a speaking and writing vocabulary large enough for your beginning job. You will need to add specialized and technical words used by the business field in which you work. The techniques you've learned in college will help you continue to increase your vocabulary.

The correct pronunciation of words is as important as their correct spelling. The way you pronounce a word indicates that you probably know how to spell it. All dictionaries provide a pronunciation key either on the fly leaf and/or at the bottom of each page.

Become familiar with the diacritical marks which are used mainly above vowels to indicate their sound. There are two accent symbols. The symbol ('), as in **moth·er** \'məth-ər\, is used to mark primary stress; the syllable following it is pronounced with greater prominence than the other syllables. The symbol (,), as in **grand·moth·er** \'gran(d)-,məth-ər\, is used to mark secondary stress; a syllable marked for secondary stress is pronounced with less prominence than the one marked (') but with more prominence than one bearing no stress mark at all.

To spell correctly is a challenge.

Few of us are naturally good spellers. Yet we must learn to spell correctly because it is demanded of us by the business world. Only in the literary world can one, such as John Lennon, one of the Beatles, write a book using his own personal style of spelling. In Lennon's book, *In His Own Write,* you will read in the chapter, "On Safairy With Whide Hunter," the following sentence: "Little did he nose that the next day in the early owls of the more-combe, a true story would actually happen." He used misspellings to obtain a comic effect. Misspellings in the business office is misplaced comedy.

In business situations, you need to employ every means to improve your skill in accurate word usage. Here are some ways to tackle the problem.

1. Train your eye so that only the correct form looks proper. Train your

hand so that you write the correct form without a moment's thought or hesitation.

2. Learn to apply clearcut spelling principles and rules that will eliminate the possibility of error in certain confusing groups of words.

3. Pronounce each word accurately. Incorrect spelling is often the result of incorrect pronunciation caused by failure to see all the letters, to recognize accented syllables, or to understand the pronunciation symbols.

4. Define each word accurately to avoid confusion with a word that sounds nearly the same.

5. Recognize prefixes and suffixes.

Prefixes and suffixes can be added to many words.

A prefix may be one or more letters added to the beginning of a word to modify or change its meaning slightly. The spelling of the root word remains the same when the prefix is added. Here are a few with their meanings:

al-, all-	quite, entirely	already, all-around
ante-	before	antedate
anti-	opposite, against	anticlimax
bi-	two, double	bimonthly
co-	with	cooperate
con-, com-	with, together	concrete, commemorate
counter-	against	counteract
de-	from, down, away	detract
dis-	contrary, apart	disapprove
e-, ex-	out of, without	explain
il-	inferior, lacking skill	illogical
inter-	among, between	interaction
intra-	within, inside	intradepartmental
mis-	wrong, wrongly	misshape
per-	through, by means of	perchance
post-	after	postdate
pre-	before	prepossess
pro-	before, in favor of, for	pronoun
re-	back, backward, again	resign
semi-	half	semimonthly
sub-	below	subsidiary
super-	above	superstructure
trans-	across, over	transport

A suffix is a group of letters added to the end of a word. The part of speech of a word is usually changed with the addition of a suffix. Occasionally, the spelling of the root word is changed. In some cases the last letter is doubled, other times it is dropped, and sometimes it is changed to another letter. Here are a few suffixes with examples:

-age	shortage	**-ant**	claimant
-al	renewal	**-ation**	information
-dom	wisdom	**-less**	needless
-ful	purposeful	**-ment**	assignment
-en	lessen	**-ous**	humorous

-ion	rebellion	**-eous**	gaseous
-ian	civilian	**-ness**	willingness
-ility	possibility	**-or**	counselor
-ize	materialize	**-er**	jobber

These word endings require careful study.

-sede, -ceed, -cede endings.   Eleven and *only* eleven words that contain more than one syllable end with the sound *seed*. Of these eleven, *one* ends in *-sede*, *three* in *-ceed*, and the *rest* (7) in *-cede*. Get these eleven words permanently straightened out. The *only* English word that ends with S-E-D-E is *supersede*. The three words that end in C-E-E-D are *succeed, proceed,* and *exceed*. All of the other words end in C-E-D-E—*accede, antecede, concede, intercede, procede, recede,* and *secede.*

supersede	succeed	accede
	proceed	antecede
	exceed	concede
		intercede
		precede
		recede
		secede

-ent, -ant endings.   Many words end in *-ent* and *-ant.* Only a few are frequently misspelled. Train your visual and muscular responses to recognize these adjectives and the nouns derived from them. Look at each word, then cover it with your hand, and write it correctly.

superintendent   _____

superintendence   _____

insistent   _____

insistence   _____

persistent   _____

persistence   _____

dependent   _____

dependence   _____

existent   _____

existence   _____

decendant   _____

decendancy   _____

-ence endings.   The *-ence* ending calls for one of the few English spelling rules. Memorize this rule; it will be a lifesaver. *Every verb ending in* **r** *preceded by a single vowel and accented on the final syllable forms its noun* *with -ence.* Study the following list of verbs. You will realize that each verb is accented on the last syllable and that the *r* is preceded by a *single* vowel.

in-FER'	de-FER'	re-CUR'
pre-FER'	oc-CUR'	de-TER'
re-FER'	in-CUR'	ab-HOR'
con-FER'	con-CUR'	

Before you can spell the noun formed by the *-ence,* you need to know whether to double the *r* or leave it alone. If the accent stays on the *same syllable* when the noun is formed, *double* the *r.*

occurrence	recurrence
incurrence	deterrence
concurrence	abhorrence

If the accent shifts back to the *first syllable* when you add *-ence, do not* double the *r.*

preference	inference
reference	conference
deference	

We have covered all except one of the words in this category that are most subject to error. The other word that gives us trouble is *perseverance.* Its correct ending is *-ance.*

-ible, -able endings. Word endings contribute confusion to our spelling. For example the *-ible/-able* endings seem to be used without rules to direct your choice. Here are five words with these endings that are generally misspelled. Memorize them.

dependable
indispensable
irresistible
irritable (verb: irritate)
inimitable (verb: imitate)

-ify, -efy endings. Consider the verb endings *-ify* and *-efy.* These are easy to conquer when you learn the following fact: Only four verbs end in *-efy: liquefy, rarefy, stupefy,* and *putrefy.*

Verb	**Derivatives**
liquefy	liquefied, liquefaction
rarefy	rarefied, rarefaction
stupefy	stupefied, stupefaction
putrefy	putrefied, putrefaction

All other such verbs end in *-ify.*

These words are often misspelled.

Recall that you were told the ability to spell correctly depends on *memory, habit,* and *educated vision. Remember* the precise combination of letters that make up a word. Then use that combination so often that it becomes *automatic.* Finally, visualize the *correct look* of the word. Every other spelling will look wrong. Study the following frequently misspelled words; apply the principles of memory, habit, and vision.

1. all right — Always two words; think of the opposite, *all wrong.*

2. emba*rr*a*ss*ed — Two *r*'s, two *s*'s.

3. rep*e*tition — Notice that *e* follows the *p*. The first four letters are the same as in *repeat.*

4. re*comm*end — *Commend* is the verb plus the prefix *re-*; therefore *one c*, *two m*'s.

5. categ*e*ry — Use an *e* after the *t.*

6. occa*s*ional — *One s*, not two; but *two c*'s.

7. se*pa*rate — Notice that *a* follows the *p.*

8. comp*a*rative — The *e* in *compare* changes to *a* and then *-tive* is added.

9. di*sapp*oint — *Appoint* plus the prefix *dis-*; one *s*, two *p*'s.

10. di*sapp*ear — *Appear* plus the prefix *dis-*; one *s*, two *p*'s.

11. coo*lly* — To make *cool* an adverb add *-ly*.

12. va*c*uum — Refers to vacant or empty space. One *c* only in *vacuum* and *vacant.*

13. gram*mar* — Poor gram**mar** will *mar* your writing and speaking.

14. defin*i*tely — Notice it is *-itely.*

15. their — *Their*—possessive case of the pronoun *they.*

    they're — *They're*—contraction of *they are.*

    there — *There*—an adverb meaning *in that place* or *at that place.*

    — Also used to begin sentences in which the subject comes after the verb.

16. too — *Too*—an adverb meaning in addition or excessive.

    two — *Two*—a number.

    to — *To*—a preposition.

17. believe
    belief — *i* before *e.*

18. wr*i*te
    wr*i*ting
    wr*i*ter — These words use only one *t* after the long *i* sound.

19. *description*
    de*scribe* — The root word here is *scribe* plus the prefix *de-*.

20. *precede* — Do not confuse with *proceed*. *Precede* means to go before in time, rank or importance.

21. benefit
    benefi*ted*
    benefi*cial* — Notice that the Latin prefix is *bene*. The tricky past tense requires only one *t*. The adjective *beneficial* changes the spelling.

22. its — *Its* is the possessive case of the pronoun *it.*

    it's — *It's* is a contraction of *it is.*

23. person*al* — Check your pronunciation of these two words; they are spelled and pronounced differently.

	person*nel*	The *personnel* department asked for my *personal* record.
24.	simil*ar*	*Similar* has the **ar** ending.
25.	*per*form *per*formance	Pronounce these words carefully; the prefix is *per-*.

These spelling hints are helpful.

The preceding guidelines should help you eliminate a great many spelling errors you are likely to make in writing. As has been stated before, correct spelling is vital in business communications where accuracy is of utmost importance. Additional hints are provided below to help you improve your ability to be accurate. Whatever you choose to do, memorize these hints or use them for reference, the knowledge you acquire will give you confidence in your ability to spell.

1. Memorize the *ie* rule.

I before *E*
Except after *C*
Or when sounded like *A*
As in *neighbor* or *weigh*.

Some *ie* words are *believe, niece, siege, field, achieve*. The following words have the *ei* because the *c* immediately precedes the vowel combination: *receive, receipt, ceiling, conceive, conceit*.

You will need to learn these *exceptions:*

e*i*ther	se*i*zure	anc*i*ent
fore*i*gn	she*i*k	consc*i*ence
he*i*ght	we*i*rd	financ*i*er
le*i*sure		
ne*i*ther		
se*i*ze		

2. Many word endings (suffixes) are merely added to the root word.

port	portable	beat	beating
change	changeable	benefit	benefiting
replace	replaceable	dye	dyeing
notice	noticeable	hinge	hingeing
agree	agreeable	lean	leaning
		report	reporting
mile	mileage	toil	toiling
		plead	pleading
portray	portrayal		
		casual	casually
annoy	annoyance	final	finally
		legal	legally
reform	reformation	sincere	sincerely
		usual	usually

cancel	canceled		
equal	equaled	agree	agreement
soak	soaked	encourage	encouragement
travel	traveled		
		kind	kindness
advantage	advantageous	sudden	suddenness
courage	courageous		
		nine	nineteen
hope	hopeful		
success	successful	nine	ninety, **but** *ninth*

3. Some word endings cause the spelling of the root word to be changed.

a. When the word ends with a consonant, **double** the consonant when adding an ending that begins with a vowel.

One-syllable word ending in a consonant preceded by a single vowel.

fit	fit*ted*
drop	drop*ped*
plan	plan*ned*
bag	bag*gage*
wrap	wrap*ping*

Two-syllable word ending in a consonant preceded by a single vowel, *if the accent is on the last syllable.*

remit	remit*tance*
begin	begin*ning*
transfer	transfer*red*
occur	occur*ring*

b. When the word ends in a silent *e,* drop the *e* when adding an ending that begins with a vowel.

come	com*ing*
debate	debat*able*
desire	desir*able*
arrive	arriva*l*
type	typ*ing*
use	us*able*
argue	argu*ing*

c. When the word ends in *y* preceded by a consonant, change the *y* to *i* before a suffix, except when the suffix begins with *i.*

busy	bus*ily*	busy*ing*
carry	carr*ier*	carry*ing*
copy	cop*ied*	copy*ing*

d.   When the word ends in *ie*, change the *ie* to *y* when adding *ing*.

lie   ly*ing*

tie   ty*ing*

4.   The addition of *prefixes* such as *de, dis, mis, non, re, un, trans, in,* and others does not change the spelling of the root word.

*dis*satisfy	*re*commend
*mis*direct	*un*natural
*mis*spell	*in*numerous
*de*scribe	*non*sense

ASSIGNMENTS

Apply your knowledge of words

A. To increase your vocabulary, develop the dictionary habit: study it; learn the history (etymology) of words; and hunt up synonyms for words you overwork. Make it a point to add new words every day. Practice using the dictionary as indicated in 1 to 5 below.

1. The preferred spelling of the word is shown in boldface type and given first. Other accepted spellings follow in heavy type. Which of the following is preferred?

   (*a*)   colour, color   (*d*)   labor, labour
   (*b*)   goodbye, good-by   (*e*)   programing, programming
   (*c*)   distill, distil   (*f*)   though, tho

2. The dictionary gives the word in syllables and shows its accent mark or marks. Distinguish between the strong and less strong accent marks, and place one or both with the proper syllable after you have syllabicated the following words.

   (*a*)   *beneficial*   _____   (*d*)   *employees*   _____

   (*b*)   *stationary*   _____   (*e*)   *convenient*   _____

   (*c*)   *managerial*   _____   (*f*)   *possibility*   _____

3. Diacritical marks (listed at the bottom of the page in most dictionaries) used in the respelling of the word show the correct pronunciation. Indicate the pronunciation of each of the following words.

   (*a*)   *data*   _____   (*d*)   *functional*   _____

   (*b*)   *dictate*   _____   (*e*)   *obsolete*   _____

   (*c*)   *category*   _____   (*f*)   *incorporation*   _____

4. The parts of speech of words are indicated by an abbreviation (noun, *n;* verb, *v;* adjective, *adj.;* adverb, *adv.;* etc.) immediately following the pronunciation. Some words can be used as two or even three parts of speech. How may these words be used?

(*a*) *consistent* _____   (*d*) *extreme* _____

(*b*) *principal* _____   (*e*) *miscellaneous* _____

(*c*) *perpetuate* _____   (*f*) *prefer* _____

5. Principal parts of verbs are shown, especially if they are irregular verbs. Look up the following verbs, write out their principal parts, and note if they can be used as other parts of speech.

(*a*) *consummate* _____

(*b*) *incline* _____

(*c*) *bid* _____

(*d*) *lend* _____

(*e*) *forecast* _____

(*f*) *send* _____

B.   The following sentences test your ability to recognize misspelled words. Underline all misspelled words you find, and write the word correctly in the blank at the end of the line. If there are no errors, write *OK*.

1. The presdent said that the indictment supersedes the original document.   _____

2. He was given explisit directions to limit his activities.   _____

3. The recommendations of the committee were presented in writting.   _____

4. It is easier and wiser to suspend judgement until the facts are known.   _____

5. The majority of the approppriation acts and resolutions were special in nature.   _____

6. Your first duty will be to pursuade the person to work.   _____

7. A predicament is a situation that may be disagreeible or comical.   _____

8. What remained was a few unrecognizible fragments.   _____

9. Advancment is slow because opportunities for promotion are infrequent.   _____

10. The responsability for the situation was put on those to whom it belonged.   _____

11. The possibility of the same problem recurring has been eliminated by the use of a management check-and-balance system.   _____

12. It was difficult to arouse him to any appreciation of monatary aspects of the situation.   _____

13. The students found it impossible to adjust to the requirments. _____

14. The exhibit deserved a more conspicious location and more favorable criticism than it received. _____

15. I feel we should procede with the original sales forecast. _____

    C. Correct any misspelled words in the following list by writing the correct form of the word on the blank line. Place an *OK* in the blank if the word is correct.

1.	catagory	_____	11. questionaire	_____
2.	bankrupcy	_____	12. ordinerily	_____
3.	assertain	_____	13. competitive	_____
4.	separate	_____	14. priviledge	_____
5.	similiar	_____	15. maintainance	_____
6.	occurrance	_____	16. occassional	_____
7.	relevent	_____	17. alright	_____
8.	personnal	_____	18. vaccuum	_____
9.	eliminate	_____	19. grammer	_____
10.	accomodate	_____	20. disappoint	_____

    D. Fill in the missing letters in the following words with either *ei* or *ie.*

1. modif___r	9. l___n	17. hyg___ne	25. l___sure
2. w___gh	10. len___nt	18. consc___nce	26. pat___nt
3. var___ty	11. cl___nts	19. gr___f	27. w___rd
4. y___ld	12. forf___t	20. conc___t	28. conc___ve
5. d___tary	13. n___ghbor	21. s___ge	29. ach___ve
6. misch___f	14. recip___nt	22. f___rce	30. rec___ve
7. d___fy	15. b___ge	23. l___utenant	
8. effic___nt	16. bel___ve	24. med___val	

    E. The following letter is to be proofread carefully to eliminate all spelling and typographical errors. Underline the misspelled words and write them correctly in the column.

1.   Dear Customar: _____

2.   Febuary is the month "forward-thinking" men all _____

3.   over Southern California start taking advanage of our   _____

4.   Advance Slection Plan . . . and when you think of the   _____

5.   advantages of early buying, it makes sense. Here's how   _____

6.   it words: _____

7.   You make your selection of a liteweight suit now   _____

8.   when our stocks are the largst ever. Have your suit   _____

9.   fited, alterred, and delivered now. Youll get the   _____

10.   best posible service from our tailer shops.   _____

11.   Pay latter! The charge will not appear on your   _____

12.   statment until May, and then your usual terms   _____

13.   will aply, up to six months if you have an optionel   _____

14.   account.   _____

15.   We cordialy invite you to come in and see the largst   _____

16.   selection of Hart Schaffner & Marx suits in the Southland.   _____

17.   Note paticularly the new HS&M and Silverwood's topical   _____

18.   suits mentioned on the atached page.   _____

19.   Get sit for your most comfortible summer ever by   _____

20.   puting our Advance Slection Plan into action now!   _____

               Sincrely yours,   _____

F.   The addition of prefixes to words is a straightforward addition. In the addition of suffixes, however, the spelling of the basic word is often changed before the suffix is added. Add the prefixes and/or suffixes given in parentheses to the following words.

1. allot (ed)   _____   6. nine (ty)   _____

2. picnic (ing)   _____   7. (il) logical   _____

3. omit (ed)   _____   8. remove (al)   _____

4. loose (ly)   _____   9. qualify (ed)   _____

5. regret (able)   _____   10. general (ly)   _____

11. benefit (ing) _____

12. interfere (ed) _____

13. insist (ence) _____

14. like (able) _____

15. occur (ing) _____

16. liquid (fy) _____

17. file (ing) _____

18. cancel (ed) _____

19. permit (ing) _____

20. change (able) _____

21. courage (eous) _____

22. acknowledge (ment) _____

23. due (ly) _____

24. (dis) satisfy _____

25. (de) scribe _____

26. (im) mature _____

G. Each of the following sentences may contain one or more misspelled or wrong words. Draw a line under the word or words that need to be changed or corrected. Place the new word(s) or the correctly spelled word(s) in the blank at the right.

1. The exam schdule will be available soon for the fall quarter. _____

2. Counceling is by appointment only. _____

3. The Registar's Office provides an official record of a student's acedemic achievement. _____

4. Students must file the registration application and perfered program card with his study list packets. _____

5. Faculty representatives will be partisipating in registration. _____

6. The degree will be granted if the requirements are fullfilled. _____

7. The paper should be typed and the format should be of journal quality. _____

8. To be admited to graduate statis in the school, a student must meet certain conditions. _____

9. These course is one of the most valueable I have had. _____

10. Are you interested in becoming a programmer? _____

11. A doctoral comittee shall consist of a minimum of five members. _____

12. We have been particulerly concerned with the student's ability to handle the course. _____

13. Incomplete forms may cause unecessary delay in prosessing and payment. _____

14. The applicant must furnish three letters of recomendation. _____

15. Allocatting teaching course load will be decided by the Chairman of the department. _____

H.   These few lines recently appeared in the *Reader's Digest*. How many misspelled words can you find?

Colledges Don't Like Pore Spelers

Its no suprise that this going to colledge bussiness takes a lot of studing, grammer and literture. If your not atheletic or captian of the team, colledges sincerly belief there students must have unusal mental equiptment. They won't take you, even if you're famly dosen't like it, just becaus you want too go.

_____ Misspelled Words.

Name _____

Date _____

PRACTICE WRITING

In your dictionary, find five or more words that are new to you. Read the definitions, check the pronunciations, and use each word in an effective sentence. If possible, use these new words tomorrow when talking or writing.

New word   *Used in a sentence*

1. _____   _____

   _____

2. _____   _____

   _____

3. _____   _____

   _____

4. _____   _____

   _____

5. _____   _____

   _____

6. _____   _____

   _____

7. _____   _____

   _____

8. _____   _____

   _____

9. _____   _____

   _____

10. _____   _____

   _____

The role of mechanical devices in business writing

Mechanical devices are aids to clarity.

The most important mechanical device used in constructing sentences is punctuation. Other mechanical aids to writing clarity include the use of hyphens in compound words and division of words, capitalization, abbreviation, and expression of numbers. Your purpose in all writing, of course, is to convey the message you have in mind to the mind of your reader. Thus, if you master the commonly accepted standards for using the mechanical devices presented in this section, you have assurance that the knowledge you acquire and use will help your reader to understand your message. Unclear letters and reports are costly for these reasons: (1) they may require the reader to seek interpretation, (2) they may result in improper action, and (3) they may create legal disputes.

Hyphens have an important role in compound words

Are you puzzled whether to hyphenate or not to hyphenate? Experienced writers solve this problem by thinking about the intended meaning of the words and by applying the generally accepted guidelines for hyphenation.

Hyphens connect two or more words that express a single idea.

A hyphen indicates a close relationship between words. Two or more words, combining to make a single thought, are usually connected by hyphens. The most important reason for using the hyphen is to make the meaning clear.

Some compound expressions, however, do not require hyphens. When deciding whether to write a compound expression as one word, two words, or a hyphenated word, you need to determine what the compound means and to recall the guidelines you have learned about correct hyphenation. Some authorities may differ on the use of the hyphen, but the guidelines presented in this section reflect current business practices. If you are in doubt about the form of a compound word, you should consult a recent dictionary.

Use hyphens with some compound nouns and adjectives.

Compound nouns. Some compound nouns are hyphenated. Others are written as single words or as two words. Compound nouns requiring hyphens often consist of one or more nouns plus an adjective or a preposition. They also may be made up of words other than nouns. A few words with hyphens are given below. (See also pages 111, 122–23, and 245–46.)

court-martial	follow-up	pay-off
mother-in-law	go-between	stand-in

Compound adjectives. Use a hyphen to join two or more words used as a compound adjective to modify a noun.

He is a *well-known* speaker on business ethics.

We need an *up-to-date* list of their clients.

First-class accommodations are available.

In the following situations the hyphen is **not** used:

1. When the compound adjective follows the noun it modifies. (The words are given separate emphasis.)

This list of clients is *up to date.*

The accommodations were *first class.*

The speaker was *well known.*

2. When one of the modifiers is an adverb ending in *ly.*

She was a *highly efficient* office manager.

The *newly hired* stenographer typed the minutes.

A *widely diversified* investment program is advisable.

3. When two or more independent adjectives precede the noun. (Each one modifies the noun separately.)

The teacher spoke about *important economic* concepts.

My new boss is an *outstanding public* servant.

She bought a *speculative common* stock.

The Green family grew mushrooms in a *cool, damp* cellar.
(Refer to Section 6, Part 2, for explanation of the use of the comma in the last sentence.)

4. When one of the words in a compound adjective is in the comparative or superlative degree.

One of the books is the *highest priced* book on management published this year.

When the compound adjective, however, merely describes the noun, it is hyphenated.

The manager bought two *high-priced* books on management principles.

Use hyphens with fractions before nouns.

Use the hyphen with fractions written as words and immediately followed by the nouns they modify.

The new law requires a *two-thirds* vote to pass.

My partner will be given a *one-half* interest in the business.

Two and *one-half* years' training is needed for the job.
(Refer to Section 3, Part 3, for use of the possessive with the word *years.*)

If the fraction is not immediately followed by the noun it modifies, do *not* use the hyphen.

Their interest in the land was *two thirds.*

The absentees represent *one half* of the group.

One third of the shipment was damaged.

Use hyphens with compound numerals.

Use a hyphen in writing compound numerals under one hundred and compounds used to express time. Do *not* use the hyphen with round numbers, such as *one hundred, one thousand, one million.*

Twenty-six people were present.

We shall see you in the office at *two-thirty.*

Spell out *one hundred thirty-two* dollars when writing a check.

Single-thought words require hyphens.

Use hyphens in unusual combinations of words or special improvised words that convey a single thought.

know-how *(noun)*	blue-pencil *(adj.* or *verb)*	X-ray *(adj.* or *verb)*
gray-blue *(adj.)*	dry-clean *(verb)*	(*X ray* as a *noun*
runner-up *(noun)*	cross-examine *(verb)*	is not hypenated.)
write-up *(noun)*	work-stopper *(noun)*	

A number of single-thought words have been combined in common usage and are written as one word. The following are examples:

coffeepot	bookkeeping	screenplay
nighthawk	nickname	photoelectric
shopworn	waterproof	businessman

Use hyphens in certain prefixes and suffixes.

Use the hyphen in writing words with certain prefixes and suffixes.

1. *Self, vice,* and *ex* used as prefixes and *elect* used as a suffix are usually hyphenated.

self-sufficient	ex-President Greenburg
self-made	Vice-chancellor Saxon
self-addressed	Governor-elect Williams

Exceptions: selfsame, selfless

Hyphens are *not* used in compounds *ending* in *self, ship, ever,* and *hood,* such as *himself, statehood, workmanship, whichever.*

2. In prefixes joined to proper names and in compounds of unusual word formations, use hyphens. The prefix is usually not capitalized unless it is a part of the proper name or title.

un-American	pre-January sale
non-Catholic	Pan-American
pro-British	ex-consul
Trans-Atlantic	ex-President Kerr

3. Some words are hyphenated to avoid consecutive vowels or triple consonants or in writing confusing combinations of letters.

bell-like	anti-imperialist
tie-up	semi-invalid
follow-up	trade-in

4. Some words beginning with *re* that are spelled the same may need the hyphen to set forth the difference in meaning between them.

re-cover (to cover again)	recover (to retrieve)
re-treat (to treat again)	retreat (to withdraw)
re-form (to form again)	reform (to change)

Study special situations.

Use hyphens in the following situations:

1. When one word in a phrase is not to be joined to the following word but is to be joined to a word appearing later in the sentence. (Such usage is referred to as the suspensive hyphen.)

long- and short-term capital gains
French- and German-speaking residents
12- and 14-story buildings

A space is always left after the suspensive hyphen whether it is handwritten or typed to show that the word is not connected to the one next to it. (See pages 245–46.)

2.   After a single letter to join it to a word when making a descriptive adjective or noun.

an A-frame cabin	an S-curve
a T-square	a U-turn

Hyphens are *not* required in these situations:

1.   With frequently used one-thought modifiers that are clear without the hyphen.

life insurance policy	civil service jobs
high school student	new car sales
social security payments	real estate convention

2.   With a proper name composed of two words and used as an adjective.

New York shows	Western Union cablegram
South American countries	New England states
Supreme Court decisions	Far Eastern customs

Note, however, that when the adjective is compounded from *two* proper nouns, the hyphen is used.

Milwaukee-Chicago route
New York-Los Angeles flight
Anglo-Saxon word

3.   With names of official positions or with civil, government, or military titles.

Purchasing Agent	Chief of Police
Attorney at Law	Lieutenant Colonel
Secretary of State	Sales Manager
Attorney General	Rear Admiral

Note: When the title represents two combined offices, it *is* hyphenated, such as *Secretary-Treasurer.*

ASSIGNMENTS

Apply your knowledge of hyphens

A. Place hyphens where necessary in the following sentences.

1. The manager received an up to date price list.
2. He wanted a two thirds interest in the new business.
3. Thirty three of the employees were given raises in salary.
4. All highly rated employees were promoted.
5. Our manager, who was well known, kept a detailed calendar.
6. He was particularly noted for his know how.
7. Some employees say our manager is a self made person.
8. The secretary treasurer of the corporation should understand corporate law.
9. There are several employees in the office, and absenteeism is one third that of last month.
10. Each employee understands the importance of a contribution to the overall know how of the firm.
11. Social Security payments are deducted from each worker's weekly pay.
12. One of the individuals in the office was given a traffic ticket for making a U turn.
13. Our supervisor took a Chicago New Orleans flight to attend an important conference.
14. Federal income tax rules have recently been changed on long and short term capital gains.
15. Our manager tries to provide work for invalids and semi invalids.

B. Place hyphens where necessary in the following sentences, and circle words that are usually written as one word. Check the dictionary if you are unsure of the preferred usage.

1. Open shelf filing is useful for large envelopes and packets.
2. General correspondence not requiring follow up should be kept no longer than one month.
3. Whether to keep papers for one, two, or three month periods depends on the nature of the content.
4. Probably, more than one half of all filed material is useless.
5. Files in large offices should be kept by expert file clerks and not by general office clerks working on a part time basis.
6. Filing should be done on a daily basis, not as a rainy day job.
7. The know how of filing then becomes important.
8. Non alphabetic filing systems have definite disadvantages.

9. The self sufficient filing clerk is a great asset to a firm.
10. Frequently, long reports in the over ten page category are filed and are unused.
11. Careful workmanship in a filing department requires checking and rechecking.
12. Good service from a filing department makes necessary up to date, labor saving, time saving, and functional equipment.
13. Most office employees can look forward to receiving Social Security payments.
14. Two hundred fifty four managers met in Houston for the convention.
15. Work hours may be regulated by federal or state statutes.
16. As an ex secretary, the supervisor will understand secretarial problems.
17. The office is only about one tenth as mechanized as the factory.
18. New equipment must fit into the long range plans of the company.
19. The office manager was well known in Los Angeles.
20. Naturally, the office supervisor must keep up to date.

C. Place hyphens where necessary in the following sentences.

1. The office uses one, two, and three part forms depending on the number of people to receive copies.
2. The new manager was intent upon a program of urgently needed reform in office methods.
3. Supreme Court decisions have had a highly effective influence on employment practices.
4. High priced equipment does not assure an efficient office.
5. One third of the employees belong to the credit union.
6. We will meet you after the office closes at four thirty.
7. The supervisor received the write up of our absentee study at nine o'clock.
8. The personnel manager interviews many high school students.
9. Are you going to take the Chicago New York shuttle plane?
10. One of our supervisors left to take a civil service job.
11. As a businessman or businesswoman you will be well paid if you have ideas that will make money for your employer.
12. In mid winter we suffer in our cold, damp office.
13. When you send for information, a self addressed envelope may insure an answer.
14. Mrs. Harper will be the stand in for the office manager.
15. After the manager attended the administrator's meeting, he visited some of the New England states.

Name _____

Date _____

PRACTICE WRITING

Compose original sentences that illustrate the correct use of hyphens, as directed below.

1. Compound adjective before the noun _____

_____

2. Compound adjective following the noun _____

_____

3. A fraction (spelled out) preceding the noun _____

_____

4. Time in hours and minutes _____

_____

5. Measurement using figures and words _____

_____

6. Two or more adjectives with a common root word _____

_____

7. An unusual compound adjective that conveys a single thought _____

_____

8. A hyphenated prefix _____

_____

9. A compound proper noun adjective _____

_____

10. A prefix with a proper noun _____

_____

Appropriate word division contributes to clarity

Word division is occasionally necessary to make the right margin of a letter, manuscript, or report as even as possible. The *hyphen* is used to indicate this division in a word. This process is sometimes called syllabication.

The syllable is the basis for all correct word division. Therefore, it is necessary to pronounce each word to determine where the syllable break occurs. The dictionary should be consulted if you are in doubt.

pres-ent *(noun)*   **but**   pre-sent *(verb)*

pref-erence *(noun)*   **but**   pre-fer *(verb)*

Try to avoid dividing words whenever possible. If it is necessary, the following guides should be followed.

Use these word division guides.

1.   Divide only between syllables.

busi-ness   knowl-edge   pag-eant   rup-ture

One-syllable words should not be divided.

through   strength   weight   rate

Words pronounced as one syllable are not divided.

shipped   talked   planned   wrecked

2.   Leave at least *two letters* at the end of a line of writing and carry over at least *three* letters to the next line. This promotes continuity of thought. Also, the last word in a paragraph or the last word on a page should not be divided. Avoid dividing the last word in more than two consecutive lines.

3.   Do not divide contractions.

shouldn't   haven't   they're

4.   Do not divide abbreviations, figures, or symbols.

memo.   U.S.A.   Y.M.C.A.   3:30 p.m. $25.25

Follow these suggestions for improving word division.

1. Divide *between* double consonants unless the double consonant is part of the root word.

begin-ning   suc-ceed   omit-ted   ship-ping   pos-sible   recom-mend
But: drill-ing   pass-ing   full-est

2. Divide *after* a one-vowel syllable that occurs within a word (sometimes called a dangling vowel syllable).

reg-u-lar: divided *regu-lar*
tel-e-vision: divided *tele-vision*
vis-i-tor: divided *visi-tor*

3. Divide *between* two consecutive vowels that are pronounced individually.

gradu-a-tion: divided *gradu-ation*
anx-i-e-ty: divided *anxi-ety*
con-tin-u-ation: divided *continu-ation*

4. Divide *before* a recognized suffix such as *able, ible,* or *ical.*

agree-able   deduct-ible   crit-ical

5. Divide one-word compounds *between* the compound elements.

letterhead: divided *letter-head*
manhood: divided *man-hood*
blackboard: divided *black-board*

6. Divide hyphenated words *only* at the hyphen.

self-/addressed   law-/abiding   one-/third part

7. Avoid dividing proper names. When a division is necessary, divide *after* the title and initials or *after* the title and first name.

Miss Jane / Morris   Mr. J. D. / Morgan

8. Do not separate degrees or other letters after a name from the surname. For example, in writing Dr. Albert M. Katz, M.D., do not carry M.D. over to the next line. If there must be a division, divide *after* the middle initial *M.,* Dr. Albert M. / Katz, M.D.

9. Do not separate dates between month and day. If some division is necessary, write January 10, / 1945 or Janu- / ary 10, 1945.

ASSIGNMENTS

Apply your knowledge of word division

A. Use the following directions in completing this exercise:

1. If the word at the end of the line is not divided correctly, write it as it should be divided on the line at the right—for example, *acceptable,* write *accept*-able. Pronounce each word to determine where to divide into syllables.
2. Write *ND* (no division) if the word should not be divided.
3. Write *avoid* if the word is preferably not divided.
4. Write *OK* if it is correctly divided.

1. We found the reports to be be-
lievable.   _____

2. The series of letters was a contin-
uation of our first mailing.   _____

3. When the visitor stop-
ped talking, I asked him to come into my office.   _____

4. We also ordered some of the let-
terhead stationery.   _____

5. Most of the letters had self-
addressed envelopes.   _____

6. When the meeting was over, I had no de-
sire to leave.   _____

7. Someone in the office said sel-
ling was an easy job.   _____

8. The secretary thinks that my i-
deas should be kept to myself.   _____

9. I hope the new schedule will be a reg-
ular policy in the office.   _____

10. Some of the employees could-
n't operate the computer   _____

11. When the vote was taken, the staff recom-
mended that Mr. White be the chairman.   _____

12. If we are interested in progress, a planned program should be arranged.   _____

13. The man who came into the office said that nobody was at the reception desk.   _____

14. If you wish to succeed in life, acquire as much knowledge as possible while in school.   _____

15. The young children today are watching too much television.   _____

    B.   Follow the directions below in checking these sentences:

    1.   On the line to the right, indicate where the division should occur if you do not agree with the one in the sentence.

    2.   If you think it is correct, write *OK*.

1. Miss Hall, my secretary, is leaving February 5.   _____

2. The letter was addressed to Mr.
John McKinley.   _____

3. I think everyone left at 5:30
p.m.   _____

4. He was the former chief of C.I.
A.   _____

5. The noted surgeon's name was Dr. David H.
Hoffman.   _____

6. The sign on the door was ALBERT M. BROWN,
M.D.   _____

7. The package of paper weighed 25 pounds, 6
ounces.   _____

8. Is the date of the letter November 25?   _____

9. The astronauts were aboard ship 15 minutes after recovery.   _____

10. The bookkeeper was conscientious, efficient, and thorough.   _____

    C.   Follow the directions below:

    1.   Divide the following words into their correct syllables for word division by rewriting the words on the line at the right and placing a diagonal where division or divisions could occur. Be sure to pronounce each word to determine where to divide into syllables.

    2.   If the word cannot be divided, write *ND*.

1. fulfilling	_____	6. confessed	_____
2. beginning	_____	7. haven't	_____
3. self-defense	_____	8. unnecessary	_____
4. trapped	_____	9. manageable	_____
5. parasite	_____	10. strength	_____

11. following _____

12. noisy _____

13. anxiety _____

14. separate _____

15. confusion _____

16. 1,500,000 _____

17. nevertheless _____

18. nothing _____

19. matter-of-fact _____

20. Y.M.C.A. _____

21. New Hampshire _____

22. September 15 _____

23. Mr. James A. Willows _____

24. collectible _____

25. apologize _____

26. Training Dynamics, Inc. _____

27. 12-inch _____

28. $1,450.50 _____

29. specifically _____

30. Wednesday _____

Capitalization is important in writing

Words are capitalized to give them emphasis and to clarify statements in which they are used. If you wish to become a skilled writer, you should learn the common practices of capitalization. There are special situations, such as in advertising and legal writing, where the usual rules are not always followed. Such deviations from common usage can be learned on the job. When you write letters and reports in business, however, you are more likely to be correct if you follow the generally accepted rules explained below. They are easy to apply and to remember.

Capitalize first words.

You are familiar with most of the conventional uses of capitals for first words in various kinds of writing. A brief review, however, may be helpful. Capitalize the following:

1. The first word of every sentence.

A package is expected.
The house is vacant.

2. The first word of a direct quotation when it is a complete sentence.

The department manager said, "Your speech was most impressive."

3. A single word or the first word of a phrase that expresses a complete thought.

Certainly.   Yes, of course.
Probably.   Not exactly.
What for?   When?

4. The first word in a complete sentence that follows a colon.

A wonderful thing happened to me today: My boss gave me a raise.

However, the first word after a colon is not capitalized if the statement introduced is a dependent element.

The office exists for two reasons: to give service to customers and to provide information to managers.

5. The first word of each item in an outline.

    A. Types of life insurance policies
       1. Whole life
       2. Endowment
       3. Annuity
       4. Term

Capitalize titles, headings, and subheads.

The first word and all other words except articles, conjunctions, and prepositions should be capitalized in titles of the following: (1) reports, (2) technical papers or briefs, (3) books, (4) articles, (5) magazines, and others not illustrated, such as speeches, poems, plays, newspapers, musical compositions.

    1. An Analysis of the United States Employment Service
    2. The Economic Aspects of Occupational Choice
    3. *Dimensions in Communication*
    4. "Are You Getting Your Words' Worth?"
    5. *California Management Review*

Titles of books and magazines should be underlined to distinguish them from smaller works, such as reports, or set in italics if the reference is printed.

Headings and subheadings in reports and articles follow the same general practice of capital letters for the first and last words and all other important words in the heading.

Capitalize special parts of letters.

The first word, all nouns, and titles are capitalized in a salutation.

Dear Professor Weeks   My dear John   Dear Friend

In the complimentary close, only the first word is capitalized.

Yours truly   Sincerely yours   Cordially yours

Capitalization in attention and subject lines follows the common practice for titles—capital letters for all important words.

Attention: All Swing-Shift Employees
Subject: The Glass Industry's Need for Closer Cooperation
Re: Automobile Insurance Policy No. 828914

In the inside address, an individual's title, the name of the department, and the company name are capitalized. Street, city, and state names are always capitalized.

Mr. James A. Smith, Director
Engineering Division
Lockheed-California Company
459 Victory Boulevard
Burbank, California

Company names in the complimentary close may be written in all capitals or capitals and lower case, but the typed signature lines should be written in capitals and lower case.

GENERAL MOTORS CORPORATION	Advance Products Co., Inc.
James A. Brown, Vice President	Elwood B. Thomas
	Sales Manager

Capitalize proper nouns.

A proper noun is always written with a capital letter whereas a common noun is usually written with a small letter. You should keep in mind these general principles: (1) A proper noun names one particular person, a group of people, a place, or a thing; (2) a common noun names one of a kind—*desk, machine, car, pencil*. The rules given below will assist you to apply these principles.

Capitalize the names and nicknames of people.

Wilbur N. Smith

Stretch Smith

Personal names and titles. Capitalize titles when used with personal names to show profession, office, rank, or family relationship.

Professor Fred Johnson	Robert Kelly, Chairman
President Richard Sigband	John Green, President
Private Henry Jones	Treasurer Henry Ureda
Cousin David	Lt. Colonel Peter Hunt

Titles may be used with the last name if identity is clear.

| President Field | Mayor Green |
| Chairman Meyers | Senator Hilton |

Many titles that precede or follow a person's name may be abbreviated to save time in writing.

Dr.   Mr.   Mrs.   Mmes.   Messrs.   Jr.   M.D.

Academic degrees

Ph.D.	Doctor of Philosophy	Henry Brown, Ph.D.
B.S.	Bachelor of Science	Jeffrey Lloyd, M.B.A.
B.A.	Bachelor of Arts	Frank Johnson, M.D.
M.B.A.	Master of Business Administration	
M.S.	Master of Science	
M.A.	Master of Arts	
M.D.	Doctor of Medicine	

Hyphenated elements, *ex-* and *-elect*, and the words *late* or *former* are not capitalized when joined to titles.

The late President Eisenhower

The main speaker was ex-Governor Thomas.

Mayor-elect Davis will take office soon.

Titles showing family relationship used in place of personal names, or to show relationship without personal names, are usually not capitalized. These titles are often introduced by such words as *a, an, my, his,* and *your*.

My mother is driving my father to the airport.

His brother works in production, and my sister is a secretary in engineering.

Company names. Names and subdivisions of companies, institutions, organizations, libraries, and foundations should be capitalized. Articles, prepositions, and conjunctions within the name are usually not capitalized.

Pan American Air Lines	Accounting Department
Northwestern University	Mathematics Department
Bay View Theater	Public Relations Office
Kiwanis Club	Education Committee
General Tire & Rubber Corporation	Treasurer's Department
Huntington Library	Special Collections Department
First Methodist Church	Escrow Department
Bank of America	

Some writers prefer to capitalize the words *company* and *corporation* when used alone to refer to a particular company. *Company* and *corporation,* however, are usually not capitalized when used alone.

Brand names. Brand names are capitalized because they name specific products. Product types are not capitalized because they refer to the general item regardless of maker or special name.

Capitalize	but	Do not capitalize
Ford		automobile
Heinz		catsup
Nescafe		coffee
Arrow		shirts

Government terms. Names of governmental agencies, departments, offices, and legislative bodies are capitalized.

Building and Safety Commission	Supreme Court
Federal Housing Administration	Office of the President
Department of Public Works	The White House
Secretary of State	

Government terms need not be capitalized when they are used as adjectives or when they refer generally to the local, state, or national government.

He is a federal employee.

The government regulates railroad operations.

If the intent, however, is to refer to a particular government, the words *federal, government, union, nation, commonwealth,* or *state* may be capitalized.

Our Government must set up ways to control environmental pollution.

Geographical terms. Geographical names that apply to particular cities, states, countries, counties, sections of the country, oceans, harbors, rivers, streets, and avenues are always capitalized.

The Los Angeles Harbor is the largest harbor in Western United States.
The city of Philadelphia has a symphony orchestra.

The words *city* and *state* may also be capitalized, as in:

City of Pasadena   State of California

In most legal documents, however, "City of" and "State of" are capitalized.
Do *not* capitalize such names as *ocean, river, harbor,* and *city,* if used alone
or in the plural.

The rapids of the Wisconsin River are more turbulent than those in
any other river in the state.
Seattle is the largest city in the Pacific Northwest.
The Long Beach and Los Angeles harbors are largely artificial.

If *compass-point names* designate particular sections of a state, country,
or the world, they should be capitalized. If they refer to directions, do not
capitalize.

Australia is in the Southern Hemisphere.
My home is in Southern Arizona, but my brother lives in the Midwest.
We drive east to get to Nevada.
The hurricane belt is in Southeastern United States.
My next trip north will be to Trenton.

Calendar names. Names of holidays, days of the week, and months are
capitalized.

Columbus Day   Tuesday
Fourth of July   September

Names of seasons are not capitalized unless personified.

winter	Old Man Winter
summer	The summer sales are held in July and August.
spring	The Spring in all her glory
fall	Sales appear to rise in the fall and decline slightly during the holiday season.

National origin. Names of races, languages, nationalities, religions, and the
adjectives derived from them are capitalized.

Canada	Canadian
Japan	Japanese
Arab	Arabic
Negro	Mormon
Baptist	Roman Catholic

Historical events. Historical events, periods, documents, and political eras
and policies are capitalized.

World War II	The Sixties
Clayton Act	Depression Era
Declaration of Independence	Cold War
Industrial Revolution	New Deal

Personified words. Occasionally, a person may wish to highlight an idea embodied in a word by turning it into a proper noun.

> In the crowded city, Evil often raises its ugly head.

Proper adjectives are capitalized. Many adjectives are derived from proper nouns. In the majority of cases these proper adjectives should be capitalized.

> Napa Valley wine   Danish pastry
> Canadian bacon   Milwaukee brick
> Mexican pottery

Some proper adjectives do change to common adjectives through frequent use, however.

> bohemian manner   french fries
> china cup   plaster of paris
> roman candle   (*paris* as a common noun)
> pasteurized milk

Certain other words should be capitalized. Divisions or parts of a published work, except page, paragraph, size, or verse references, are usually capitalized.

> Refer to Volume I, Chapter II, page 6.
> The quotation is from Act I, Scene 2, page 20.

Titles for specific courses, but not general divisions of knowledge, are capitalized.

> All business administration students must study college mathematics.
> The students are to take Mathematics 2C.
> Anyone who has been here six months is eligible for the Management Development Course.

Sums of money may be spelled out in some legal documents, commercial papers, and contracts in order to avoid misunderstanding and errors. In such instances, the principal words in the sum should be capitalized.

> Thirty days after date we promise to pay the Westwood Bank the sum of Two Hundred Ten Dollars.

The personal pronoun *I* and the interjection *O* are capitalized. *O* and *oh* are used interchangeably, but *oh* is capitalized only at the beginning of a sentence.

> When, O when, will he call?
> The first time I met him he was alone.

All words referring to the Deity are usually capitalized.

> It may be an act of God.
> The Bible is His word.
> **But:** The gods are good to us.
> *Standard Reference for Secretaries and Administrators* is the new secretary's bible.

PART **3**

ASSIGNMENTS

Apply your knowledge of capitalization

A. As you read the following sentences, circle the letters that should be capitalized.

Example: The collection letter read as follows: My dear mr. Dover and ended with yours truly.

1. Management silence is the achilles heel of employee relations.
2. The right-to-work laws are of direct concern to employees.
3. The taft-hartley act marked the beginning of strong unions.
4. psychology, economics, and law are important subjects for study in industrial relations.
5. The law is quoted in volume I, chapter II, page 6.
6. The late president roosevelt was responsible for much labor legislation.
7. An m.b.a. degree in management is probably essential for leadership positions in organizations today.
8. Most company cafeterias serve pasteurized milk.
9. professor fogel teaches in the industrial relations area.
10. The secretary of labor is the official most concerned with the welfare of workers.
11. Planning is important to space organizations, city governments, and the U.S. state department.
12. The main topics in the speech outline included (1) thinking, (2) efficiency, and (3) systems.
13. Few ex-presidents of our country are alive at one time.
14. The japanese have signed numerous trade agreements since world war II.
15. milwaukee brick is famous in the midwest.

B. As you read the following sentences, circle the letters that should be capitalized.

1. The "journey for perspective" students went to australia in the southern hemisphere.
2. professor churchman's book, *the systems approach,* is the first nontechnical study of this science.
3. My uncle and your father are labor arbitrators.
4. hunt's catsup is world famous.

5. You may quote me, "no one is to take mathematics 2C or business administration 402 without my approval."

6. Have you studied economics? I took economics 101 and also economics 135.

7. The fall semester usually begins in september.

8. huntington library contains valuable documents for the study of history.

9. The note for my tuition read, "four hundred dollars."

10. The letter from my accountant read as follows: dear Mr. Keithley and ended cordially yours.

11. His letter said, "pay your federal income tax installment before june 15."

12. It also said, "be sure to keep careful records of your current-year expenses."

13. My accountant lives in the city of pasadena, but he travels a great deal in western united states.

14. When I address him in a letter, should I use dear friend, my dear howard, or dear Mr. Backer?

15. A friend of mine is editor of the *california management review*.

16. The editor's name is Woodrow W. Case, but we call him woody as a nickname.

17. If your school has a computer, it probably uses it for the following purposes: to process student records, to instruct, and to keep accounting records.

18. The great lakes cities have become international harbors since the construction of the st. lawrence seaway.

19. If you travel to the great lakes region, you will be amazed at the industrial development, not only in the american sector but also on the canadian side.

20. The building and safety commission of the city of Los Angeles is responsible for the inspection of all new buildings.

C.   Many companies, such as the Pacific Gas and Electric Company, prefer to capitalize the titles of the company's officers. You will notice this use of capitals especially in quarterly letters and the annual report to stockholders. Assume that you are an employee of a company that prefers the full use of capitals. As you read the following paragraphs, circle the words that should be capitalized.

1.   Last tuesday, the board of directors elected John S. Jones, chairman of the board, and
2.   Sherman I. Smith, president and chief operating officer.
3.   On thursday, Ross O. Hunt was elected a member of the board of directors to fill the
4.   vacancy caused by the death of Mr. James B. Brown. Mr. Hunt is chairman of the board
5.   and chief executive officer of cross zeller corporation.
6.   All incumbent members of the board of directors were reelected, and the selection by
7.   them of haskins and sells as independent public accountants for next year was ratified.
8.   At the organization meeting following the annual meeting, John B. Booth, formerly
9.   vice president and assistant general manager; K. D. Christen, formerly vice president—finance;
10.   and R. W. Joyce, formerly vice president—commercial operations, were elected senior vice
11.   presidents. Richard K. Peters, formerly general counsel, was elected senior vice president
12.   and general counsel.

D.   Correct the capitalization in the following list by rewriting. If the word is correct as it appears on the list, write *OK* in the space.

1.   english   _____

2. on Page 145 _____

3. Harvard business review _____

4. sherman anti-trust act _____

5. professor Williams _____

6. President-Elect _____

7. Christmas day _____

8. Economics 120 _____

9. b.a. degree _____

10. rotary club _____

11. Ohio and Illinois rivers _____

12. Vermont Syrup _____

13. wednesday _____

14. volume I _____

15. the northwest U.S. _____

16. Orange Bowl Game _____

17. father _____

18. MIT medical center _____

19. Chapter IV _____

20. secretary of the treasury _____

E. Correct the capitalization in the following list by rewriting. If the word is correct as it appears on the list, write *OK* in the space.

1. French fries _____

2. the sum of two hundred dollars (*legal use*) _____

3. city of Oakland _____

4. the fourth of July _____

5. state employee _____

6. go north to Oregon _____

7. lions club   _____

8. Winter sales   _____

9. Planning department   _____

10. Wisconsin Cheese   _____

11. Saturday   _____

12. My, o my!   _____

13. Peter Lorenzo, M.B.A.   _____

14. shorty Jones   _____

15. english for modern business   _____

16. Section 8, Page 315   _____

17. San Fernando valley   _____

18. Rose Bowl Game   _____

19. the seventies   _____

20. My Dear David   _____

Name _____

Date _____

PRACTICE WRITING

Compose a letter to Richard D. Irwin, Inc., Homewood, Illinois, asking them for information about the types of books they publish. You are interested in securing the latest books in business and economics that have been written by authorities in those fields. You would appreciate receiving their catalog, price list, and order blank.

_____

_____

_____

_____

_____

_____

_____

_____

_____

_____

_____

_____

_____

_____

_____

_____

_____

_____

_____

_____

PART **4**

Abbreviations are used in business

Abbreviations are usually reserved for special writing—statistical and technical material, tabulations, footnotes, memorandums, interoffice communications, invoices, and routine work—where brevity is necessary. In letter writing, abbreviations should be used sparingly. Also, be consistent in your use of abbreviations in each piece of writing, using only the forms generally accepted by the business world. (See Appendix 2, page 421.)

Learn acceptable uses of abbreviations.

Abbreviations are acceptable in most writing in the following situations.

Titles before proper names.   Use *Mr., Mrs., Ms., Dr.* when the surname is given. *Drs.* is used with surnames of two or more doctors. If the names include the given names, use *Dr.* with both. *Ms.* may be used when it is difficult to determine whether a person addressed is a *Miss* or *Mrs.* or if the individual prefers it.

Mr. John Jones	Mrs. Brown, Miss Brown, Ms. Brown
Mrs. Jean Erickson	Drs. Case and Smith
Dr. J. H. Case	Dr. John Case and Dr. Bruce Smith

In writing addresses, when the complete name follows the abbreviation, you may use *Rev.* for Reverend, *Prof.* for Professor, *Hon.* for Honorable, *Sen.* for Senator.

Rev. Carl Hill	Prof. George Little	Sen. H. J. Bliss

If the surname only is given, spell out the title: Professor Little, Reverend Hill, Senator Bliss, The Honorable Judge Jones. Also, in text material these titles should be spelled out with the complete name or the surname only.

Titles after proper names.   When the name precedes the abbreviations, use *Jr.* for Junior, *Sr.* for Senior, *Esq.* for Esquire, *M.D.* for Doctor of Medicine, *L.L.D.* for Doctor of Laws, *Ph.D.* for Doctor of Philosophy, *C.P.A.* for Certified Public Accountant.

399

Harry H. Ring, M.D.	Ray Ellis, Esq.
Henry Jacobs, Ph.D.	John Kelly, C.P.A. (or CPA)
William Jones, MBA (or M.B.A.)	David Olson, L.L.D.
Martin Pierce, Jr.	John Marble, DBA (or D.B.A.)

Dates, numbers, and time references. Use only accepted forms of abbreviations. (See Appendix 2 and your dictionary for preferred forms.)

8 a.m.　　10 p.m.　　100 B.C.　　No. 25　　Vol. 11, p. 6　　pp. 10-30

Names of organizations. Abbreviations are commonly used for the names of business firms; government agencies; and labor, professional, and civic organizations.

YWCA or *Y.W.C.A.* for Young Women's Christian Association
UN or *U.N.* for United Nations
AFL-CIO for American Federation of Labor/Congress of Industrial Organizations
NAM or *N.A.M.* for National Association of Manufacturers
TWA for Trans World Airlines
I.R.S. or *IRS* for Internal Revenue Service

These words are preferably spelled out.

Abbreviations in company names. Spell out *and* in company names unless the sign for *and* (&) is used in the corporate name. Also, spell out *company* unless the abbreviation *Co.* is used by the company.

H. J. Wright and Company	Peters & Smith Shoe Company
John Moses Company	Alberts Music Co.

Spell out the words *corporation, incorporated,* and *limited* when used with company names, except when abbreviated in the corporate names.

Green Shoe Corporation	United Gas Corp.
Smith and Pierce, Incorporated	Jones Iron Works, Inc.
Grace Lines, Limited	Reed Dunham, Ltd.

Note the comma before Incorporated and Limited and Inc. and Ltd.

Street names. Spell out the words *street, avenue, east, west, north,* or *south* in writing street names. Use the abbreviations for these words sparingly, except for compound directions after street names—e.g., *N.E.* (Northeast) and *S.W.* (Southwest). It is preferable also to use words for numbered street names *First* through *Tenth.* Use figures for those above ten.

656 East First Street	5800 Fifth Avenue
1072—17th Avenue	321—23rd Street
15396 Eighth Avenue, N.E.	952 West 15 Street

State and city names. Spell out names of states in text material unless it is necessary to abbreviate because of lack of space. The *District of Columbia,* however, is abbreviated as Washington, D.C. Do not abbreviate the names of cities except in names combined with *Saint.*

St. Louis	St. Augustine

In addressing material for mailing, the U.S. Postal Service prefers that all state names be abbreviated for use with official ZIP Code numbers.

See Appendix 2, page 421, for a list of the preferred abbreviations for use with ZIP Codes.

Days and months.   Spell out days of the week in business letters, reports, bulletins, and so forth.

Monday   Saturday   Friday

Spell out months of the year.

January   April   October

See Appendix 2, page 421, for acceptable abbreviations of days and months for statistical work.

Note: Preferably, spell out the words *and so forth* in most business letters and text material. The abbreviation *etc.* may be used in memorandums, tabulations, and invoices.

Some abbreviations are followed by periods.

1.   A period usually follows each part of an abbreviation that stands for a single unit. No space is left after the intervening periods.

f.o.b. — free on board

ft. — foot or feet

lb. — pound

i.e. — that is

c.o.d. — cash on delivery

a.m. — ante meridian

p.m. — post meridian

2.   Retain the period after an abbreviation followed by other sentence punctuation.

We sent the goods c.o.d.; they should arrive today.

The meeting is at 1:30 p.m., and you should be present if at all possible.

3.   A period following an abbreviation at the end of a sentence serves as the end-of-sentence punctuation. If the abbreviation is enclosed in parentheses, an additional period is then necessary outside the parentheses to complete the sentence.

The Finance Committee will meet at 9:30 a.m.

The price of the car is $4,000 (f.o.b.).

4.   When an abbreviation ends an interrogative or exclamatory sentence, a question mark or an exclamation point follows the last period in the abbreviation.

Do you wish the goods sent c.o.d.?

I will be there at 8:30 p.m.!

5.   Do not space after the periods within an abbreviation, but do space after titles appearing before a name and between a person's initials.

Ph.D.   M.D.   c.o.d.   e.g.   U.N.

But: J. H. Simmons   Dr. R. H. Perry   Gov. Albert Green

Some abbreviations are not followed by periods.

Periods are not used when writing the following abbreviations.

1. Symbols for chemical terms.

H_2O for water O for oxygen H for hydrogen

2. Symbols for radio and television broadcasting stations and systems, and business firms.

KFI   WISN   ABC   CBS   NBC   RCA   TWA

3. Special symbols for military and government agencies.

FCC — Federal Communications Commission
USN — United States Navy
FDA — Food and Drug Administration

4. Dates with ordinal endings—*d, st, th.* Ordinal endings are shortened forms for writing dates, but they are not abbreviations. They are used only in writing dates when the day precedes the month. (*Note:* The ordinal ending *d* is preferred to writing *nd* or *rd* in *2d* and *3d.*)

1st   2d   3d   4th   3d of May   31st of December

5. IOU and SOS. These are shortened forms but are not considered abbreviations.

Some abbreviations are capitalized.

Capitalize abbreviations only if the unabbreviated form would be capitalized or if the abbreviation has become an established form.

No. 1 — Number One
NEA   — National Education Association
Ph.D. — Doctor of Philosophy
Sgt.   — Sergeant (with surname)

Abbreviations can be made plural.

1. Most abbreviations form their plurals by adding *s* to the singular.

yr.   yrs.   gal.   gals.
co.   cos.   yd.   yds.

2. The singular and plural forms of some abbreviations for units of weight and measure are the same.

ft. (for *foot* or *feet*)   min. (for *minute* or *minutes*)

3. Abbreviations made up of separate uncapitalized letters form their plurals by adding an *apostrophe* and *s.* Capitalized abbreviations form their plurals by adding the *s* or *'s.*

c.o.d.'s   a.m.'s   f.o.b.'s   C.P.A.s   M.D.s   Ph.D.s

4. The plurals of some single-letter abbreviations are formed by doubling the letter.

p. (for *page*)   pp. (for *pages*)
f. (for *the following page*)   ff. (for *the following pages*)

Apply your knowledge of abbreviations

A. Cross out any incorrect punctuation or abbreviation. Place the correct form and punctuation on the line to the right. If there are no errors in the sentence, write *OK* on the line.

1. You must be at the meeting promptly in the Administration Bldg. _____

2. Our company sold the trucks for $15,000 (f.o.b.). _____

3. Do you know when Mrs. Hayes was hired? _____

4. Radio Station K.N.B.C. is an excellent station. _____
5. Did you know the tank holds 8 gal. of liquid per 2 fts of depth. _____

6. There are ten more c.o.d.'s that we should receive. _____

7. The artist was born in 650 a.d. _____

8. Sen. Holman gave the report to Prof. Wilson. _____

9. Refer to page 34 in checking no. 8 & 9. _____
10. The announcer at K.N.X. said that the Hon. James Jones was home from Washington. _____
11. The teacher told us to open our books to chap. II, p. 82–83. _____

12. Sen. Brown will speak at our meeting on Wed., December 3d. at 3 PM. _____

13. The sales mgr. told the file clerk to check for the missing material.   _____

14. Dr. F. J. Johnson lives in Wash., D.C., but frequently lectures in Saint Louis.   _____

15. The money for the stock is due on May 23d and should be paid to the Bank of Amer., 788 W. 3d St., Dallas, Tex.   _____

_____

_____

B. Cross out any incorrect form of abbreviation and rewrite it correctly on the line to the right. If there are no errors in the sentence, write *OK* on the line.

1. The meeting was conducted by the chairman of R.C.A.   _____

2. My secretary wrote to the company office in Chicago, Ill.   _____

3. Our office is located in Los Angeles, Calif.   _____

4. The printed address on the stationery was 1320 4th St., S. Diego, Cal. 90369.   _____

_____

5. Our car will be sent FOB Detroit by Gen. Motors.   _____

6. Did you know the meeting started at eight p.m.?   _____

7. The conference is set for 4:30 p.m. tomorrow in the bank bldg.   _____

8. Did you check the data given in the report on P.P. 22–23?   _____

9. The boss's full name is George H. Rand, Junior.   _____

10. My supervisor changed the meeting date to Tues., Nov. 30.   _____

11. The meeting will include prof. Brown and rev. Hill.   _____

12. You will find the needed information in vol. II, PP. 4–8.   _____

13. A representative from the YMCA will participate.   _____

14. My nephew, who has an L.L.d. degree, is a lawyer.   _____

15. He lives at 412 Hartzel St., Saint Paul.   _____

C.   In the following paragraphs, correct all errors or omissions in abbreviations and punctuation by crossing out the incorrect form and writing the correct form in the column to the right.

1.   Pres. Jones appointed Profs. Buffa and

Mason to the Gen. Elections Board. He also   _____

appointed Mr. Geo. Smith, Robert Johnson,

and Fred Goodman, M.D. They were asked   _____

to meet on Mon., Sept. 5, to review some

material from the Calif. Retirement System.   _____

_____

2.   The meeting will be held in San. Fran.,   _____

Calif., and will include Gov Murphy, Sen.

Goodlad, and Rep. Smith. The location of   _____

the meeting is at 22 E. 9th St., in the

Harper Bldg. on the Univ. campus.   _____

_____

D.   Write one acceptable abbreviation after each word or phrase in the following list. Distinguish between capitals and small letters. (Use Appendix 2, pages 421–23, or a dictionary if necessary.)

1.	cash on delivery	_____	11.	year	_____
2.	yards	_____	12.	August	_____
3.	account	_____	13.	free on board	_____
4.	discount	_____	14.	for example	_____
5.	balance	_____	15.	following pages	_____
6.	amount	_____	16.	gallons	_____
7.	numbers	_____	17.	feet	_____
8.	enclosure	_____	18.	Certified Public Accountant	_____
9.	and so forth	_____	19.	District of Columbia	_____
10.	department	_____	20.	that is	_____

Name _____

Date _____

PRACTICE WRITING

Using the following information, write a short paragraph announcing a special job-counseling event sponsored by the organization indicated below. Correct any errors in abbreviation or punctuation when you include the information in your announcement.

Event: Job-Counseling Seminar
Place: Yg. Men's Ch. Assoc., 132 N. 4th St., Prescott, Ar.
Director: Jas. Wm. Gunn, Junior
Time: 9:30 AM to 5 p.m.
Date: Tue., April 17th
Speaker: J. Philip Monroe, PH.D.
Topic: "How to Succeed in the Petroleum Industry"

_____

_____

_____

_____

_____

_____

_____

_____

_____

_____

_____

_____

_____

_____

_____

PART **5**

Numbers are included in business writing

In today's business world, *figures* are used more frequently than *words* in writing numbers. One reason for this is that figures can be read more quickly and accurately than words. Nevertheless, the careful writer should be familiar with the guides that have been set up for writing numbers and should use good judgment in their application. Whether you use figures or spelled-out numbers, however, an important rule to follow is to be *consistent* in the use of the method you choose.

In writing business forms, figures should be used. In writing letters, reports, and articles, the following guides will help you make your finished copy clear, concise, and effective.

Learn these guides for writing numbers.

As words.

1.   Spell out a number if it begins a sentence.

Twelve of the packages were lost.
Five of the officers were present.

Note: If the number is large, it is better to rearrange the sentence and use figures.

Awkward: *Two thousand twenty-five people* live in this area.
Better: The number of people in this area is *2,025.*

2.   Spell out numbers *ten* and under as a general rule. Use figures for numbers *above ten*.

There were nine to ten persons at the meeting.
The secretary typed 25 letters.

Round numbers (even units of ten, hundreds, or thousands) should be written in words.

The store had one hundred clerical workers.
She bought fifty self-addressed envelopes.

407

3.   Spell out numbers expressing indefinite amounts.

About thirty-five people showed up.

He collected *almost* one hundred dollars.

He is *approximately* thirty-nine years old.

4.   When two numbers follow one another in a sentence, spell out the smaller number and write the other in figures. *Exception:* When using numbers written with three or more words, then use figures for both.

He ordered 23 ten-inch boxes.

He ordered ten 23-inch boxes.

He ordered 125 210-lb. barrels.

5.   Spell out numbers referring to decades and centuries.

The play was about the gay nineties.

We are living in the twentieth century.

Note: Expressions such as Gay Nineties and Twentieth Century may be capitalized for emphasis.

6.   Spell out dates in formal invitations.

. . . on Sunday, the twenty-third of June.

7.   Spell out common fractions that are used alone in a sentence. If the fraction is an adjective modifier, use a hyphen.

One half of the stock is lost.
    (noun)
The recipe called for one-third water.
    (adjective)
The stock fell three tenths of a point.
    (noun)

Note: If the fraction is part of a larger number, write the number in figures.

The correct size is 12½.

The magic number is 15¼.

8.   Preferably, spell out references to time if the word *o'clock* is used.

Our plane leaves at six o'clock.

Note: Never spell out the time with *a.m., m., p.m.* (lower case is preferred).

Our date is at 6.30 p.m.

As figures.

1.   Use figures for a series of numbers within a sentence even though some of the numbers are under ten. Be consistent. Do not write some of the numbers in figures and some in words.

There were *107* freshmen, *210* sophomores, and *8* seniors present.

2.   Use figures for writing dates.

The letter was dated June 30.

The invoice was stamped April 1.
  (**Not:** April 1st)

Note: If the day precedes the month, it should be written with the ordinal ending.

The deposition was taken on the 13th of July.

3. Use figures with the abbreviations *a.m., p.m.,* and *m.* Lower case is preferred.

Work hours are 8:30 a.m. to 5:30 p.m.
The plane left at 12 m.

4. Use figures, preferably, for writing percentages.

The bank paid 5 percent.
  [The sign for percent (%) may be used in writing memos and tabulations.]

5. Use figures for writing exact age.

The new vice president is 39 years of age.
His exact age is 39 years, 2 months, 3 days.

6. Use figures for writing page numbers and divisions of books.

page 35   pp. 305–17
Chapter 10, Part 3.   Volume 3

7. Use figures for dimensions, measures, and distances.

The rug was 9 by 12 feet.
The distance was 63 miles.
The 150-acre farm yields 30 bushels of wheat an acre.

8. Use figures for decimals and market quotations.

General Motors 5s at 102½
2.75   0.6   0.23

9. Use figures for temperatures, election returns, and chemical terms.

92 degrees or 92° H_2O 450 votes

Numbers referring to money are in figures or words.

1. Use figures in writing sums of money. Omit the decimal point and ciphers in even amounts; but in a list of even and uneven sums, use both the decimal point and ciphers.

$15.50 $100   20 cents $5

2. In writing legal papers, spell out amounts of money, followed with the figure in parentheses. Capitalize words expressing amounts of money.

The cost of the project will be Three Hundred Fifty Dollars ($350).

3. Spell out numbers expressing indefinite sums of money.

The agent collected *about* two thousand dollars.

Addresses always use figures except in two instances.

1. Use figures for writing building numbers, except for the number *One*.

1536 Kestor Street

One Park Avenue

2. Spell out street names from *one* through *ten*. Use figures for any street name above ten. (See page 400).

652 First Street   2500—15 Street *or* 2500—15th Street

359-A Ninth Street

5

ASSIGNMENTS

Apply your knowledge of number usage

A. Cross out any incorrect number forms, and write the correct forms in the column to the right. Write *OK* if the number is written correctly.

1. The report contained four hundred fifty-three questions to be answered. _____

2. We sent fourteen 12-inch desk computers to the accounting department. _____

3. The larger of the two numbers is 15¼. _____

4. Seven o'clock is the time of our meeting. _____

5. Seventy-five men were present for the conference. _____

6. Our next meeting will be the 23 of June. _____

7. The chairman said that 1/2 of us should go with him. _____

8. About 50 of those men came to the first meeting today. _____

9. We will meet in Murphy Hall at 1:30 p.m. _____

10. Employee absences weren't like this in the 19th century. _____

B. Cross out any incorrect number forms, and write the correct forms in the column to the right. Write *OK* if the number is written correctly.

1. Let me know when the chemical solution reaches one hundred degrees. _____

2. We live at eighty five West Howard Drive. _____

3. My new partner is about 45 years old.   _____

4. Our total assets consist of twenty-five shares of stock, fifteen
   promissory notes, and 3 government bonds.   _____

5. The mayor must receive at least 1,350 votes in the primary
   election to be held on June third.   _____

6. Our new product, the four-by-twelve wood panel, is probably
   what caused our stock to go up 1/2 point.   _____

7. Our inventory shows there are 27 packages of cards and
   twelve packages of envelopes.   _____

8. 12 employees in the training program completed the
   requirements by June fifteenth.   _____

9. Low temperature this morning was thirty-two degrees.   _____

10. The president of our firm is sixty-three years of age.   _____

    C. Cross out any incorrect number forms and write correct forms in the right-hand column. Write *OK* if number is written correctly.

1. No eight-inch widths are available for the 6 orders we received.   _____

2. We received almost $200 for the educational TV fund.   _____

3. Our contract reads "One Thousand Ten Dollars ($1010)."   _____

4. Most of this amount came from 50-cent donations.   _____

5. Whenever a fraction is part of a larger number, write the
   number in figures, as 8⅘.   _____

6. All donations are welcome for this worthy cause, whether
   they are ten dollars, five dollars, or twenty-five cents.   _____

7. I am leaving for six West 16th Street, not East twenty-sixth
   Street.   _____

8. Only fourteen machines were delivered before June fifth.   _____

9. The building located at 1536—10th Street has about
   ninety-four acres of floor space.   _____

10. 25 typewriters were delivered on March first for the Business
    Education Department.   _____

    D. Correct any errors in the use of numbers in the following paragraphs by crossing out the incorrect form and writing the correct form in the column to the right.

1. The company purchased 15 twenty-five carton crates   _____

   of IBM cards. That should be enough to complete 50   _____

   programs for the week. 18 employees will be working   _____

on this project. The job will entail punching five
thousand three hundred fifty cards.

    _____

    _____

2.   There are about 45 students in this class. The class
adjourns at twelve m. Our mid-term will be on the
twenty-second of October and the final examination
will be on January 20th.

3.   After the president was re-elected by a margin of
seven hundred fifteen votes, the company stock rose
three points to 85. Our interest rate is currently ten
and one half percent. It would be advisable to check
our dividend policy on Part three, page thirty-one, of
the company manual. The company manual is an
eight-by-ten hardcover text.

4.   This university was founded in the 19 century. It did
not grow substantially, however, until the era of the
Roaring 20's. It is now made up of 25 departments,
fifteen colleges, and seven schools. The Business
Administration Department has an office staff
consisting of three administrative assistants, 11
secretaries, fifteen clerk-typists, and three clerks.

5.   If you will refer to Chapter II, page six, of the General
Electronic Corporation Manual, Number five, you will
find a brief summary of corporate activities. On
September sixth, the stockholders voted one hundred
to 13 in favor of company policy. They elected to
float a new seven % Series 10 bond and to increase

the quarterly dividend from twenty-five cents to 30   _____

cents. The stock is now selling at forty-two and five   _____

eighths.   _____

6.   The company's nineteen eighty earnings   _____

reached two million dollars, or nine dollars   _____

and fifty cents a share, an increase of   _____

thirty-three and one-third percent over   _____

nineteen seventy-nine earnings of one   _____

million five hundred thousand dollars.   _____

Details may be found on page twenty-nine.   _____

7.   The company's sixteen year unbroken record   _____

of dividend increases is unique. In nineteen   _____

eighty-one it was twenty-five percent above 1980.   _____

For the sixteenth straight year payments   _____

increased, rising fifty cents a share to two   _____

dollars and fifty cents.   _____

8.   Capital appropriations increased thirty   _____

percent to a seasonally adjusted thirty   _____

billion five hundred million dollars in   _____

the first quarter of 1981 from twenty-three   _____

billion five hundred million dollars in the last   _____

three months of nineteen eighty.   _____

9 of fifteen industries surveyed increased   _____

their investment plans, but only 6   _____

planned substantial increases.   _____

9.   The nine by twelve paper is expensive   _____

     for the nineteen eighty-two yearbook.   _____

     Standard size is eight and a half by   _____

     eleven. There will be 8 sections with   _____

     a total of two hundred pages. Graduates   _____

     will total three hundred fifty with   _____

     twenty more graduating in summer school.   _____

     The school has about 50 teachers and 5 administrators   _____

     and is part of a district that has 12 high   _____

     schools. At graduation, the temperature   _____

     will be at least eighty-five degrees.   _____

Appendices

Spelling of 500 troublesome words with recommended syllabication

abrupt	aggres-sive	auto-mation	cen-sus	con-trol
absence	align-ment	aux-il-iary	change-able	con-trol-ling
absorb-ent	all right		char-ac-ter	con-tro-versy
abun-dance	allege	bal-ance	charge-able	con-ven-ience
accede	allot-ment	bal-lot	chiefly	corre-late
accel-er-ate	allot-ted	bank-ruptcy	cli-en-tele	cor-re-spond-ence
accept-able	already	ban-quet	col-lat-eral	cour-te-ous
acces-si-ble	alu-mi-num	bar-gain	col-lect-ible	credi-tor
acces-sory	amend-ment	basi-cally	col-lege	criti-cism
acci-den-tally	analy-sis	behav-ior	col-umn	criti-cize
accom-mo-date	ana-lyze	believ-able	com-mis-sion	curi-ous
accom-mo-da-tion	ana-lyz-ing	bene-fi-cial	com-mit-ment	cyl-in-der
accom-pa-ny-ing	anec-dote	bene-fited	com-mit-tee	
account-ant	apolo-gize	book-keeper	com-modi-ties	data
accu-mu-late	appa-ra-tus	bound-ary	com-para-tive	deci-sion
accus-tom	appar-ent	bril-liant	com-pe-tence	deduct-ible
achieve-ment	appear-ance	bro-chure	com-peti-tor	defend-ant
acknowl-edg-ment	appoint-ment	budget	com-puter	deferred
acquaint-ance	appre-cia-tion	bul-le-tin	con-cede	defi-cient
acquire	appro-pri-ate	bureaus	con-ceiv-able	defi-cit
acquit-tal	approval	busi-ness	con-du-cive	defi-nite
across	archi-tect		con-fer-ence	dele-gate
ade-quate	argu-ment	cal-en-dar	con-fi-dent	delin-quent
adjourn-ment	arrange-ment	cam-paign	con-gratu-late	depend-ent
adjust-ment	assign-ment	can-celed	con-science	describe
admis-si-ble	assist-ance	can-cel-la-tion	con-sci-en-tious	descrip-tion
admit-tance	assur-ance	can-di-date	con-scious	desira-bil-ity
advan-ta-geous	attend-ance	career	con-secu-tively	despite
adver-tise-ment	attor-neys	care-ful	con-sen-sus	develop
advis-able	audi-ble	cash-ier	con-spicu-ous	devel-op-ment
affect	author-ity	cata-log	con-tinu-ous	diag-no-sis
affili-ate	author-ize	ceil-ing	con-trib-ute	dif-fer-ent

dis-ap-pear
dis-ap-point
dis-burse-ment
dis-crep-ancy
dis-sat-is-fac-tion
dis-tinct
dis-tribu-tor

effect
effi-cient
eight
elec-tronic
eli-gi-ble
elimi-nate
embar-rass
enclo-sures
endorse-ment
enforce-able
enter-prise
envelop (verb)
enve-lope
envel-op-ment
envi-ron-ment
equipped
equiva-lent
erro-ne-ous
espe-cially
envi-dently
exag-ger-ate
exceed
excel-lent
exhaust
exhi-bi-tion
exist-ence
exor-bi-tant
expe-ri-ence
expla-na-tion
exten-sion
extraor-di-nary

fac-sim-ile
fal-lacy
famil-iar
fas-ci-nate
fea-si-ble
Feb-ru-ary
finally
finan-cially
flex-ible
for-ci-ble
for-eign
for-feit
forty

fran-chise
ful-fill
fun-da-men-tal

gauge
genu-ine
ges-ture
gigan-tic
gov-ern-ment
gram-mar
guar-an-tee
guid-ance

handi-capped
hand-some
hap-haz-ard
heav-ily
hec-tic
height
hin-drance
humor-ous
hur-riedly

ille-gal
illegi-ble
illit-er-ate
imag-ine
imi-ta-tion
imme-di-ately
inau-gu-rate
inci-den-tally
indel-ible
inde-pend-ent
indis-pen-sa-ble
induce-ment
inflam-ma-ble
inhab-it-ant
ini-tia-tive
instal-la-tion
insur-ance
inte-grate
intel-li-gi-ble
inten-tion-ally
inter-cede
inter-est
inter-fere
inter-fered
inter-pre-ta-tion
inter-rupt
irregu-lar
irrele-vant
irrevo-ca-ble
issuing

jeop-ard-ize
jour-ney
judg-ment
jus-ti-fi-able
jus-ti-fied

knowl-edge

label-ing
labo-ra-tory
lac-quer
ledger
legiti-mate
lei-sure
lia-ble
liai-son
library
license
lien
lik-able
liq-ui-da-tion
lis-ten
live-li-hood
lone-li-ness
lovely
lux-ury

main-te-nance
man-age-able
man-age-ment
ma-neu-ver
man-ual
manu-fac-turer
manu-script
mathe-mat-ics
medi-ocre
mer-chan-dise
mile-age
mini-ature
mis-cel-la-ne-ous
mis-spell
mod-ern
morale
mort-gage
mov-able

natu-rally
nec-es-sary
neces-sity
nicely
nine-teenth
ninety
ninth

notice-able
nui-sance

oblige
obso-lete
occa-sion-ally
occurred
occur-rence
offi-cial
omis-sion
omit-ted
oper-ate
oppo-nent
oppor-tu-nity
oppose
oppo-site
opti-mis-tic
ordi-nance
origi-nate

pam-phlet
par-al-lel
par-cel
par-tial
par-ticu-larly
peace-able
pecul-iar
per-ceive
per-for-mance
per-ma-nent
per-mis-si-ble
per-se-ver-ance
per-sist-ent
per-son-ally
per-son-nel
per-suade
phi-loso-phy
phy-si-cian
planned
plausi-ble
pleas-ant
pos-ses-sion
prac-ti-cal
pre-cede
pre-ce-dence
pre-ced-ing
pre-domi-nant
pre-fer
pref-er-able
pre-limi-nary
pres-sure
preva-lent
prin-ci-pal

prin-ci-ple
privi-lege
proba-bly
pro-ce-dure
pro-ceed-ings
proc-ess-ing
pro-fes-sion
prof-ited
pro-gram-ming
promi-nent
prom-is-sory
pro-nun-ci-ation
pro-por-tion-ate
psy-chol-ogy
pub-licly
pur-sue
pur-su-ing

quan-tity
ques-tion-naire

real-ize
receipt
receiv-able
recipi-ent
rec-om-mend
rec-om-men-da-tion
rec-on-cile
recur-rence
ref-er-ence
referred
reg-is-ter
reim-burse-ment
rele-vant
relief
relieve
remit-tance
repe-ti-tion
replies
rep-re-sent-ative
req-ui-si-tion
ret-ro-ac-tive
reveal
revi-sion
ridicu-lous
rotary

safety
sal-able
sat-is-fac-tory
scar-city
sched-ule
sec-re-tary

seize
sen-si-ble
sepa-rate
serial
serv-ice-able
ship-ment
siege
sig-nifi-cance
simi-lar
simul-ta-ne-ous
siz-able
skep-ti-cal
spe-cifi-cally
speech
split-ting
sta-tion-ary
sta-tion-ery
sta-tis-tics
strength
strictly

study-ing
sub-sidi-ary
sub-sidy
sub-stan-tial
sub-stan-ti-ate
sub-sti-tute
suc-ceed
suc-cess-ful
suc-ces-sor
suf-fi-cient
suing
sum-mary
super-in-ten-dent
super-sede
super-vi-sor
sur-plus
sur-prise
sur-vey
sus-cep-ti-ble
sus-pi-cious

sys-tem
sys-tem-atic

tact-ful-ness
tan-gi-ble
tar-iff
tech-ni-cal
tech-nique
tele-vise
tele-vi-sion
tem-pera-ment
tem-po-rary
ten-ant
ten-dency
ter-ri-ble
ter-ri-tory
their
theory
there-fore
thor-oughly

trans-fer-able
trans-ferred
treas-urer
truly
tying
typi-cal

unani-mous
undoubt-edly
unfore-seen
unique
unu-sual
usable
usage
use-ful
using

vac-uum
var-ies
ver-sa-tile

visi-ble
visi-tor
vol-ume

waiver
war-ranty
weather
Wednes-day
wel-fare
whether
wit-nessed
writ-ing
writ-ten

yes-ter-day
yield

zeal-ous

APPENDIX **2**

Abbreviations

STATES, TERRITORIES, AND UNITED STATES POSSESSIONS

Alabama	AL†	Kentucky	KY	Ohio	OH
Alaska	AK	Louisiana	LA	Oklahoma	OK
Arizona	AZ	Maine	ME	Oregon	OR
Arkansas	AR	Mariana Islands*		Pennsylvania	PA
California	CA	Marshall Islands*		Puerto Rico	PR
Canal Zone	CZ	Maryland	MD	Rhode Island	RI
Caroline Islands*		Massachusetts	MA	Samoa*	
Colorado	CO	Michigan	MI	South Carolina	SC
Connecticut	CT	Minnesota	MN	South Dakota	SD
Delaware	DE	Mississippi	MS	Tennessee	TN
District of Columbia	DC	Missouri	MO	Texas	TX
Florida	FL	Montana	MT	Utah	UT
Georgia	GA	Nebraska	NB	Vermont	VT
Guam	GU	Nevada	NV	Virginia	VA
Hawaii	HI	New Hampshire	NH	Virgin Islands	VI
Idaho	ID	New Jersey	NJ	Wake Island*	
Illinois	IL	New Mexico	NM	Washington	WA
Indiana	IN	New York	NY	West Virginia	WV
Iowa	IA	North Carolina	NC	Wisconsin	WI
Kansas	KS	North Dakota	ND	Wyoming	WY

* Spell out.
† The all-caps two-letter state abbreviations have been authorized for use with the U.S. Postal Service ZIP Code.

ABBREVIATIONS FOR DAYS AND MONTHS

Sunday	Sun.	January	Jan.	August	Aug.
Monday	Mon.	February	Feb.	September	Sept.
Tuesday	Tues.	March	Mar.	October	Oct.
Wednesday	Wed.	April	Apr.	November	Nov.
Thursday	Thurs.	May	May	December	Dec.
Friday	Fri.	June	June		
Saturday	Sat.	July	July		

COMMON ABBREVIATIONS USED IN BUSINESS
(For a more complete list consult the dictionary)

@	at
abbr., abbrev.	abbreviation, -ed
acct., a/c	account
ack.	acknowledge, -ment
a/d	after date
addl.	additional
ad lib.	at one's pleasure; freely
adm.	administration, -tive
adv. chgs.	advanced charges
advtg.	advertising
agr.	agreement
agt.	agent
a.m., A.M.	before noon
amt.	amount
ans.	answer, -ed
appl.	application
approx.	approximate
appt.	appointment
apt.	apartment
art.	article
assn.	association
asst.	assistant
atten., attn.	attention
atty.	attorney
ave.	avenue
avg., av.	average
bal.	balance
bbl.	barrel(s)
bbls/day, b/d	barrels a day
bf.	boldface
B/L	bill of lading
bldg.	building
blvd.	boulevard
bu.	bushel(s)
bul.	bulletin
bus.	business
Bus. Mgr.	Business Manager
C.	Celsius (centigrade), hundred
cap.	capital, capacity
caps.	capital letters
cat.	catalog
cc, cc.	carbon copy, cubic centimeter
C/D	Certificate of Deposit
cert., ctf.	certificate, -tion, certified
ch.	chapter, channel (TV), chemical, chart
chg.	charge
ck.	check
clk.	clerk
cm	centimeter

cml.	commercial
Co.	Company
c/o	in care of
c.o.d.	cash on delivery
com., comm.	committee, commission, communication
Corp.	Corporation
dept.	department
dis., disc.	discount
e.g.	for example
ea.	each
enc., inc.	enclosure, inclosure
e.o.m.	end of month
et al.	and others
etc.	and so forth
ex., exch.	exchange
exp.	express
ext.	extension, exterior, extract
F.	Fahrenheit, franc(s), French
f., ff.	and following page(s)
fac.	facsimile
fig., Fig.	figure
fl.	fluid, floor
fl. dr.	fluid dram
fl. oz.	fluid ounce
f.o.b.	free on board
frt.	freight
ft.	foot, feet
fwd.	forward
g	gram (*metric*)
gal.	gallon(s)
gds.	goods
govt.	government
gr.	grain, gross
gr. wt.	gross weight
guar.	guarantee; -ed
hdbk.	handbook
hdqrs., hq.	headquarters
hm	hectometer (*metric*)
hosp.	hospital
hp.	horsepower
hr.	hour
ht.	height, heat
ibid.	in the same place
i.e.	that is
in.	inch(es)
Inc.	Incorporated
inc.	increase, income
incl.	inclusive, including
ins.	insurance, inspector

inst.	instant, installment	PBX, P.B.X.	Private Branch Exchange (*telephone*)
inv.	invoice	pd.	paid
invt.	inventory	pfd.	preferred (*stock*)
ital.	italics	pkg.	package
jt.	joint	p.m., P.M.	after noon
kc.	kilocycle	p.p.	parcel post
km	kilometer	pr.	pair, pairs
kw.	kilowatt	P.S., p.s.	postscript
l	liter (*metric*)	qt.	quart, quantity
la., lge.	large	R.D.	Rural Delivery
lab.	laboratory, labor	recd.	received
lb., lbs.	pound(s)	retd.	returned
l.c.	lower case	Rev.	Reverend
lds.	loads	rm., Rm.	ream, Room
liq.	liquid	R.N.	Registered Nurse
loc. cit.	in the place cited	RSVP, r.s.v.p.	respond, if you please
ltr.	letter	Rte.	Route
lv.	leave	Ry.	railway
m.	noon, meter, mile	sec., secy.	secretary
mdse.	merchandise	sect., sec.	section
memo.	memorandum	sq. ft.	square foot (feet)
mfg.	manufacturing	Sr.	Senior
misc.	miscellaneous	St.	Street, Saint, Strait
mi.	mile(s)	supt.	superintendent
min.	minute(s)	u.c.	upper case
mkt.	market	viz.	namely
mo.	month	vol., Vol., vols.	volume, volumes
MS, M.S., ms.	manuscript	vs., v.	versus
No., Nos.	number(s) (*before figures only*)	wam	words a minute
N.B., n.b.	note well	whsle.	wholesale
oz.	ounce	wk.	week
p., pp.	page, pages	wt.	weight
pat.	patent, patented	yd, yds	yard, yards
payt.	payment	yr.	year

Prepositions with special words

Many words used in combination with prepositions require a specific preposition to convey logical meaning. Learn the proper application of these combinations. You may need to check your dictionary for the correct definition of the word accompanying the preposition.

accede to	We cannot *accede to* the taxpayer's request for an extension of time.
accessory { of	He was an *accessory of* the criminal.
to	He was an *accessory to* the act.
accommodate { to	He finds it hard to *accommodate* himself *to* new situations.
with	We *accommodated* him *with* a loan of five dollars.
accompany { by	He was *accompanied by* counsel. (a person)
with	The letter was *accompanied with* an affidavit. (a thing)
accord { to	There shall be *accorded to* each man what he earns.
with	I am in *accord with* the findings.
accountable { for	The division manager is *accountable for* his actions.
to	I am *accountable to* the manager for my actions.
accused { by	He was *accused by* the plaintiff of having filed a false statement.
of	He was *accused of* perjury.
acquiesce in	The president has *acquiesced in* the decision.
acquit { of	He was *acquitted of* the crime.
with	He *acquitted* himself *with* honor.
adapted { for	The work simplification guide was *adapted for* our use.
from	The movie was *adapted from* the book.
to	He finds it difficult to *adapt to* new procedures.

adequate { for / to
His salary was not *adequate for* his needs.
His ability was *adequate to* the job.

adverse to
The counsel was not *adverse to* discussing the compromise.

averse to
He was not *averse to* hard work.

advise of
The employees were *advised of* the new regulations.

affix to
A stamp was *affixed to* the container.

agree { in / on / to / with
We *agree in* principle with those who favor the plan.
They cannot *agree on* the delegation order.
They state that they *agree to* the compromise.
The taxpayer and his counsel *agree with* us that he owes an additional sum.

amenable to
He was *amenable to* our argument.

analogous to
This situation is *analogous to* the one we faced last year.

annoy { by / with
The clerk was *annoyed by* the frequent interruptions.
The supervisor showed that he was *annoyed with* the recalcitrant employee.

apparent { in / to
His attitude is *apparent in* his actions.
The trouble is *apparent to* everyone in the office.

append to
A rider was *appended to* the bill.

appreciation { for / of
The student had a real *appreciation for* the arts.
She expressed *appreciation of* their hard work.

appreciative of
We are *appreciative of* their efforts.

authority { in / on / to
Dr. Warren is an *authority in* his field.
Mr. Simpson is an *authority on* linear programming.
He has *authority to* sign this document.

basis { for / in
The supplier said he had a sound *basis for* agreement.
His argument has no *basis in* fact.

commensurate with
His salary was *commensurate with* his abilities.

comply with
We must *comply with* the manager's request.

concur { in / with
We *concur in* the decision of the survey committee.
One member did not *concur with* the others.

conform to
All agents must *conform to* the regulations.

consist { in / of
His value *consists in* his ability to work with others.
The handbook *consists of* principles of supervision.

consistent { in / with
We should be *consistent in* applying the law.
His actions are not *consistent with* his statements.

correspond { to / with
His description of the incident *corresponds to* what we believe to be the case.
We have been *corresponding with* his counsel.

demand { from / of
What did he *demand from* them in payment?
They have *demanded* an accounting *of* the company funds.

depend on		Mrs. Tucker depended on her subordinates for information.
differ	from	My estimate of the total tax due *differs from* his.
	in	We *differ in* our opinions on the matter.
	on	They *differed on* the amount to be assessed.
	with	I *differ with* him about the evaluation method to be used.
discrepancy	between	There is a *discrepancy between* the two accounts.
	in	There is a *discrepancy in* his account.
displeased	at	The supervisor was *displeased at* the employee's conduct.
	with	The supervisor was *displeased with* the employee.
eligible	for	She is *eligible for* the job.
	to	Everyone is *eligible to* apply for the job.
equivalent	in	His office and mine are *equivalent in* size.
	of	This amount is the *equivalent of* full payment.
	to	Each payment is *equivalent to* a week's salary.
excluded from		This item may be *excluded from* gross income.
exempt from		This type of income is *exempt from* tax.
expect	from	What return do you *expect from* your investment?
	of	What does the vice president *expect of* his assistant?
familiar	to	The taxpayer's name is *familiar to* me.
	with	He is quite *familiar with* the proceedings.
find for		The jury *found for* the defendant.
furnish	to	Adequate supplies were *furnished to* them.
	with	Please *furnish* us *with* background information on this matter.
habit of		He made a *habit of* waiting until the report was due before he began writing it.
identical with		That case is *identical with* the one I am working on.
identify	by	The witness was *identified by* the tattoo on his arm.
	to	The witness *identified* the suspect *to* the officer.
	with	He was *identified with* the opposing members.
ignorant of		He was *ignorant of* his rights.
improvement	in	The *improvement in* his writing was soon noted.
	on	His second draft was an *improvement on* the first.
inconsistent	in	He was *inconsistent in* his review.
	with	This procedure is *inconsistent with* established policy.
infer from		We *infer from* his statement that he plans to discuss the adjustment further.
influence	for	His *influence* was always *for* harmony.
	by	We were all *influenced by* the president's statements.
	on (upon)	The rumor of an organizational change had an *influence on (upon)* production.
	over	The supervisor had a strong *influence over* his staff.
	with	He referred frequently to his *influence with* those in authority.

inform of	Supervisors should keep their subordinates *informed of* any changes in procedure.
inherent in	A capacity for growth is *inherent in* all people.
insert in	This phrase should be *inserted in* the draft.
intercede { for	My lawyer *interceded for* me.
with	He *interceded with* the board in my behalf.
invest { in	The taxpayer said he had *invested* the money *in* stocks.
with	He was *invested with* full power to act.
irrelevant to	This statement is *irrelevant to* the matter under discussion.
irrespective of	They decided to appoint him *irrespective of* the criticism that might result.
liable { for	He is *liable for* damages.
to	The employee is *liable to* his employer.
liberal { in	He was very *liberal in* his views.
with	He was *liberal with* praise.
necessity { for	There is no *necessity for* a reduction in force.
of	We are faced with the *necessity of* reducing travel expenses.
oblivious of	He was *oblivious of* the effect that his remote manner had on his employees.
precedent { for	Is there a *precedent for* this action?
in	His decision established a *precedent in* law.
recompense for	He was fully *recompensed for* the time he spent on the work.
reconcile { to	We have become *reconciled to* our fate.
with	Our views cannot be *reconciled with* his.
similarity { in	I agree that there is much *similarity in* their appearance.
of	The *similarity of* the cases caused confusion.
to	This timesaving device shows a *similarity to* one I have.
talk { of	The traveler *talked* long *of* his experiences.
to	The lecturer *talked to* a large audience.
with	The lawyer *talked with* his client.
transfer { from	He has been *transferred from* his former position.
to	They *transferred* him *to* another department.
unequal { in	The contestants were *unequal in* strength.
to	They were *unequal to* the demands placed on them.
use { for	He had no *use for* the extra table.
of	She made good *use of* her opportunity.
wait { at	I will *wait at* the back of the conference room until I can talk with the conference leader.
for	He seemed to be *waiting for* someone.
on (upon)	This matter must *wait on (upon)* my leisure.

Glossary of grammatical terms

Active voice. Active voice is the form of the verb that reveals the subject performing the action stated by the verb.

Adjective. An adjective is a word or word group that modifies or describes a noun or pronoun.

Adjective complement. See *Complement*.

Adverb. An adverb describes, interprets, or limits any verb form, an adjective, or another adverb. It may be a single word or a group of words, such as clauses, prepositional phrases, and infinitives.

Adverbial clause. Dependent clauses that modify a verb (usually the verb in the main or independent clause).

Adverbial phrase. An adverbial phrase is a prepositional phrase that modifies a verb, an adjective, or another adverb.

Agreement. Agreement is a term used with pronouns and indicates that they agree with the noun they replace in person, number, and gender.

Antecedent. The antecedent is the word to which the pronoun refers.

Antonym. An antonym is the exact opposite of another word—*fair* is the antonym of *unfair*.

Appositive. An appositive is a noun or pronoun, usually in a group, that explains or means the same as the noun or pronoun it follows.

Miss Summers, a competent *secretary*, explained the operation of the machine.

Article. The words *a, an,* and *the* are called articles and are members of the group of words known as determiners. *A* and *an* are indefinite articles that designate any member of a class or group. *The* is a definite article that points out some particular person or thing.

Clause. A group of words containing a subject and a verb is known as a clause. See *Independent clause* and *Dependent clause*.

Collective noun. A collective noun names a group of objects or persons. When the group acts as a unit, the collective noun is considered singular. When the individuals or things within the group act individually, the collective noun is considered plural.

The *board* was unanimous in *its* decision.

The *board* disagree on the next project *they* should undertake.

Comma splice. When two independent clauses are joined by a comma *only,* the error is called a comma splice.

Commands. In commands the subject of the sentence is asked to do something. The subject *you* is understood, not stated.

Count the stationery inventory.

Requests, where the subject politely asks for something to be done, are similar to commands.

May we have your answer before noon.

Commands and requests are called imperative sentences.

Common noun. A common noun names a member

of a general class—*chair, store, typewriter, envelope.*

Comparative conjunction. Conjunctions paired with specific words, such as *either/or,* are called comparative conjunctions because they emphasize comparison between two things.

Comparative degree. The comparative degree is used to indicate a comparison between two things. Most adjectives form the comparative degree by the addition of *r* or *er.* Others form it by the addition of the words *more* or *less,* and a few are spelled quite differently from the root word.

> Our building is *newer* than the one across the street.
>
> He is *less* eager for the promotion than he indicated.
>
> I felt bad yesterday but I feel *worse* today.

Complement. Complement is the general term used for nouns, pronouns, or adjectives that follow linking verbs. See *Noun or pronoun complement* and *Object complement.*

Complete subject. The complete subject is made up of the word, phrase, or clause that names the person, place, or thing about which something is said, plus all determiners and other modifiers. For sentences written in normal order, all words before the verb comprise the complete subject.

> *The typist sitting at the fourth desk* | turns out more work than any other typist.

Complex sentence. A complex sentence is made up of one independent clause and one or more dependent clauses.

> The report arrived after it was too late to change the plans.

Compound sentence. A compound sentence is made up of two or more independent clauses.

> The enclosed brochure should be read carefully, and then it should be filed under machine maintenance.

Compound subject. A compound subject consists of two or more subjects. See *Subject.*

> *Ideas* and *suggestions* must be presented in writing.

Compound verb. A compound verb consists of two or more verbs. See *Verb.*

> A secretary *takes* dictation and *transcribes* her notes.

Compound-complex sentence. A compound-complex sentence is made up of two or more sentences, one of which is a complex sentence.

> After the reports were made, the committee voted to accept them; and the secretary made a notation to that effect in the minutes.

Conditional sentence. A conditional sentence tells about an event that is dependent upon another event taking place. It is concerned with the "if-then" idea. *Should* is used with *I* or *we;* and *would* is used with *you, he, she, it, they.*

Conjugation. Conjugation is a systematic series of the forms or tenses of a verb.

Conjunction. A conjunction is a joining word that connects sentence parts. See *Coordinate, Correlative or comparative,* and *Subordinate conjunctions.*

Contraction. A contraction is composed of two words in a shortened form, by the omission of one or more letters. All contractions are written with an apostrophe where the letters are missing (cannot—can't).

Coordinate conjunction. The coordinate conjunctions, *and, but, or, nor,* and sometimes *yet* and *so,* are used to join sentence elements of equal value—nouns to nouns, verbs to verbs, phrases to phrases, etc.

Dangling modifier. Any descriptive word or group of words, such as infinitives and phrases, that does not clearly modify a particular noun or pronoun is considered to be dangling.

Declarative sentence. See *Statements.*

Demonstrative pronoun. These pronouns point out specific persons or things: *this, that, these* and *those.*

Dependent clause. A clause that contains a subject and verb and is introduced by a subordinator.

> *Before you leave,* please check with Mr. Thomas.

Determiner. A determiner, such as the articles, points to a noun. Other determiners are *my, your, her, this, its, every, none, their, both, many, some, several, all,* etc.

Direct object. See *Object.*

Double comparison. The use of two words in the comparative or superlative degrees to modify a noun. Such expressions as *more harder* and *most fastest* are *never* used. Only one word in the proper degree should be used. See *Comparative degree* and *Superlative degree.*

Double negative.   The use of two negative words to modify another word is considered poor English. Such combinations as *don't never, can't hardly, scarcely never* should be avoided.

Emphatic verb.   An emphatic verb is formed with a main verb and the auxiliary verb *do*. Both negative and positive sentences may be written with an emphatic verb.

I **do think** that you should write the letter.

He **did not want** to write the letter.

Exclamations.   A sentence that expresses strong feeling or emotion and ends with an exclamation point.

Exclamatory sentences.   See *Exclamations*.

First-person pronoun.   A pronoun that refers to the person speaking, such as *I, we, me, us, my, our, mine,* and *ours,* in the first person.

Fragment.   A group of words that cannot stand alone as a sentence is called a fragment. Occasionally, fragments are used in business writing, especially in promotional materials.

Future perfect tense.   The future perfect tense indicates action that will be completed at some definite future time and before some other future action takes place. The helping verbs *shall have* and *will have* are used with the past participle.

The reports will have been distributed before the convention.

He will have distributed the reports before the convention.

Future progressive tense.   Future progressive tense indicates continuous action in the future. *Shall* and *will* plus a form of the verb *be* and a main verb (present participle) are combined to make up the tense.

He will be going to the meeting on Friday.

Future tense.   The future tense indicates state of being or action that will occur in the future. The auxiliaries *shall* and *will* are used with the verb in simple future. *Should* and *would* are used in conditional sentences that refer to future time.

He **will** talk about inflation at the convention.

He **would** make faster progress if he would study data processing.

Gender.   Gender is the placement of nouns in classes called masculine, feminine, or neuter. The choice of words that modify, replace, or otherwise refer to the noun must be in the same class.

The manager gave the letter to Miss Jones so that *she* might have it duplicated and returned to *him*.

Gerund.   See *Verbal noun*.

Homonyms.   A word like another in sound and possibly spelling but different in meaning.

Helping verbs.   Helping verbs are parts of verb phrases and are used to assist the main verb to express the correct action.

She **might be able** to go if Monday is a holiday.

Imperative sentence.   See *Commands*.

Indefinite pronoun.   Third person pronouns, such as *all, any, someone, each, everyone,* and *another,* do not name specific persons, places, or things.

Independent clause.   An independent clause is the main or principal clause in a sentence. A simple sentence has one independent clause. See *Clause*.

Indirect object.   An indirect object names the final receiver of the object of a transitive verb.

Mrs. Sheldon gave *him* the message.

Indirect question.   An indirect question is inserted in a statement in the form of a dependent clause. The sentence ends with a period.

The salesman asked *when he might expect an answer.*

Infinitive.   The basic verb form is in the infinitive— *to talk, to write, to spell.* The infinitive may be used as a noun, adjective, or adverb and may have both a subject and object. Many times *to* is omitted because the thought flows more smoothly without it.

Mr. Norton wanted *to have* the meeting postponed.

Infinitive phrase.   An infinitive phrase is composed of the infinitive, its object or complement, its subject, and any modifiers.

To listen attentively to a boring speaker is an ability I need to develop.

Interrogative pronoun.   Interrogative pronouns ask questions—*who, whose, whom, which, what.*

Interrogative sentence.   See *Questions*.

Intransitive verb.   An intransitive verb does not have an object, even though it may show action.

Inverted sentence. In inverted sentences, the subject comes after the verb or predicate, or after a word group, such as a phrase or clause. See *Normal word order.*

Below the street will be our parking *garage.*
After thinking it over, *he* decided to cancel the policy.
Missing is our profit *margin.*

Irregular verb. Verbs whose principal parts do not fit the standard patterns of forming the past tense, past participle, and third person singular present tense are called irregular verbs. See *Regular verb.*

Linking verb. The linking verbs are the forms of the verbs *be, appear, become, feel, taste, smell, look, seem, sound.* These verbs are followed by complements, either nouns or adjectives.

Mrs. Todd **seems** happy in her new position.
Mr. Tull **will become** vice president on July 1.

Main verb. The last word in a verb phrase is the main verb.

Modifier. A word, known as an adjective or adverb, that makes the meaning of another word more precise is called a modifier. Phrases, such as prepositional, infinitive, verbal noun, and participial, and clauses also function as modifiers.

Mood. Mood is the ability of verbs to indicate factual, commanding, or unrealistic messages. The three moods are *indicative, imperative,* and *subjunctive.*

Neuter gender. Nouns for which *it* can substitute are called neuter—that is, they are neither feminine nor masculine. See *Gender.*

Nominative case. The form of the pronoun when used as a subject or complement *(I, we, you, he, she, it, they).*

Normal word order. In normal word order the subject comes first in the sentence followed by the predicate.

Noun. Words that name persons, places, things, ideas, or qualities are called nouns.

Noun clause. A noun clause is a dependent clause that acts as a subject, object, or complement.

Noun modifier. A noun that modifies another noun is a noun modifier.

The *rules* committee is drafting a new set of by-laws.

Noun or pronoun complement. Nouns or pronouns that follow the linking verbs and that mean the same as the subject are called complements.

Mrs. Heath is the department *manager* of Administrative Services.
It is *I.*

Number. Number refers to whether a word is singular or plural.

Object. An object is a noun or pronoun that follows a transitive verb. It identifies the person or thing receiving the action. Besides the transitive verb, other verb groups, such as infinitives, participles, and verbal nouns, may have objects.

She handed the *letter* to me.
To hit the *keys* correctly you need a light *touch.*

Prepositions also have objects.

He came directly from his *office.*

Object complement. An object complement represents the same person or thing as the object, or it describes the object.

The employees elected her their *representative.*
John thought Mary *pretty.*

Objective case. Objective case refers to the group of personal pronouns that are used as objects or indirect objects of verbs, objects of prepositions, subjects and/or objects of infinitives, and objects of verbal nouns and participles. *Me, us, him, her, them* are objective case pronouns.

Parallel construction. To achieve parallel construction, sentence elements that are joined must be of the same form, i.e., noun/noun, verb,/verb, subject/subject, object/object, etc.

Participial phrase. A participial phrase is used as an adjective and is composed of the present or past participle of the verb, its object and other modifying words.

The machine *broken beyond repair* was sold for scrap.

Participle. Verbs have two participle forms—the present and the past. The present participle is the *ing* ending of the verb, and the past participle uses the *ed, d, en, n,* and *t* endings of verbs. Irregular verbs often have participle forms that differ in spelling from the infinitive form of the verb.

Passive voice.   In passive voice, someone or something as the subject of the sentence is acted upon.

He has been employed by General Motors as a supervisor.

Past perfect tense.   The past perfect tense is the form of the verb used to indicate that action begun in the past was completed at some stated or implied time in the past. The helping verb *had* is used with the past participle to form the past perfect tense.

Past progressive tense.   The past progressive tense of the verb shows continuous occurrence of an event in the past.

Last month Mr. Case was interviewing applicants for the bank.

Past tense.   As one of the five basic tenses of a verb, the past tense indicates state of being or action begun in the past and finished in the past. The regular verb adds *d* or *ed* to the present tense to form past tense.

Perfect tense.   The perfect tense, a secondary tense, is used to show action completed in present, in past, or in future time. The helping verb *have* is used with the past participle of the verb to form the perfect tenses. See *Past perfect, Present perfect,* and *Future perfect.*

Person.   Person refers to the relationship between the subject and the verb. The person speaking is called a first-person subject; the person spoken to is a second-person subject; and the person or thing spoken about is a third-person subject.

Personal pronoun.   A personal pronoun refers to a person or thing. *I, me, us, my, mine, our, ours* are first person; *you, your, yours,* second person; *he, him, his, she, her, hers, it, they, them, their, theirs,* third person. The *self* pronouns, *myself, himself,* are also classified as personal pronouns.

Phrase.   A phrase is a group of closely related words that does not contain a subject and a verb.

Plural.   Plural is a term that implies more than one person or thing.

Plural verb.   A plural verb agrees with a plural subject. The only difference between it and a singular verb is found in the spelling of third-person singular. See *Singular verb.*

Positive degree.   An adjective in its basic form is in positive degree. No comparison is intended by the adjective; it merely describes the word it modifies.

Possessive noun.   A possessive noun shows ownership and is always written with an apostrophe (except for pronouns). Almost all singular possessive nouns end in *'s,* and plural nouns end in *s'.*

Possessive case.   Nouns and pronouns that show ownership are in the possessive case.

Possessive pronouns.   These pronouns show ownership: *my, mine, our, ours, your, yours, his, her, hers, its, whose, their, theirs.*

Predicate.   The predicate of a sentence or clause is made up of the verb, its modifiers, and any complements or objects.

Preposition.   A preposition is one of a particular group of words that joins a noun, pronoun, or a word group used as a noun to form a phrase that modifies some other word in the sentence.

Prepositional phrase.   A prepositional phrase is composed of a preposition, its object, and any determiners and modifiers of the object.

Mrs. Sheldon took the letter *from the file in her office.*

Present participle.   See *Participle.*

Present perfect tense.   The present perfect tense indicates that action begun in the past is completed in the present. The helping verb *have* is used with the past participle to form the present perfect tense.

I *have finished* the inventory of supplies.

Present progressive tense.   The tense used to describe continuous action in the present is the present progressive tense.

Mr. Fields *is talking* to Mr. Parker on the telephone.

Present tense.   Present tense points to action or state of being in progress right now.

He *dictates* in spurts.

Progressive tense.   In describing continuous action in the past, present, or future, the progressive tense is used. It is formed by the auxiliary verb *be* plus the present participle. See *Past progressive* and *Present progressive.*

Pronoun.   A word that takes the place of a noun.

Proper noun.   A noun that names a particular person, place, or thing is a proper noun and is always capitalized.

Questions.   A sentence in which the subject asks for information or for any other kind of answer is called a question. It ends with a question mark, and requires an answer from the receiver.

When will Mr. Willis return?

Regular verb.   Regular verbs are those verbs that make the third-person singular present tense by adding *s* or *es* to their infinitive form and that make the past tense and past participle forms by adding *d* or *ed* to their infinitive form.

Relative pronoun.   A relative pronoun connects a dependent clause with a main clause and agrees in person, number, and gender with its antecedent in the independent clause. Relative pronouns are *that, which, who, whom, what,* and compounds of these pronouns, such as *whoever* and *whichsoever.*

Requests.   See *Commands.*

Second person.   The person spoken to is known as second person—*you, your,* and *yours.*

Sentence connectors.   Words like *therefore, however, consequently* are called sentence connectors. They require special punctuation when used to connect two sentences. A semicolon must come at the end of the first sentence.

Sentence structure.   See *Simple, Compound, Complex, Compound-complex sentence.*

Sentence types.   See *Commands, Exclamations, Questions,* and *Statements.*

Sentence patterns.   The arrangement of words in sentences follows three basic patterns: Subject + Intransive verb, Subject + Transitive verb + Object, and Subject + Linking verb + Complement. There are variations within these patterns, and a few sentences do not fit any of the basic patterns. The order of the principal parts of a sentence makes up its pattern.

Simple sentence.   A simple sentence contains only one independent clause and no dependent clauses.

Singular.   A word that denotes only one is known as singular.

Singular verb.   The singular form of the verb is used with a singular subject. In the third-person singular (he, she, it), the addition of *s* or *es* to the verb is the singular form. The first- and second-person singular are the same.

I ask
you ask
he, she, it asks

Split infinitive.   If a word comes between the *to* and the verb, the infinitive is said to be split.

Statements.   A sentence that makes a statement, declares a fact, or expresses an opinion is known as a statement. It always ends with a period even when it contains an indirect question.

Our products are sold in all 50 states.
He asked whether our products are sold in all 50 states.

Subject.   The noun, pronoun, phrase or clause naming the person speaking, the person being spoken to, or the person, place, or thing being spoken about is called the subject of a clause whether independent or dependent. See *Complete subject* and *Compound subject.*

Subject complement.   The noun, pronoun, or adjective following a linking verb that names or describes the subject of the clause is sometimes called a subject complement. See *Complement* and *Noun or pronoun complement.*

Subordinate clause.   A dependent clause introduced by a subordinator is known as a subordinate clause. See *Subordinators.*

Subordinators.   Words that relate a dependent clause to an independent one are called subordinators. Such words as *after, as, because, before, if, since, until, when, where, that, which, what, whoever, unless* are used as subordinators. These words are also known as subordinate conjunctions, conjunctive adverbs, or relative pronouns.

Superlative degree.   The superlative degree is used to show a comparison of three or more things. For regular adjectives and adverbs, the addition of *est* to their positive form results in the superlative degree. For irregular adjectives and adverbs, many times *most* or *least* is used with the positive degree. Other irregular modifiers change their spelling for the superlative degree.

Suspensive hyphen.   The use of a hyphen with one part of a compound adjective where the second word of the compound is dropped to eliminate repetition. The second word appears in an immediately following compound adjective.

Ten- and 20-pound kegs of nails are available.

Tense.   Tense refers to the various forms of the verb that indicate a particular time. The tenses are present, past, future, and the secondary perfect tenses.

Third person.   Third person refers to the person, place, or thing spoken about. Nouns are in third person, and third person pronouns are used with noun antecedents. See *Person* and *Personal pronoun.*

Third-person singular.   Third-person singular is the form of the verb that agrees with a singular noun or third person pronoun subject. In regular verbs, third-person singular is formed by adding *s* or *es* to the verb. See *Personal pronoun.*

Time relationship.   See all definitions of tense: present, past, future, and perfect.

Transitive verb.   The transitive verb requires a word

or words to complete the meaning or to receive the action. It forms a pathway from the subject to the object. All verbs that require an object are called transitive verbs. Some verbs may be used as both transitive and intransitive.

Verb.   A word that expresses action or state of being is known as a verb.

Verb phrase.   A verb phrase consists of a verb plus its helpers.

She *should have received* a promotion last year.

Verbal noun.   Verbal nouns, also known as gerunds, change verbs into nouns by giving names to actions.

They are formed by adding *ing* to the verb.

Dictating is a skill.

Verbal noun phrase.   The verbal noun plus its object and modifiers makes up the verbal noun phrase.

Dictating a long letter without notes takes years of practice.

Voice.   Voice is a quality shown by transitive verbs. There are two voices: active and passive. *Active voice* is used when the subject performs the action. *Passive voice* is used when the subject is acted upon.

Mary *typed*   **versus**   The letter *was*
the letter.   *typed* by Mary.

Index